Vaisikasutra

Courtesans in the Ancient India

Vaisikasutra
Courtesans in the Ancient India

Santosh Ghosh

KALPAZ

ISBN: 978-93-5128-206-8

Price: ₹ 1090

First Published, 2016

Published by

Kalpaz Publications
C-30, Satyawati Nagar,
Delhi – 110052
E-mail: kalpaz@hotmail.com
Ph.: 9212142040

Printed at: G. Print Process, Delhi

Cataloging in Publication Data—DK

Courtesy: D.K. Agencies (P) Ltd. <docinfo@dkagencies.com>

Ghosh, Santosh, 1943- author.

Vaisikasutra : courtesans in the ancient India / Santosh Ghosh.

pages cm

Includes bibliographical references.

ISBN 9789351282068

1. Courtesans—India—History. 2. Courtesans in literature.
3. Sanskrit literature—History and criticism. I. Title.

DS425.G46 2016 DDC 934 23

Contents

Chapter Six

Chapter Seven

Prologue

In my latest book *Music in the Ancient World* (Delhi: 2012) I have briefly described with the fact that through the ancient history and literature the art of Music begun in singing and dancing of Magical Women with regard to a professional character, showing exceptional female beauty and test and called them a *harlot, ganika, vesya, rupajiva, pumscali, dasi* and *courtesan*. The term is generally applied to the act of practiced by women referred to as "the oldest profession." This result motivated me and inspired to searching by and large in processes and spent through the years together for a remarkable composition.

In the treatment of such subject my first contribution: *Whoredome in Ancient Mesopotamia* publish in issue of Calcutta Book Fair 2015 of PURBASHA EKHON (Bilingual Bangla, English), International Literary Magazine launched from India and Norway.

Our ancient classic authors created how can any literary craftsman who would hold up his contemporary as *mirror*, suppose to a courtesan life, their customs and practice of the art music performed for their won interest of professions. They also created their won female body for sale of *sexual love* (all are doubtful pleasure!) for a male partner.

There are quite number (I have a record about hundred of books) of books on erotic, and relation with the courtesans and few are also regarded as Pornography while this volume is at all not a tome, neither it's a bedside *pillow* book. The compiler selected twenty nos. of stories and each story told by our prominent (Sanskrit and Parakrit) ancient writers. So its expected this book is for the general readership. Also the book is intended both the Indian and foreign readers. It may even interest a special approach throughout the ancient from the known to unknown.

Therefore, this book desirous of reading for adult, mature and serious readers. Also who studies in academic level, student of college and university for scholarly engaged in research work. The present volume designed to contribute to the solution to sum extent of the historical problem during their time. Our ancient authors throws light in as the story, drama, monologue-play and poetry and indicate on the changing their views towards *obscenity* skillfully in proper way. These are a different form of a tolerable reflection for a popular and quite intelligible production pertaining from other author.

Vaisika Sutra of my book: There is no scope to comparison with and other author's title and book. Vaisika Sutra in fact regenerated from the ancient texts and entirely thought for the courtesans culture and practical life. However, the Editor unable to make very extensive use of the treasures of this school of Vaisikha Sutra presenting by various ancient authors. Vaisika Sutra's evidenced in many more pieces were still incomprehensible, and certainly a very different kind of study needed to fill up the great gap in the history of Indian Literature.

In conclusion, there are more logical ground for saying that the "biological and instinctive peculiarities of man and women, the economic domination of man-made society and a host of other *mirror* factors produced the casual act of *sex* procured by man for women a consideration this *act* unchanged even todays."

Acknowledgements

I owe a profound debt of gratitude to Sir P. T. Nair of celebrated historian Kolkata, Sri Ashim Mukapadhya, Asstt. Librarian and Information Officer National Library, Kolkata. Also Dr Gargi Gangapadhya, Professor, Ramakrishna Sarada Mission Vivekananda Vidyabhavan for any careful and penetrating suggestion, without which the book would have been a great deal worse than it is.

I also wish to acknowledge the help and services that I receive from the staff of the National Library, Kolkata, the Bangiya Sahitya Parishad, Kolkata.

The author extremely grateful to Sri Mohitosh Paik in computer assembling and DTP job of intire book and Sri Prasanjit Ray, computer operator. Credited to very different kind of illustrate of pictorial construction of related theme of this book. And without my wife Nandita and my journalist daughter Sayantani's help of very many kinds, this book would never have been written, or revised or completed.

Preface

This work *Vaisikasutra : Courtesans in the Ancient India* need, no preface for those reader who are familiar with the books of ancient classical Sanskrit Literature which have made accessible by the great scholars both the Western World and Indian Pandita. To those not familiar with the ancient literature it may be stated that the bulk of its content (stories) is derived to searching from the old canon, commentary in the old style hand writing (Palm-Leaf) manuscript. Wherever the compiler has admitted modernisation he has done so with due consideration and always in the spirit of a Legitimate development. Additions and modifications contain nothing but ideas for which prototype can be found somewhere among the traditions of classical Sanskrit Literature, and have been introduced as popular writing style, is sure to be welcomed by the general audience.

Sri Santosh Ghosh, being a devotee of this work, has traced the philosophy of Vaisikhasutra of the Courtesans in the Ancient India, meticulously with the help of the writings of the best of the authorities, without interposing himself anywhere so that his readers are left free to form their own judgement upon the subject. Since last two decade he present numerous articles and books. From our publication house, we have also produces 'Telecommunicatinos 20th Century' (Bangla : 2002) and Sepoy Mutiny from Telegraph Messages (2008) in English broke new ground on that subject. His 'Music in the Ancient World' (2012) also turn a new leaf in this vast subject.

As we look with pride the present book : Vaisikhasutra : Courtesan in the Ancient India will be publish by Kalpaz publication, Delhi, India. I believe, this book takes the olden stories and brings them into the Golden Book.

Sukumar Gupta

Introduction

Introducing Vaisika Sutras of Courtesans in the Ancient India

This book carries on the theme of *Vaisika* of courtesans in the Ancient India, which are based on directly study of the science of erotics. In Ch. XXII (Natya Sutra) devoted to Vaisika of *nayaka* (actor) Bharat speaks: "A Vaisika is so called because he excels (Visesaya) in all arts or become his dealings are in connection with a courtesan (*Vesya*).

As devoted to Vaisika Courtesan (*actress*), their nature of love Bharat says, of three class of the *Vaisiki* type, the courtesan, the *madanatura* (love sick) or one craving for company and showing it openly disporting herself, the *anurakta* (devoted) or the courtesan who is attached to a particular love and the *virakta* estranged or the courtesan who is averse.

The Kamasutra of Vatsyayana acknowledges his debt to numerous of earlier writers on the subject and gives an account of the origin of the science. He tell us that amongst the other authorities, Dattaka wrote on prostitutes; at the request of a prostitute of Pataliputra, another writer Ganika-putra on mistresses. In six chapter relating respectively to virgin, brides, wives, mistress, prostitutes, technique of sexual union and secret instruction.

The way of Dattaka is mentioned in Kamasutra, it can be safely assumed that Dattaka preceded Vatsyanyana by a couple of centuries. Dattaka was an author, famous poet, the author of Vaisikasutra or *Vaisikadhikaram*.

The story of Dattaka is very interesting. A Brahmana from Mathura migrated to Pataliputra. A son was born to him at his old age the mother died at Child-bed, and the father gave the child to a Brahmani, who named him Dattaka (because he was given to her). The boy grew up, acquired a knowledge of all the sastra and the fine art. On account of his great skill in the exposition of the sastras he become famous as Dattakachrya. Attaining maturity, he was anxious to learn the ways of world, which, he thought, could be best learnt from public women. So he want to their quarters everyday and learned their ways. So thorough did he learn, that at last they used to come to him for advice in matters erotic art. Then *virasena* and other noted courtesans of Pataliputra requested him to write a treatise on the art of winning lovers.

In fact, the Kamasutra of Vatsyayana was not the first to describe and instruct in the courtesans art and culture. Dattaka who live before Vatsyayana and wrote a special guide for courtesans. In the Jaina literature, were supposed to have acquired a knowledge of the seventy-two traditional arts. These list contains many items of the sixty-four mentioned in the Kamasutra. *Prabandhacintamani*, counts 72 accomplishments. So, many of our ancient writer follows Dattaka or their age old writers on the erotics.

The wide spectrum of ancient accounts – political treatise, theatricals play, guide to love making in Buddhist and Jaina religious text and art and in the Sanskrit and Parakrit Literatures, stories, drama monologue play, poetry indicate the degree to which the image of the *ganika* stirred the lives and thoughts of Indians during ancient time. No wander the image of the *ganika* strides through antiquity literature as dazzling female, combining as she does a glamorous, yet dangerous, but cultivated persons.

The subject of this Manuscript for publication is the conception of literary obscenity as found in law and practice and its cultural and social effects. My primary concern is the restraint which the conception exercise on serious ancient literature and consequently on intellectual freedom and reproduction from original document.

The Vaisika sutra on courtesans in ancient India, present something delightfully natural and charming in the *Hothouse* of Sanskrit belles-letters. Herein each story attempts to depict the life and style of courtesans as whole. This complex emotion has inspired the stories in this form of unique book, where readers will find reflections of their own feeling, thoughts and attitudes not only courtesan, but also their male partner, their character, qualities and reputation inscribe. As such the importance of these stories from the standpoint of Hindu social history in various part of India is immense. They are also very important documents from the literary aspect.

In this collection, majority of stories, specially the Bhanas supplying us of some data relating to the history of Indian philosophy and religions. The most important among these, relate to the evolution of the *vaisisikha-darsan* (For the parivrajika, a female religieux) though she professed to be a follower of the vaisikha doctrine says that her teacher has forbidden her to be in speaking terms with anyone who clings to the six *padarthas* (categories), the original basis of this. From the retort of the vita is it learned that the two more padarthas, *yoga* and *moksa* were then already added to the vaisikha doctrine. An inquiry about the cause of this, may give us important light about the religious and philosophical thought of the time.

The tradition of earliest of these works in the Manipravalam School in *Vaisikha Tantram* written in the thirteenth century. It is fairly typical of the work that appealed to the upper class reading public of those days. It contains about 200 quatrain in Sanskrit metres and is in the form of professional advice given to a prostitute or courtesan by her mother.

These instruction are of a practical nature calculated to please the pampered tastes of a leisured class. But each quatrain is composed with care and due weight is given to the rule of rhetoric. For instance, the mother tells the daughter, who is to get ready of the family vocation as courtesan, that "old age is a sea to be crossed by means of the wealth earned during one's youth." Several quatrains of this type are quoted in *Lilathilakam* by way of illustration for the several rules of grammar and rhetoric. An example may be quoted here;

> All breezes are not breezes
> The real breeze is the one.
> That bathes is the nearby river,
> dances among the growing coconut trees.

Cresses the uniquely beautiful body
of mistress Rohini.
And comes in kindness to thrill
me by blowing over me.

Perhaps the most representative of these early manipravalam works are the tales of courtesans *(Achicharitams)* and the message of poems *(Sandesakavyas)* not survival.

These poignant, intriguing, beautiful, comical and gesture of charming courtesans stories telling by greatest ancient Buddha-Jaina commentator, Sanskrit poet, dramatist, writers of all time, will definitely leave reader's mind with memorable, lingering touch of romance.

For those who want to trace the stories of this book to its fountain-head, a table of reference has been added, which indicates as briefly as possible the main source of the various chapters of the content:

Ascetics and Courtesans ".... and a harlot must exchange abuse,...The (the harlot) must say: 'you, who have misbehaved! Who have violated your vow of continence"! Jan Gonda's studies on the prostitution in Rigveda, 'Ascetics and courtesans', we hardly know much about their life and accomplishment.

'The canter of the *Samaveda* and courtesan' of Somadeva (1070 A.D.) included in the above article with a additional ancient source.

Jataka: Stories of Courtesans Jataka (C450 B.C.), the best known portion of Buddhist *nikaya* revised by Buddhaghosa. He wrote a great commentary on the verses. Jataka tell us numerous stories about courtesans. We have selected only three of them:

Kanavera Jataka: This was a story told by the master at Jetavana, about a Brother who was tempted by thoughts of the wife he had left. The circumstances that led up to the story will be set forth in the Indriy Birth! The Master, addressing this Brother, said, "once before, through her, you had your head cut off." And then he related a legend of the past. This is the story of famous courtesan Sama and the star of a robber.

Sulasa – Jataka: The Master told this while dwelling in Jetavana, concerning a female servant of .... Anathapindika's request, he (master) told the tale of old. This is the story of a thief and the courtesan Sulasa.

Atthana – Jataka: The Master told this tale an ungrateful courtesan, who charge of thousand pieces a night from a Merchant. One day he forget to bring her fees and was driven away by her maids. When the king learnt this, he ordered that bring him back. She entreated him but he refused to return.

Kamma Katha – Sagara: According to the Jaina tradition as represented in the Vasudevahindi (Vh), there are many stories which describe previous lives of various persons to illustrate the omnipotence of the law of *Kamma*. Jaina literary activity continued took place in 453 A.D. after the council of *valabhi*. It's valuable in reconstructing the cultural history of Jaina India.

Marriage of Carudatta and his entry into a Prostitute's House: An interesting episode sketch of married life of Carudatta. The marriage was take place with beautiful Mittavati. But she is not happy, her husband's act, ... he doesn't visit her at night. In response to this news, Caru's mother arrange for her son to be taken into the house of a prostitutes. This episode seems to be a part of the narration connecting Caru's entry to a prostitute's house.

Samba and his lover for a Courtesan's Daughter: We can only surmise that it was something to do with the uncertainties surrounding *Madanamanjuka's* origin, and the religious implications involved in her purification. The story named as it occurs in a justifying, history of courtesans, in the Vasudevahindi, this appears with regard to *Suhiranna*, in no way do any doubts of purification threaten the real hero Vasudeva. Samba and Suhiranna episode formed a part of the Jaina *Harivamsa Purana* originally.

Brahman's Courtesan Lover (Story of Rupanika): Story is set in Mathura the birth place of Krishna. It is most famous collection from the *Bharat Kathasaritasagara* composed by Somadeva Bhatta. Rupanika, a prostitute, cherished selfless love for a poor Brahman a persisted in it even against the explicit desire of her mother.

Finally we find, the king as the arbiter of caste relation, here legalises the Brahmin *Lohajangha's* marriage with a prostitute.

Caturbhani (Four Play): The discovery of the four one-act monologue (Bhana) plays under the title of Caturbhani has brought to light the talent of Sanskrit dramatist in the domain of humorous and farcical writing. The four plays which are of the some type present variety, satire, comic, relief and free colloquial style.

This type of play has only one actor, who appears as a Vita (Rake). He is represented as setting out on some mission of dubious respectability in the course of which he walks through the town and meets and holds conversations with a variety of characters. As he is the only character on the stage this is done by his pretending to see and hear other people of whom he asks "What do you say" (*Kim bravisi*), and then himself quoting their word. The name of city in which the action takes place and a description of its beauties as the "hero" walks through it is a regular feature of the composition.

The plot of such plays is slight but within its limited scope there is much of variety. The satirical and comic pictures of various classes of people – the sky-gazing poet, the penniless impotent, the dried-up mistress, the mendicant consoling a courtesan with the words of the Buddha, the grammarian with his effections, the hypocritical Buddhist – are indeed enjoyable. The Vita is the central character in such plays. Here is four Bhanas:

Ubhayabhisarika (The Mutual Elopment) of Vararuci, is set in Kasumapura (Pataliputra): "Oh, now lovely looks this main street of Kusumapura; sprayed and scrubbed, bright with masses of many-hued flowers, it invites one to come and live here! .... So, now I beg you to bring us together – you who are the eternal spring time of Kusumapura, the most trusted friend of the courtesans, you must help me." Dating of Ubhayabhisarika, is some where first century B.C., the second century A.D., believed it might be the earliest Indian play content.

In the Ubhayabhisarika attributed to Vararuci, the Vita (Rake) is request by his friend to propitiate his offended lady. But when, after a series of way side adventures which furnish the themes for the monologue, he reaches the house of the lady, he finds that the lovers, urged by the beauty of the season, had already set out in search of each other and managed a touching reunion with his help.

Padmaprabhrtaka (The Lotus gift) of Sudraka (248 A.D.), is laid in Ujjayini: "Oh, the supreme glory of the city of Ujjayini, the belle of the land of Avanti, opulent with all kinds of accountrements, the ornamental cosmetic pointing on the check of the Jambu-continent face of the Earth"!

Sudraka is famous with the authorship of surviving play the *Mrechakatika*. Here we present of Bhana-play of padmaprabhrtaka of Sudraka, was a king as well as a scholar versed in many science from mathematics to harlotry, who lived one hundred years and ten days.

Sudraka's Padmaprabhrtaka, besides mentioning such characters as *Pithamarda, Vita, Sakyabhiksuki, Malakaradarika* and the friend of the type *Sahapamsukridita* given by Dattaka, describes a series of courtesans in different situations, whom we can identify as *prosita-bhartaka, Kalahantarita* and *Vasakasajjika*, greater theoretical consciousness characterises.

Padataditaka (The Kick) of Syamilaka is less explicit and refers: "Honestly, how extraordinarily beautiful the town of *Sarvabhauma* is! Ruled by King Sarvabhauma and its magnificence revealed in all her jewels, it is the ornament on the forehead of Jambudvipa", or it's set in Ujjayani, the ancient capital city of the Gupta empire. It must have been composed before 550 A.D.

Padataditaka of Syamilaka records an interesting episode which throws, welcome light on the institution. Story presenting the *milieu* of courtesan-love, Syamilaka may be taken as a special glorification of the character called *Vita* and his role.

An assembly of Vita is to consider the question of expiation and purification referred them by Vishnunaga, for the indignity he has suffered by allowing an intoxicated courtesan to kick him, in playfulness, on such a sacred spot of his head!

Some worth is think that it is not Vishnunaga, but the girl who should under go a purification ceremony for setting her foot upon such a beast. One man suggests that he should rub and shampoo her dishonoured foot, another that he should save his head, a third that he should wash is head with the water with which the washes her feet and drink the same.

In the end it is agreed on the proposal of the Presiding *Vita* that the girl should put more sense into her lover by setting her foot on the president's own head in the sight of Vishnunaga.

Dhurta-Vita-Samvada (Message from a clever vita) of Ishvaradatta is set in Kusumpur (Pataliputra): "It is fitting indeed that the name of Kusumpura should be established throughout the world simply as the city, a distinction not shared by any other city." Kusumpura meaning: *City of flowers*. Dhurta-Vita-Samvada, it was written during the *Murunda* regime in Magadha in third century A.D.

The Dhurta-Vita-Samvada is however, more interesting in many ways. The nominal *hero* of this monologue-play, a claver and experienced Vita finding the rainy season too depressing, comes out to spend the day in some amusement. He can not offer dice and drinking – even his clothes have been reduced to one garment – so he wends his way towards courtesan's house – street, meeting various kinds of people and altimately reaching the house of the roguish couple Visvalaka and Sunanda where he passed the day in discussing certain knotty problems of erotics put to him by the former.

In the Bhana, Dhurta-Vita-Samvada, there is a regular discussion on the relative efficancy of the different means of removing *Mana*; Ishvaradatta criticises *Padapatana, Sapatha,* and *Hasa* (a variety of *Rasantara*) and advocates another variety of Rasantara viz. sudden, and forcible kissing of the lady.

Again, apart from occurrence here of *Manavati*. Pronaya-Kalaha, Abhisara etc., we have specific discussion as to whether a *Samanya-nayika* has real love or not? The relative efficacy of the various means of bringing a lady's mana to an end, and many point on which aspect of love differ in the case of a *vesya* from those of a *Kulavadhu*.

Kuttanimahatmayam (Kuttanimata) of Damodargupta was the leading star in the sky of Sanskrit gnomic and didactic poetry. He was the first minister (*Dehi-sochib*) of king Jayapida (8th Century) of Kashmira. Kalhan in *Rajatarangini* mention: The learned scholar *Udbhatta*, for whom had been fixed a daily allowance of one lakh of *Dinars*, was the president of the Assembly of King (IV: 495). He made the poet name Damodaragupta, the author of the *Thought of a procuress*, the leading minister among political advisers as Bali appointed Sukra (IV: 496).

Bali, the king of the *Asuras* or Titans, had as his preceptor the wise Sukracharya who knew the secret of immortality. The work Kuttanimahatmyam was discover in the Combay Temple Library by professor Dr. P. Peterson in 1838. The poet is just as anxious to show his knowledge of the Alankarasastra, Vaisikasastra of Dattaka and the Kamasastra of Vatyasayana.

Damodargupta was a shrewd story teller. He adopted a unique device for achieving wide range the progress of the story within stories. Its poetry, here its diverting in prose style. The story proceed with a introductory part of the tale:

The way of the Courtesan: Malati, a prostitute of Varanasi, addressed herself to a procuress Vikarla for instruction how to attract lover. The procuress give her shrewd lessons how to ensnare a lover (in particular Chintamani, son of a high official), and how to win a man's love and fortune. Many of her advices are didactic verse illustrated by amusing, cunning love tales, e.g. with other prostitutes.

Henceforth, Kuttanimahatmya depends for its development of another two stories, one of

Haralata: The women of Lust (Story of Sundersena and Haralata): Kasumpur (Pataliputra)'s Brahmana Purandara's handsome and learned son Sundarasena come to Varanasi and spent about one and half year enjoying various kind of pleasures in the company of his beloved Haralata, a prostitute. Just then he received a missive from his father rebuking him for having fallen in the trap of an prostitute in complete disregard of his high family tradition and asking him to return home immediately.

Gunapatalia, his friend advice resolved to obey his father. Haralata accompanied them up to a banyan tree where Sundarsena bade her good bye and proceeded further. He had hardly covered a little distance when he learnt from a fellow-traveller the liding of the said demise of Haralata.

Haralata's story told by Vikarala to Malati, that she may tell in to the son of the Bhatta. Above the two stories, it would be clear, not in any way connected with one another. Likely third one:

Story of Manjuri from Harlot to Heroine: Again Vikarala narrated the story of Prince Samarabhatta and Manjuri. Samarabhatta visited Varanasi in a temple and offered worship. He was suitably received in an assemblage of dancers, actors and actresses, musicians including business magnets. On his inquiry about the state of music and dance art in Varanasi, the Master (*nartakacarya*) pointing out that the courtesans were 'interested more in their clients than in the pursuit of fine art'.

He, however, introduced the prince to a pretty dancing girl, her name Manjuri. Nartakacarya, requested to Samarabhatta to witness the first show of the *Ratnavali* performed by his pupils. The prince, seeing the performance, particularly Manjuri's role as *Sagarika* very much appreciated. He rewarded the dance-master and returned to his residence. But he was deeply enamoured of Manjuri, and when she was just describing her physical charms to his minister, there appeared Manjuri's messanger who narrated graphically her mistress's affected love-lorn condition, thereby blazing is sexual appetite still further.

On hearing Samarbatta's favourable reply, Manjuri, come to the prince's residence, gratified him with a variety of love plays and deserted him after squeezing all his wealth.

In conclusion, the way of the courtesan, Malati's mission fruitful.

Sringaramanjuri: Around the year 1010 A.D. there ruled a king on the throne of Dhara. He was known by the name of Raja Bhojadeva. He belonged to the Paramara dynasty and ruled for forty four years. It was said of him that during his rule "he accomplished, ordered, give and knew what was not in the power of anybody else." Of his many accomplishments one was his gift for story-telling them stories that had a lesson to convey. To this group of stories belong the stories of Sringaramanjuri.

These are stories of courtesans, their accomplishment and stratagem, and how they employed them for winning over kings and nobles. An essential part of a courtesan's training was the study and understanding of *ragas* (human emotions and feeling).

The Sringaramanjuri provides us a graphic description of the bowd Visamasila, the mother of Sringaramanjuri. She had a strong liking to seduce paramours, she was deceitful like a strong cat, was expert in the art of *Vaisika*, she played tricks on others but was never cheated herself, she scolded her daughter to narrated a numerous stories, and each emphasising the king of love of courtesans shows:

Fall of Ravidatta: Ravidatta was born in a Brahman family, had acquired knowledge of many arts including the art of love. His father advised him not to go near harlot and rogues or pleasure garden. However, after the death of his parents Ravidatta to go and watch the festive procession of Kama. In a garden he saw a beautiful girl and at once fell in love with her. She is a courtesan Vinayavati, who sent a message of love to Ravidatta. The young man fell a victim to the allurements.

Ravidatta from the beginning presenting to her costly gifts and large amounts of money and completely disregarded the warning of his elders. Vinayavati disvested him of his wealth and render him a pauper. Then she sent him a message that a merchants of Suvarnadipa wanted to purchase her love for a large amount of money and she asked him, not to come to her house. The lover was disconsolate and decided to visit her place. In there he was insulted by the servant. Vinayavati refused to recognise him.

Visamasila, stated to her daughter Sringarmanjuri: I shall relate to you the stories of other courtesans, who employed their knowledge of the art to climb the dizzy height of glory! Listen:

The Matchless Courtesan Devadatta: A poor Brahman Suradharman trouble by his poverty, reached the Ocean and clad in a leather jacket (*Charmachandataka*) worshipped it daily. He received the gift of an invaluable jewel from the Ocean. Feigning madness, he hid the jewel carefully and reached Ujjayani where Devadatta, a beautiful courtesan live. Devadatta at once guessed that he passed some invaluable treasure. But when she asked him anything he uttering no other word then, "Mother Know."

The courtesans played various tricks mention in the *Vaisika*, to seduce their lover. It is advised that if a *faked life* does not succeed, one should take recourse to play *fake death*. The motif has been brought out in this story.

When Suradharman, realising that she had guessed his secret, he decided to leave her, whatever he deep love her. Even so he left her. On his journey in wayside, Devadatta send message that Devadatta had died pining for him. Realising that he had committed a sin and returned to her house and saw her coffin. Thereupon, he ready to give up his life, he handed over the jewel to her. Devadatta got up and welcomed the 'hero'. She employes this trick and taking away all the wealth of her paramour and drives him out of the house.

Vaisikasutra pointing out the secrets: As a man remains courteous from the danger of a tiger so should a prostitute be in showing her tree love to any one. In this world because of this love a number of paramours have been cheated.

Lavanyasundari: "Self-sacrifice is strongest armour of a courtesan who sets her heart at acquiring wealth", said Visamasila to her daughter. Alike the story of Lavanyasundari wife of a oilman Ghuda. Listen:

Lavanyasundari was young, beautiful and dutiful wife of a oilman Ghuda lived in the city of Ahicchatra. The city ruled under the king Vairamukuta enjoying the pleasures of kingship. One day during his usual prowl along the street. He show a glimpse of Lavanyasundari, who stood near the window. The king was struck by her matchless beauty and he resolved to possess her by hook or crook.

The king arrested the oilman under the pretext that he had practiced adulteration in oil. The king asked for a hundred elephant as price for his release within six months. Lavanyasundari guessed the king's motive. She explain to her husband, "It is an idle dream of the king to possess me. If you do as I tell you without questioning my conduct, I shall procure hundred elephants and save you from the clutches of the cruel king. The oilman agreed.

Now Lavanyasundari thought of king Sahasanka who ruled in Ujjayini, who could give her the hundred elephants if she resolved to please the king and she did with a great valour and adventure as a charming courtesan.

Just finishing the story Visamasila narrate: "It was more amazing than the stories of the DEVAS told by the great RISHIS, but bear in mind, that Lavanyasundari was not motivated by greed. She wanted to secure first the hundred elephants so that she could save her husband's life and secondly she wanted to uphold the dignity of the courtesan's profession as she did. Now listen another story":

Love is Dangerous: It is the story of the adventures of the merchant Ratnadatta of Pundravardhan. He secured the permission of his father to go abroad for a service of king Pratapmukta. On the journey he would depend on his skill in gambling and live on the house of the courtesans. In the course of journey he reached in Vidisa. Where he live in the house of courtesan Lavanyasundari. There he passed the night making love.

Ratnadatta decided to proceed onwards accompanied by Lavanyasundari. Then he reached Manyketa with Lavanysundari he resided in the house of a courtesan Chitralekha.

One day while Ratnadatta was away hunting for a job, the king of Manyaketa to notice Lavanyasundari and fell in love with her. The king sent a messenger and asked to bring her to him, unless Chitralekha lose her nose and ears and even her life. Lavanyasundari heard the threat she went to the king of her own accord. The king enjoyed her company and sent her on the next day with a hundred thousand coins. She accepted the gift on condition that she should be allowed to leave at her own will.

"When a courtesan begin to love in earnest, she lays the foundation for her own destruction, as did Lavanyasundari of Vidisa", said Singaramanjuri's mother. She plead, "So a courtesan should always protect herself from love as from a tiger." Listen another story of king Vikramaditya.

Muladeva Distrusts Women: In Avanti ruled the great king Vikramaditya. There also lived a gentleman scoundrel Muladeva. He was cleaver, a master of roguery. Also an object of king's affections. Many years' experience had taught Muladeva not to trust any women. According to belief of Muladeva, women are fickle minded by nature.

King object and said, women is an instrument to the attainment of the three goals of man's life. She is the abode of happiness, the root of fame, wealth and offspring.

Then Muladeva decided to take, a wife at least to verify the truth of all the ennobling qualities and attribute to a women. Muladeva's married life was not unhappy, yet his suspicions about women he shortly found not only his wife but also the Chief Queen doing sinful and wicked conduct. Finally, Muladeva prove it before the king in presence of both his wife and the Queen.

"Of all these shades, the sentiment of love is being held as the noblest, but few understand how fickle, false and untrue this sentiment is. Love has brought death and dishonour to the high and low; it has disgraced the family of king like Vikramaditya and the householder; it has even put to shame the saintly man." Said Visamasila to Sringaramanjuri.

Courtesan in Bombay: "The Dancing or *Nach Girls* of Bombay are either Hindus or Muhammadans, and are known by the name of *Kalavantis* or women possessed of the *art of Kala* of dancing and singing." These castes and classes most of the professional classes of musicians on which information is available resided in the western part of the Bombay presidency and especially in the Kanara, Ratnagiri and Poona districts and in Goa.

There were a significant number of member to be included in Bombay Presidency census report between 1880-1901. These has been described in detail in the publications in a article 'Bombay Dancing Girl' by K. Raghunathji in the Indian Antiquary (A Journal of Oriental Research) Vol. XIII 1884. Again, Bombay Dancing Girl published in 1890 in book form by the photograph print. Now its almost out of print and rare document. We have change the title as 'Courtesans in Bombay'.

The women courtesans in order to stress the degree of respect they were shown as artists and in order to separate them from the *Vesya* (Prostitutes) who have had a peripheral relationship to the arts in Indian History. Raghunathji's article may have been base on observations on the courtesans tradition in India, both Hindu and Muslim.

I am Standing Water but I am very thirsty

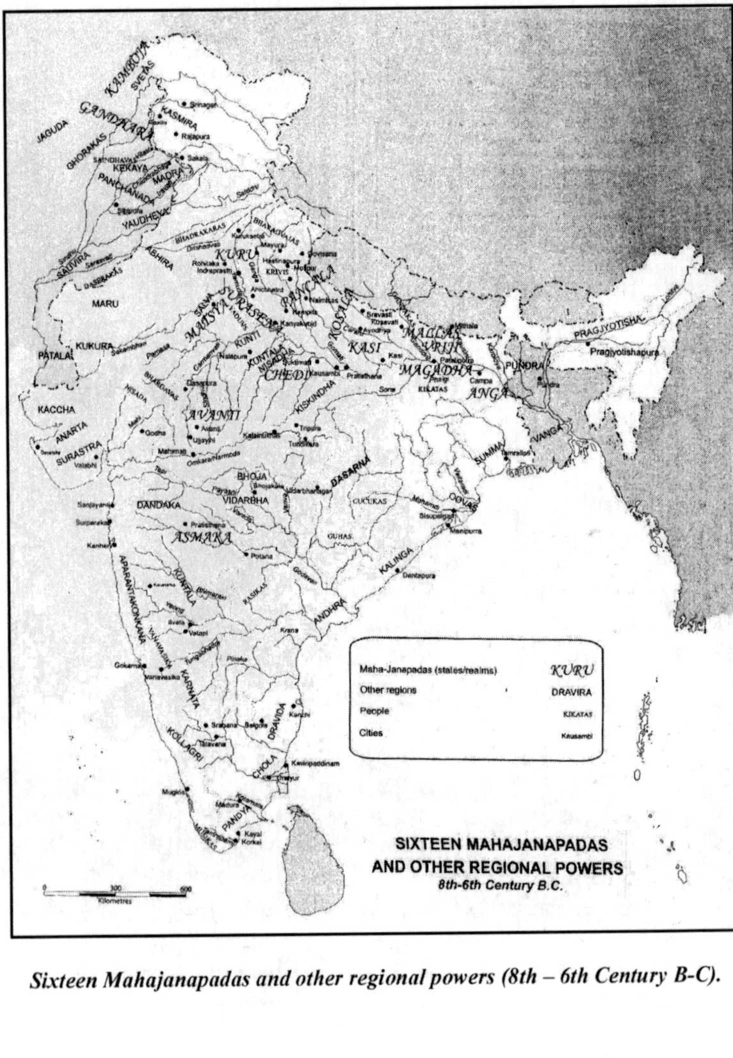

Sixteen Mahajanapadas and other regional powers (8th – 6th Century B-C).

Chapter One

Ascetics and Courtesans

Jan Gonda

Among the Srauta rites which are described in detail by the authors of the *Srautasutra-s* and discussed in other Vedic texts is the Mahabharata. Constituting, in all probability, an ancient and essentially popular old festival of the winter solstice, when the strengthening of the sun was a religious duty, it comprises a number of interesting acts and features, some of which are in nature and purpose as clear as possible. The wives of those engaged in sacrificing start a song in order to obtain offspring. The *hotr* priest has to mount a swing and is swung to and fro to bring the heavenly blessing, gained when he rises in the air, into contact with the earth; girls dance round the fire with water pitchers the contents of which they empty (a well-known rain rite). There is, further, a mimic fight between an Aryan (of fair complexion) and a (dark-skinned) Sudra for the possession of a white, round skin which is no doubt correctly said to be a manifestation of the sun (Kathaka):

tad yad aryena varnena saudram varnam jyapayanty,
etam eva tad, dvisato bhratrvyasya vrnjate

'in that they cause the Sudra class of men to be conquered by the Aryan, thereby they keep this [the sun] from their enemy, their rival' (*Jaim. Br*).

Here the 'divine history' is imitated in order to secure its inherent power, because formerly, i.e. in the mythical *'Urzeit'*, the gods withheld the sun in the same manner from the *asura-s*. According to the *Apast Sr.,* the Sudra has to revile, the Aryan to extol, activities which are, in the *Taitt. S.* commented upon as follows:

ya akrosati punaty evainant sa,
yah prasamsati putesv evannadyam dadhati

he who reviles purifies them [i.e. those participating in the rite], he who extols places food in them after they are purified. The ritual function of abuse and contumelious speech is well known: like blame and disparagement it averts misfortune and the evil powers or leads them astray; it 'purifies', guards against envy and jealousy: scoffing, vilifying and derisive discourses are, the *Satap. Br.* says, 'the attainment of all [things desired]' *(Katyayana Sr).*

These observations lead us to another episode of the Mahabharata ritual which must arrest our attention. A *brahmacarin*—i.e. an Aryan who devotes himself to, concentrates upon, the study of *brahman*, i.e. the Veda, who absorbs the power inherent in it and is thereby initiated into a new life, acquiring a special powerfulness—and a harlot must exchange abuse. The words to be used are handed down by Drahyayana *(Sr. S.):*

sa bruyat duscaritinn avakirnin iti;
dhik tva jalmi pumscali gramasya marjani
purusasya sisnapranejani iti

(the harlot) must say: "you, who have misbehaved! who have violated your vow of continence!"; the *brahmacarin* must answer: "shame upon you! depraved one! harlot! who washes off the village community, who washes off man's member!" These words must in a ritual way be pronounced three times (*Drahy*).

There can be no doubt about the general purpose of this altercation: the mutual insult is offered 'for fertility purposes'. Sexual abuse, smutty talk, insinuations suggesting cohabitation or debauchery and allusions to sexual life in the human sphere are a frequent and widespread means of promoting the fertility of the soil or fecundity in general. During the procession organised, in ancient Greece, as a part of the rites and festivities in honour of Demeter—which were no doubt originally to secure the regular return of germination and ripening—an obligatory slanging match took place from the causeway between Athens and Eleusis. Designedly coarse and foul jests were, for instance during certain ancient Greek religious feasts and holy days, on Shrove Tuesdays, during spring festivities, etc., in various regions of Europe, the verbal equivalent and not rarely the complement of phallic rites and ritual cohabitation which served the same purpose and for which the former might be a substitute.

An ancient description of the Indian Holi festival— 'every brothel…is crowded with customers…; an almost incessant volume of polluted and polluting outcries rises to the skies, might be parallel-ed by many instances of actual and verbal debauchery on comparable occasions in Europe and other parts of the world. Hence also the ribald dialogue between the priests and the women when, in the Asvamedha rite, the chief queen is uniting with the killed horse (*Satap. Br.*). Here it is remarkable that whereas the priests and the 'chamberlain' alternately address the four queens and a girl, it is only the latter who answers; according to part of the texts, instead of the queens her female attendants, daughters of noblemen, reply.

Now, two questions arise: first, are there any indications that in this episode of the Mahabharata rite also, sexual abuse was a substitute for the act itself, and in the second place, how are we to explain the curious couple who at first sight should be surprised at being associated, as partners, by the priestly authorities in the performance of this part of the rite?

In connection with the first question mention must be made of the direction given by one of the authorities immediately after the altercation: 'the harlot and an inhabitant of Magadha enjoy each other carnally, (*Ap. Sr.*). This injunction is based on *Taitt. S.*, where this ritual coition is motivated:

yanti va ete mithunad ye samvatsaram upayanti
antarvedi mithunau sam bhavatah
tenaiva mithunan na yanti

'those who perform the year rite lose their virility [lit. "are separated from copulation"]. There are a pair uniting within the [*maha*] *vedi*— i.e. within the sacrificial ground – verily, they [i.e. the performers of the rite] do not lose their virility.'

The sense is clear: the inhabitant of Magadha and the courtesan have to meet in order to avert the impending impotence of those who perform the rite; the coition of the couple is to preserve and support the virility of the sacrificial community unimpaired. According to one of our sources, the *Kathaka* the purport of this act is to secure the procreative force of the year (*yan mithunam caranti sam-vatsarasyaiva prajananasyopaptyai*). Von Schroeder's suggestion or conclusion that it is the *brahmacarin* who immediately after the altercation has sexual intercourse with the women cannot be substantiated, but this does not prevent us from conjecturing that the inhabitant of Magadha may in the course of time have been substituted for an ascetic *brahman or brahmacarin*. The institution of substitutes is—for instance, in the case of human sacrifices, or when the king must be put to death either at the end of a fixed period or on the appearance of any symptom of bodily decay—well known in the history of religions. In ancient Mesopotamia, for instance, the king had certain unpleasant ritual duties performed by a substitute or 'mock-king'.

Hauers J.W. was no doubt so far right that the texts referring to this rite should not be harmonised or artificially reduced to conformity; they rather point to different stages of development, geographical varieties, etc. Whereas A. B. Kath, obviously refers to a plurality of those cohabiting—as is attested in the case of fertility festivals in many countries, ancient and modern — and *Laty, Sr.* observes that a pair belonging to any class must unite sexually, outside the sacrificial ground, other texts are rather vague: *Taitt. S.*, 'there are a pair uniting…'; *Katy.*, 'cohabitation takes place' *Ait. Ar.*, 'cohabitation of living beings (*bhutanam*) takes place'. Whereas the pair meant in *Apast. Sr. S.* cohabited within the *mahavedi*, the couple mentioned by Latyayana had to perform the same act outside, probably because they did not possess the 'sacredness' inherent in the Magadha and the *pumscali*. That the rite was not much appreciated by the civilised and was abolished early appears from *Sankh. Sr.* where it is called an ancient custom which, being fallen into disuse, is not to be executed (*tad etad puranam utsannam na karyam*).

The Magadhas on the other hand were, no doubt largely because they were not fully brahmanised and felt to be 'uncultivated', of little repute throughout Vedic literature. They were obviously considered to be foreigners, because in the *Atharvaveda* fever is wished away to their country and to other distant regions in the north and the east. There is a curious tradition preserved by *Laty. Sr.* and *Katy. Sr.* the equipment characteristic of the *vratya*—who in all probability was an Aryan, who having neglected the rites and becoming impure by visiting foreign countries, was deprived of the membership of the Aryan community — is given, when the latter is re-admitted into that community, to a merely nominal brahman—if this is the sense of *brahmabandhu*—living in Magadha. In doing so the Vratya transfers his 'guilt' or unworthiness to the person who accepts his possessions (*Panc. Br.*), the giver being henceforth qualified to participate in the Aryan rites. In this connection the commentary attributed to Sayana (on *Panc. Br.*), even speaks of *vratyas* belonging to or born in the country of Magadha (*magadhadesiyebhyo vratyebhyah*). The conclusion seems therefore to be that the Magadhas were outsiders. Now in many countries, strangers or foreigners were looked upon as ritually impure and as bearers of unknown power, for which reason they were duly 'respected' by keeping one's distance. Dangerous tasks such as certain affairs connected with harvest were not rarely assigned to them; that is why fertility and purificatory rites often require the lifting of certain taboos with regard to them. Instances showing that they were even killed as representatives of the 'corn-spirit' or were forced to be a substitute for a man who had to die are not rare. As is well known, the ritual defloration, intended to remove the danger of initial intercourse as well as guarantee the efficiency of sex qualities is frequently performed by a priest or a foreigner, for they are regarded as the potent ones. These beliefs and customs explain also the important role played by foreigners in sacred prostitution. In Tibet the institution of guest prostitution which, being indigenous also in many regions of Asia, is also a facility offered to and accepted by monks, is considered a sort of ritual defloration, to which —if Father M. Hermanns is right— almost all girls are subjected without scandalising their relatives. The role of the inhabitant of Magadha, either in his own right as an 'outsider' or, perhaps, as a substitute for the like-wise potent ascetic *brahmacarin*—offensive rites may be replaced by a more mitigated or even 'symbolic' form—seems therefore perfectly intelligible.

It may be added that a man of Magadha is also coupled with a prostitute (*pumscali*) in which is a rather obscure passage dealing with some attendants and the attire of a *vratya*. When the latter moves to the east, faith is the prostitute; when he goes to the south, dawn; to the west, cheer or comfort; to the north, lightning, the words *sraddha, usah, ird* and *vidyut* being grammatically feminine. In the same order Mitra, the *mantra*, laughter, and thunder are said to be the Magadha, or man of Magadha, the words expressing these ideas being masculine. As lightning and thunder are a well-known pair and laughter may be well associated with cheer or comfort, the harlot and the inhabitant of Magadha were obviously conceived as a pair or a couple. Since the name Magadha-s occurs to denote professional bards or panegyrists — e.g. *Vajas. S.*, where they are, by the way, again associated with prostitutes, the latter being connected with Kama, 'sexual love', the former with 'excessive crying and shouting' which is no doubt explicable from the apotropaeic and cathartic function of noise, music, singing, shouting, etc.—and since itinerant actors were, also in ancient India, not always incorrectly, under the suspicion of loose morality, their wives being hardly distinguished from concubines and prostitutes, this couple as described in the text, may be regarded as based on reality.

The same companions are moreover said to attend the *vratya* in *Baudhayana Sr. S: brahmabandhur amagadho magadhavakyo brahmabandhur apumscalu pumscalu-vakya* 'a male person related to the brahman-s [a nominal brahman, a brahman by birth only], who, though not a Magadha [in the proper sense], is called a Magadha, and a female related to the brahman-s, who though not a prostitute [in the proper sense], is called a 'prostitute'. Both attendants probably had a 'sacred' function.

Whatever the function of the *brahmabandhu* in connection with the *vratya*, he is—probably as a 'substitute'—to perform a ritual duty in *Gobhila Gr. S.*

In describing the Pumsavana rite this text mentions four persons to be considered for the pounding of the *nyagrodha* shoot which is placed in the nostril of the expectant mother: a *brahmacarin*, a wife keeping her vow (of chastity), a *brahmabandhu* and a young girl. In contradistinction to Hauer who is of the opinion that the *brahmacari* has to perform the task in 'orthodox' 'spheres' or regions, the *brahmabandhu* outside the sphere of influence of 'orthodoxy', it would appear to me that the girl and the *brahmabandhu* were to be entrusted with the pounding, if the bearers of the power of chastity were not available. Since a girl may be considered to represent potential sexuality, the *brahmabandhu* may have been credited with the same quality. It may be surmised that this 'connection of brahmans' was by his very birth qualified to perform, as a substitute, ritual acts such as those under discussion.

Let us now turn to the second question. Why must the sexual intercourse be carried out by a *brahmacarin* and a prostitute? Now, with regard to the latter the answer has already been given by those scholars who collected a profusion of material to show that, according to a widespread belief there exists an indubitable solidarity between woman and agriculture, an intimate connection between female fertility and the fecundity of the soil, between cohabitation and fertilisation of the fields, between sexual life in the human sphere and the growth of plants and crops. In many parts of the world the intercourse of the sexes was believed to be, and consciously employed as, a means of ensuring the fruitfulness of the earth. A brief reference to one well-known custom may suffice here: in some parts of Java married couples visit their fields by night and there engage in sexual intercourse for the purpose of promoting the growth of the crop.

From this conviction it follows as a logical consequence that the more unrestrained the sexual intercourse, the more effective it is considered to be, so that all forms of frequent, prolonged or customary cohabitation, including 'prostitution' and collective orgies may be specially conducive to the fertility of nature, the growth of the crops, welfare and happiness, and that, in view of the intimate relation between women and the fertile soil in general, prostitutes are, from a social and economic, and therefore also from a religious point of view valuable members of the community. From a large collection of relative data and text-places collected by J. J. Meyer it indeed appears that for example in Africa prostitutes living all over the country are believed to promote the fertility of the fields in large areas. The rain-compelling ceremonies and festivals connected with the crops of various peoples, for instance, of the Indian Naga tribes, are characterised by general orgies of licence. Meat prepared by the inhabitants of a brothel possessed according to *Carakasamhita*, curative properties and even the earth dug away from the house-door of a prostitute was held to have absorbed her beneficent potency: *Visnudh. Pur., Bhavisyott. Pur.* This earth was according to a Puranic tradition used to rub into part of the body of a king when being consecrated. In many countries harlots were or still are 'objects of luck': compare, e.g. *Visnusmrti,* where fire, courtesans, full jars, flag-staffs, etc., belong to the same category and according to the *Visnudharmott. Pur., ganikas (ca) mahabhagah*, 'highly distinguished courtesans', are together with white flowers, full jars, aquatic animals, cows, gold, etc., included in a survey of the auspicious objects.

Representing sexuality they radiate luck and prosperity and this is, not only in India, one of the reasons why they are so often present at festivals, fertility ceremonies, religious holy days, etc.: the *Bhav. Pur.* informs us that 'prostitutes together with wanton women, causing well-being and prosperity, go from house to house, bestowing unguents for the feet [so that they may walk in happiness]'

(*vesya vilasinisardham svastimanga-lakarini grhad grham vrajanti ca padabhyangapradayini*).

There exist numerous theories to explain the origin of so-called sacred prostitution: it might have been an offering to the deity in order to appease him or to secure blessings for the country and its inhabitants; it provided sexual hospitality to strangers, the good result of the act being enhanced by the co-operation of the god's mortal wives. These factors may have counted, but the most essential feature of this institution may have been that unrestrained cohabitation was performed on the holy premises of the temple in order to preserve virility and fertility and to ensure the increase of man and beast and fruitfulness of the ground.

In explanation of the co-operation of the *brahmacarin* in the above Vedic rite it may be remembered that chastity was so characteristic of those who devoted themselves to the study of, and realisation of their identity with, Brahman that *brahmacarya* may often be translated by 'state of chastity and continence'. Now ascetics are, in India and elsewhere, on the one hand credited with supranormal powers (e.g. MBh) and persons who observe chastity are believed to be able to effect marvellous events and to exert influence upon the unseen. It was on the other hand a reasonable assumption that by their very chastity they accumulated in themselves the sexual power, that they made themselves, so to say, reservoirs of that most important energy which in case of need could be discharged suddenly and completely so as to produce quite uncommon results.

What is, in connection with the subject of this article, of special interest is the custom of observing sexual continence during a certain period before undertaking an important task, performing a rite, engaging in occupations of religious or social consequence—an idea which was not foreign to medieval European legends and poetry in which the hero had to be pure and chaste. Mention may be made of a few instances to illustrate that continence was or even is, also prac-tised with a view to promoting the fertility of the earth. To this day some of the Indian tribes of Central America abstain from sexual intercourse for the purpose of thereby promoting the growth of the crops. Thus, we are told that before sowing the maize the Kekchi Indians sleep apart from their wives, and eat no flesh for five days. Among the Lanquineros and Cajaboneros the period of abstinence extends even to thirteen days. In other countries the same rule is observed during the whole of the time that a man is engaged in sowing, gardening, performing fertility rites, etc. For four days before they committed the seed to the earth the Pipiles of Central America kept apart from their wives 'in order that on the night before planting they might indulge their passions to the fullest extent; certain persons are even said to have been appointed to perform the sexual act at the very moment when the first seeds were deposited in the ground'. Cohabitation at that time was even enjoined upon the people by the priests as a religious duty, in default of which it was not lawful to sow the seed. From the moment that they sowed the maize till the time that they reaped it, the Indians of Nicaragua lived chastely, abstaining also from certain eatables and drinks. That man is, under certain circumstances, willing to restrain his sexual propensity for the sake of food, victory in war or the realisation of other ardent desires may also appear from Indian instances. Chastity is, for instance, frequently observed, among the Nagas (between the Brahmaputra and the Bay of Bengal) by persons intending to hunt dangerous animals, in other communities also by warriors. Chastity, another authority declares in connection with the ceremonial behaviour of the Lhota Nagas, is necessary for men on the night of certain ceremonies, for those engaged in certain important enterprises or occupations, the night before the sowing ceremony and so on. In a considerable number of cases we read also in the Vedic texts that the intending sacrificer must not only fast, sleep on the ground, etc., but also abstain from sexual intercourse. It is undesirable that the consecrated man should lose any potency. Attention may in this connection also be drawn to the horse which is to be sacrificed in the Vedic Asvamedha rite and which is after its death made to copulate with the chief queen: it has during the year of his rovings to be kept away from mares. We might also remember the ancient Indian king himself who must pass the first night of this rite between the legs of his favourite wife without uniting with her.

That there lies great power in sexual purity—a widespread belief which is still alive in modern times even in Europe—is very frequently attested by Sanskrit texts: 'they who keep the vow of chastity accomplish their wishes merely by conceiving them, for instance [the desire to produce] rain, to bestow children…' (*Apast. Dh.*). In the well-known tale of Rsyasrnga who, living in a hermitage, had never seen a woman, it is in the version presented by the *Mahabharata* that his mere presence brings the rain down in streams during a terrible drought in Angaland: *tapaso yah prabhavena varsayamasa. (M. Bh.).* The same version has him—after the rain has come—marry the king's daughter, although it was, curiously enough, a youthful courtesan who had enticed him into the kingdom. It has, no doubt on good grounds, been supposed that in a more original form of the legend it was the princess, Santa, herself who had gone to the forest for the wonder-working youth. And so it reads in Asvaghosa's *Buddhac.* In the *Harivamsa* it is Santa who executes the strategem in company with courtesans (*Har. Visnup.*). That the *Mahabharata* was, however, also acquainted with Santa's role as a seducer appears, where she is stated to have allured the young penitent. I would therefore consider the courtesan to be a 'substitute' for the princess herself in the younger version of the legend. According to a plausible assumption of L. Von Schroeder, it was the sexual union of the couple, not the ascetic's arrival, which in a more original version brought about the rain. There exist indeed 'less polished' Buddhist versions of the same story which make the rain fall as soon as the young ascetic has carried out the copulation. In one of them, the prose story of the *Nalinika Jataka*, the princess, here called Nalinika, overcame through her seductions the virtue of the youth in his hermitage, without bringing him to her father's capital. Yet, the god 'was so delighted that he caused rain to fall throughout the whole kingdom'. An interesting detail is that before the seduction proper the couple engaged in a conversation which for obvious reasons has been omitted in Francis' translation.

There is perhaps also an indication of a direct fertilisation of the earth by a sacred person. In AV, which however is of considerable obscurity, the *brahmacarin*—who is immoderately extolled—is said to pour seed (semen, *retas*) 'upon the surface, on the earth'; 'roaring and thundering the ruddy white-goer has introduced in the earth his great virile member'. Could these words lead us to the conclusion that the circles in which this stanza originated were not completely unacquainted with rites such as are, for instance, executed in some parts of Indonesia where men go naked to their plantations at night and seek to fertilize their clove trees precisely as they would impregnate women, while calling out for 'more cloves', or of the Russian custom where a priest was rolled by women over the sprouting crop?

In this train of thought deities who promote fertility must also be provided with consorts. Hence, for instance such annual rites as the marriage of Sangamesvar, 'the Lord of the sacred river junction', a function of Siva, and Parvati in the Bijapur district and similar rites among tribes of lower culture, e.g. the Kharwars of Chotanagpur. Here is also one of the roots of the frequent representation of the marriage of Siva and Parvati in Indian sculpture.

Following O. C. Ganguly, (*Rupam*, July, 1926) who made an attempt at explaining the so-called obscene sculptures occurring on Hindu temples, other scholars, among whom is also T. Bhattacharyya, collected sufficient material to show that these couples of lovers were 'auspicious symbols'. A passage of uncertain date in the *Agni Pur.* referred to by Bhattacharyya and one in Varahamihira's, *Brhatsamhita* (6th cent. A.D.): 'the remaining part [of the door-jambs] should be decorated with auspicious birds, *svastika* designs, jars, *mithunas* [pairs of lovers], foliage and creepers, etc.', show that this feature of temple sculpture was also known to and enjoined by the theorists. Curiously enough some texts belonging to a later period speak in this connection also of amorous sports of ascetics (*tapasvilila* or *tapakrida*).

The *Mayamata* and the *Silparatna*, for instance, implicitly allow nude figures and the amorous sports of ascetics on all buildings with the exception of dwelling-houses. The *Suprabhedagama*, enjoins the representation of Siva's sports, of Hari's sports (*Sivakrida*, etc.) and in addition to these, that of the 'sports of ascetics'. Though making the correct comment that in actual sculptures we find the figures of these gods engaged in love-making innumerable times, Bhattacharyya is of the opinion that it is difficult to understand why ascetics, famous for their religious pursuits, 'should have been made to perform such repulsive acts'. But why should, then, no objection be made to the representation of gods as amatory couples? Whatever the secondary or 'symbolical' interpretation given of these reliefs—the union of *purusa* and *prakrti* or essence and substance, the ultimate union of the soul with the divine, their more practical function as magico-religious 'lightning-conductors'—it may safely be assumed that these representations of amatory couples—which, as is well known, occurred also on Buddhist monuments even from early times and are sometimes very profusely applied—originate in 'fertility belief, this term being taken in a wide sense, including also the belief in the luck-bringing functions of these reliefs. In this line of thought the representation of an ascetic was for reasons which have already been discussed no doubt hardly less valuable than that of other mighty beings, namely, gods and demi-gods. So the actual occurrence of ascetic figures—the head shaved and a ring of beads in hand—in temple sculptures may have its roots in the same train of thought which led people to perform the fertility rites discussed in this article. It should not however be forgotten that temporary liaisons between ascetics and *apsarases* and stories in which the former are seduced by the latter are not rare in Sanskrit literature. Moreover was not Siva himself enjoying his retreat in the Himalaya whither he retired to be engaged in asceticism and to practise yoga before being subdued by Kama's power and Parvati's loveliness and before engendering the mighty figure of Kumara who alone could destroy the enemies of the gods?

The combination or alternation of chastity and licentiousness is a feature not rarely found in cults of fertility gods. It is, for example, handed down with regard to some instances of sacred prostitution to be performed with foreigners which came within the horizon of ancient Greek authors that this custom was far from being incompatible with chastity in and before wedlock. Obviously the effect of the 'sacred prostitution' was considered to be greater if those young women—who acted as representatives of the goddess herself, repeating what she had done before in the relevant myth—normally abstained from unpermitted sexual indulgence.

A short note may be added on the nudity which is not infrequently characteristic of these figures. This detail may, in my opinion, also be explained from their 'magico-religious' background. The partial or complete nakedness of an officiant was in many countries regarded as an essential condition for the performance of rites intending to influence the unseen powers. How closely connected this topic is with ritual cohabitation may appear from a variety of rites and customs found in many parts of the world. The organs of generation are clearly regarded as the seat of a specific power which can on the one hand be used positively to add efficacy to a rite, and on the other hand become a prophylactic against evil. Hence also the prevalence of phallic motives in amulets, the belief that witches, when engaged in their practices, go about naked; the nudity of the Sumerian priests when celebrating has in this connection often been referred to. In India, among both Hindus and aboriginal tribes nudity was often required in rites for curing paralysis in cattle or stopping rain. A legend current in the Himalaya tells that the wives of the Rsis used to dance naked before Siva-Mahadeva. Fertility deities were sometimes worshipped by circumambulating a tree in a nude state. These dances might be accompanied by obscene songs. In many countries ceremonies to obtain rain were often carried out in a state of complete nudity. 'In time of drought the Meitheis, headed by their raja, strip themselves of all their clothes and stand in the roadways of Imphal cursing one another to the full extent of expressive language'. Siva's phallus is on the other hand, like the great monolithic phalli of ancient times, supposed to have influence over the fall of rain and the fertility of the fields. These monuments often are to perpetuate the radiating force of the idea underlying ritual act.

The Chanter of the Samaveda and the Courtesan; In another place a Brahman who had got eight gold *mashas* (Both *masha* and *pana* (mentioned above) are really ancient native Indian weights: 16 *mashas* = *pana*. As the *pana* was usually of copper or silver, it seems probable that the gold *masha* only exists in fiction) as a present, a chanter of the Sama Veda, received the following piece of advice from a man who was a bit of a *roué*:— "You get enough to live upon by your position as a Brahman, so you ought now to employ this gold for the purpose of learning the way of the world in order that you may become a knowing fellow." The fool said: "Who will teach me?" Thereupon the *roue* said to him: "This lady (Courtesan) named Chaturika: go to her house." The Brahman said: "What am I to do there?" The *roue* replied: "Give her gold, and in order to please her make use of some *sama*" (The *vita* or *roue* meant "conciliation," but the chanter of the Sama Veda took it to mean "hymn"). When he heard this, the chanter went quickly to the house of Chaturika ; when he entered, the lady advanced to meet him and he took a seat. Then that Brahman gave her the gold and faltered out the request: "Teach me now for this fee the way of the world." Thereupon the people who were there began to titter, and he, after reflecting a little, putting his hands together in the shape of a cow's ear, so that they formed a kind of pipe, began, like a stupid idiot, to chant with a shrill sound the Sama Veda, so that all the *roues* in the house came together to see the fun; and they said: "Whence has this jackal blundered in here? Come, let us quickly give him the half-moon on his throat." Thereupon the Brahman, supposing that the half-moon meant an arrow with a head of that shape, and afraid of having his head cut off, rushed out of the house, bellowing out: "I have learnt the way of the world." Then he went to the man who had sent him and told him the whole story. He replied: "When I told you to use *sama* I meant coaxing and wheedling. What is the propriety of introducing the Veda in a matter of this kind? The fact is, I suppose, that stupidity is engrained in a man who muddles his head with the Vedas." So he spoke, bursting with laughter all the while, and went off to the lady's house and said to her: "Give back to that two-legged cow his gold-fodder." So she, laughing, gave back the money, and when the Brahman got it he went back to his house as happy as if he had been born again.

Chapter Two

Jataka: Stories of Courtesans

Kanavera-Jataka

"'Twas the joyous time," etc.—This was a story told by the Master at Jetavana, about a Brother who was tempted by thoughts of the wife he had left.—The circumstances that led up to the story will be set forth in the Indriya Birth.—The Master, addressing this Brother, said, "Once before, through her, you had your head cut off." And then he related a legend of the past.

Once upon a time, when Brahmadatta was reigning in Benares, the Bodhisatta was born in a village of Kasi in the home of a certain house-holder, under the star of a robber. When he grew up to be a man, he gained his living by robbery, and his fame was blazed abroad in the world, as a bold fellow and as strong as an elephant. And no man could catch him. One day he broke into a rich merchant's house and carried off much treasure. The townsfolk came to the king and said, "Sire, a mighty robber is plundering the city: have him arrested." The king ordered the governor of the city to seize him. So in the night the governor posted men here and there in detachments, and having effected his capture with the money upon him, he reported it to the king. The king bade the governor cut off his head. Then the governor had his arms tightly bound behind him, and having tied a wreath of red kanavera flowers about his neck and sprinkled brickdust on his head, had him scourged with whips in every square, and then led to the place of execution to the music of the harsh-sounding drum. Men said, "This rapacious robber who loots our city is taken," and the whole city was greatly moved.

At this time there lived in Benares a courtesan named Sama, whose price was a thousand pieces of money. She was a favourite of the king's, and had a suite of five hundred female slaves. And as she stood at an open window on the upper floor of the palace, she saw this robber being led along. Now he was comely and gracious to look upon, and stood forth above all men, exceedingly glorious and god-like in appearance. And when she saw him being thus led past, she fell in love with him and thought within herself, "By what device can I secure this man for my husband?" "This is the way," she said, and sent by the hand of one of her female attendants a thousand pieces of money to the governor, and "Tell him," she said, "this robber is Sama's brother, and he has no other refuge except in Sama. And ask him to accept the money and let his prisoner escape." The handmaid did as she was told. But the Governor said, "This is a notorious robber, I cannot let him go free after this sort. But if I could find another man as a substitute, I could put the robber in a covered carriage and send him to you." The slave came and reported this to her mistress.

Now at this time a certain rich young merchant, who was enamoured of Sama, presented her every day with a thousand pieces of money. And that very day at sunset her lover came as usual to her house with the money. And Sama took the money and placed it in her lap and sat weeping. And when she was asked what was the cause of her sorrow, she said, "My lord, this robber is my brother, though he never came to see me, because people say I follow a vile trade: when I sent a message to the governor he sent word that if he were to receive a thousand pieces of money, he would let his prisoner go free. And now I cannot find any one to go and take this money to the governor." The youth for the love he bare her said, "I will go." "Go, then," said she, "and take with you the money you brought me." So he took it and went to the house of the governor.

The governor hid the young merchant in a secret place, and had the robber conveyed in a close carriage to Sama. Then he thought, "This robber is well known in the country. It must be quite dark first.

And then, when all men are retired to rest, I will have the man executed." And so making some excuse for delaying it awhile, when people had retired to rest, he sent the young merchant with a large escort to the place of execution, and cutting off his head with a sword impaled his body, and returned into the city.

Thenceforth Sama accepted nought at any other man's hand, but passed all her time, taking her pleasure with this robber only. The thought occurred to the robber: "If this woman should fall in love with any one else, she will have me too put to death, and take her pleasure with him. She is very treacherous to her friends. I must no longer dwell here, but make haste to escape." When he was going away, he thought, "I will not go empty-handed, but will take some of the ornaments belonging to her." So one day he said to her, "My dear, we always stay indoors like tame cockatoos in a cage. Some day we will disport ourselves in the garden." She readily assented and prepared every kind of food, hard and soft, and decked herself out with all her ornaments, and drove to the garden with him seated in a close carriage. While he was disporting himself with her, he thought, "Now must be the time for me to escape." So under a show of violent affection for her, he entered into a thicket of kanavera bushes, and pretending to embrace her, he squeezed her till she became insensible. Then throwing her down he spoiled her of all her ornaments, and fastening them in her outer garment he placed the bundle on his shoulder, and leaping over the garden wall made off.

And when she had recovered consciousness, rising up she went and asked her attendants, what had become of her young lord. "We do not know, lady." "He thinks," she said, "I am dead, and must in his alarm have run away." And being distressed at the thought, she returned thence to her house, and said, "Not till I have set eyes on my dear lord, will I rest upon a sumptuous couch," and she lay down upon the ground. And from that day she neither put on comely garments, nor ate more than one meal, nor affected scents and wreaths and the like. And being resolved to seek and recover her lover by every possible means, she sent for some actors and gave them a thousand pieces of money. On their asking, "What are we to do for this, lady?" She said, "There is no place that you do not visit. Go then to every village, town and city, and gathering a crowd around you, first of all sing this song in the midst of the people,"—teaching the actors the first stanza,— "And if," said she, "when yon have sung this song, my husband shall be one of the crowd, he will speak to you. Then you may tell him I am quite well, and bring him back with you. And should be refuse to come, send me a message."

And giving them their expenses for the journey, she sent them off. They started from Benares, and calling the people together here and there, at last arrived at a border-village. Now the robber, since his flight, was living here. And the actors gathered a crowd about them, and sang the first stanza:—

"Twas the joyous time of spring,
Bright with flowers each shrub and tree,
From her swoon awakening
Sama lives, and lives for thee.

The robber on hearing this drew nigh to the actor, and said, "You say that Sama is alive, but I do not believe it." And addressing him he repeated the second stanza:

Can fierce winds a mountain shake?
Can they make firm earth to quake?
But alive the dead to see
Marvel stranger far would be!

The actor on hearing these words uttered the third stanza:

Sama surely is not dead,
Nor another lord would wed.
Fasting from all meals but one,
She loves thee and thee alone.

The robber on hearing this said, "Whether she be alive or dead, I don't want her," and with these words he repeated the fourth stanza:

Sama's fancy ever roves
From tried faith to lighter loves:
Me too Sama would betray,
Were I not to flee away.

The actors came and told Sama how he had dealt with them. And she, full of regrets, took once more to her old course of life.

The Master, when his lesson was ended, revealed the Truths and identified the Birth:— At the conclusion of the Truths the worldly-minded Brother attained to fruition of the First Path:— "At that time this Brother was the rich merchant's son, the wife he had left was Sama, and I myself was the robber."

Sulasa – Jataka

"*Here is a golden necklace*" etc.—The Master told this tale while dwelling in Jetavana, concerning a female servant of Anathapindika. The story is that one feast-day, when she was going with a number of fellow-servants to a pleasure-garden, she asked her mistress Pannalakkhanadevi for an ornament to wear. Her mistress gave her an ornament of her own, worth a hundred thousand pieces. She put it on and went along with the other servants to the pleasure-garden. A certain thief coveted the ornament, and with the design of killing her and taking it he began talking to her, and in the garden he gave her fish, flesh and strong drink. "He does it, I suppose, because he desires me," she thought, and at evening when the others lay down to rest after their sports, she rose and went to him. He said, "Mistress, this place is not private; let us go a little farther." She thought, "Anything private can be done in this place: no doubt he must be anxious to kill me and take what I am wearing: I'll teach him a lesson:" so she said, "Master, I am dry owing to the strong drink: get me some water," and taking him to a well asked him to draw some water, showing him the rope and bucket. The thief let down the bucket. Then as he was stooping to draw up the water, the girl, who was very strong, pushed him bard with both bands and threw him into the well. "You won't die that way," she said, and threw a large brick upon his head. He died on the spot. When she came back to the town and gave her mistress the ornament, she said, "I have very nearly been killed today for that ornament," and told the whole story. The mistress told Anathapindika, and he told the Tathagata. The Master said, "Householder, this is not the first time that servant girl has been endowed with wits rising to the occasion; she was so

before also: it is not the first time she killed that man; she did it once before," and at Anathapindika's request, he told the tale of old.

Once upon a time when Brahmadatta was reigning in Benares, there was a beautiful woman of the town, called Sulasa, who had a train of five-hundred courtesans, and whose price was a thousand pieces a night. There was in the same city a robber named Sattuka, as strong as an elephant, who used to enter rich men's houses at night and plunder at will. The townsmen assembled and complained to the king. The king ordered the city-watch to post bands here and there, have the robber caught and cut off his head. They bound his hands behind his back and led him to the place of execution, scourging him in every square with whips. The news that he was taken excited the whole city. Sulasa was standing at a window, and looking down on the street she saw the robber, loved him at sight and thought, "If I can free that stout fighting-man, I will give up this bad life of mine and live respectably with him." In the way described in the Kanavera Birth she gained his freedom by sending a thousand pieces to the chief constable of the city and then lived with him in delight and harmony. The robber after three or four months thought, "I shall never be able to stay in this one place: but one can't go empty-handed: Sulasa's ornaments are worth a hundred thousand pieces: I will kill her and take them." So he said to her one day, "Dear, when I was being hauled along by the king's men, I promised an offering to a tree-deity on a mountain-top, who is now threatening me because I have not paid it; let us make an offering." "Very well, husband, prepare and send it." "Dear, it will not do to send it, let us both go and present it, wearing all our ornaments and with a great retinue." "Very well, husband, we'll do so."

He made her prepare the offering and when they reached the mountain-foot, he said, "Dear, the deity, seeing this crowd of people, will not accept the offering; let us two go up and present it." She consented, and he made her carry the vessel. He was himself armed to the teeth, and when they reached the top, he set the offering at the foot of a tree which grew beside a precipice a hundred times as high as a man, and said, "Dear, I have not come to present the offering, I have come with the intention of killing you and going away with all your ornaments: take them all off and make a bundle of them in your outer garment." "Husband, why would you kill me?" "For your money." "Husband, remember the good I have done you: when you were being hauled along in chains, I gave up a rich man's son for you and paid a large sum and saved your life: though I might get a thousand pieces a day, I never look at another man: such a benefactress I am to you: do not kill me, I will give you much money and be your slave." With these entreaties she spoke the first stanza:—

> Here is a golden necklace, and emeralds and pearls,
> Take all and welcome: give me place among thy servant girls.

When Sattuka had spoken the second stanza in accordance with his purpose, to wit—

> Fair lady, lay thy jewels down and do not weep so sore:
> I'll kill thee: else I can't be sure thou'lt give me all thy store:—

Sulasa's wits rose to the occasion, and thinking, "This robber will not give me my life, but I'll take his life first by throwing him down the precipice in some way," she spoke the two stanzas:—

> Within my years of sense, within my conscious memory,
> No man on earth, I do protest, have I loved more than thee.
>
> Come hither, for my last salute, receive my last embrace:
> For never more upon the earth shall we meet face to face.

Sattuka could not see her purpose, so he said, "Very well, dear; come and embrace me." Sulasa walked round him in respectful salutation three times, kissed him, and saying, "Now, husband, I am going to make obeisance to you on all four sides," she put her head on his foot, did obeisance at his sides, and went behind him as if to do obeisance there: then with the strength of an elephant she took him by the hinder parts and threw him head over heels down that place of destruction a hundred times as high as a man. He was crushed to pieces and died on the spot. Seeing this deed, the deity who lived on the mountain-top spoke these stanzas:

> Wisdom at times is not confined to men:
> A woman can shew wisdom now and then

Wisdom at times is not confined to men:
Women are quick in counsel now and then.

How quick and keen she was the way to know,
She slew him like a deer with full-stretched bow.

He that to great occasion fails to rise
Falls, like that dull thief from the precipice.

One prompt a crisis in his fate to see,
Like her, is saved from threatening enemy.

So Sulasa killed the robber. When she descended from the mountain and came among her attendants, they asked where her husband was. "Don't ask me," she said, and mounting her chariot she went on to the city.

After the lesson, the Master identified the Birth: "At that time the two then were the same two now, the deity was myself."

Atthana – Jataka

***"Make Ganges calm" etc.*—The Master told this tale while dwelling in Jetavana, concerning a backsliding Brother. The Master asked him, "Is the story true, Brother, that you are backsliding?" "Yes, lord." "What is the cause?" "The power of desire." "Brother, womankind are ungrateful, treacherous, untrustworthy: of old wise men could not satisfy a woman, even by giving her a thousand pieces a day: and one day when she did not get the thousand pieces she had them taken by the neck and cast out so ungrateful are womankind: do not fall into the power of desire for such a cause," and so he told an old tale.**

Once upon a time when Brahmadatta was reigning in Benares, his son, young Brahmadatta, and young Mahadhana, son of a rich merchant of Benares, were comrades and playfellows, and were educated in the same teacher's house. The prince became king at his father's death: and the merchant's son abode near him. There was in Benares a certain courtesan, beautiful and prosperous. The merchant's son gave her a thousand pieces daily, and took pleasure with her constantly; at his father's death he succeeded to the rich merchant's position, and did not forsake her, still giving her a thousand pieces daily. Three times a day he went to wait upon the king.

One day he went to wait upon him in the evening. As he was talking with the king, the sun set, and it became dark. As he left the palace, he thought, "There is no time to go home and come back again: I will go straight to the courtesan's house:" so he dismissed his attendants, and entered her house alone. When she saw him, she asked if he had brought the thousand pieces. "Dear, I was very late today; so I sent away my attendants without going home, and have come alone; but tomorrow I will give you two thousand pieces." She thought, "If I admit him today, he will come empty-handed on other days, and so my wealth will be lost: I won't admit him this time." So she said, "Sir, I am but a courtesan: I do not give my favours without a thousand pieces; you must bring the sum." "Dear, I will bring twice the sum to-morrow," and so he begged her again and again. The courtesan gave orders to her maids, "Don't let that man stand there and look at me: take him by the neck, and cast him out, and then shut the door." They did so.

He thought, "I have spent on her eighty crores of money; yet on the one day when I come empty-handed, she has me seized by the neck and cast out: Oh, womankind are wicked, shameless, ungrateful, treacherous:" and so he pondered and pondered on the bad qualities of womankind, till he felt dislike and disgust, and became discontented with a layman's life. "Why should I lead a layman's life? I will go this day and become an ascetic," he thought: so without going back to his house or seeing the king again, he left the city and entered the forest: he made a hermitage on the Ganges bank, and there made his abode as an ascetic, reaching the Perfection of Meditation, and living on wild roots and fruits.

The king missed his friend and asked for him. The courtesan's conduct had become known throughout the city: so they told the king of the matter, adding, "O king, they say that your friend through shame did not go home, but has become an ascetic in the forest." The king summoned the courtesan, and asked if the story were true about her treatment of his friend. She confessed. "Wicked, vile woman, go quickly to where my friend is and fetch him: if you fail, your life is forfeit."

She was afraid at the king's words; she mounted a chariot and drove out of the city with a great retinue; she sought for his abode and hearing of it by report, went there and saluted and prayed, "Sir, bear with the evil I did in my blindness and folly: I will never do so again." "Very well, I forgive you; I am not angry with you." "If you forgive me, mount the chariot with me: we will drive to the city, and as soon as we enter it I will give you all the money in my house." When he heard her, he replied, "Lady, I cannot go with you now: but when something that cannot happen in this world will happen, then perhaps I may go;" and so he spoke the first stanza:—

Make Ganges calm like lotus-tank, cuckoos pearl-white to see,
Make apples bear the palm-trees' fruit: perchance it then might be.

But she said again, "Come; I am going." He answered, "I will go." "When?" "At such and such a time," he said and spoke the remaining stanzas:—

When woven out of tortoise-hair a triple cloth you see,
For winter wear against the cold, perchance it then may be.

When of mosquito's teeth you build a tower so skilfully,
That will not shake or totter soon, perchance it then may be.

When out of horns of hare you make a ladder skilfully,
Stairs that will climb the height of heaven, perchance it then may be.

When mice to mount those ladder-stairs and eat the moon agree,
And bring down Rahu from the sky, the thing perchance may be.

When swarms of flies devour strong drink in pitchers full and free,
And house themselves in burning coals, the thing perchance may be.

When asses get them ripe red lips and faces fair to see,
And shew their skill in song and dance, the thing perchance may be.

When crows and owls shall meet to talk in converse privily,
And woo each other, lover-like, the thing perchance may be.

When sun-shades, made of tender leaves from off the forest tree,
Are strong against the rushing rain, the thing perchance may be.

When sparrows take Himalaya in all its majesty,
And bear it in their little beaks, the thing perchance may be.

And when a boy can carry light, with all its bravery,
A ship full-rigged for distant seas, the thing perchance may be.

So the Great Being spoke these eleven stanzas to fix impossible *(atthana)* conditions. The courtesan, hearing him, won his forgiveness and went back to Benares. She told the matter to the king, and begged for her life, which was granted.

After the lesson, the Master said, "So, Brethren, womankind are ungrateful and treacherous"; then he declared the Truths, and identified the Birth:— After the Truths, the backsliding Brother was established in the fruition of the First Path:— "At that time the king was Ananda, the ascetic was myself."

Vasantasena's Vesyalays, Maholi, National Museum New Delhi.

Chapter Three

Kamma Katha : Sagara

Marriage of Carudatta and his Entry into a Prostitute's House

(CARUDATTA'S NARRATIVE)

Once my mother went to the house of her brother, Savvattha, who had a beautiful daughter named Mittavati. At meal time my mother was asked to stay on, but she wanted to return home, saying that she had a lot of work to do. My uncle remarked, "Why are you being so cold? Even if you cannot put up with your sister-in-law you should at least favour me."

She replied, "If you give me your daughter then our affection will continue, otherwise it will break off now."

He bowed down and said, "Who else has the right over my daughter except you? If you are pleased with me, then she is yours."

Hearing this my mother became happy. After having her meals she returned home. She told the elder members of the royal house about her brother's promise.

At that time my father was in the royal house. Flowers and perfumes were given to well-wishers of the family. When my father returned he was congratulated and praised for obtaining the girl.

In answer to my father's question my mother replied that her brother Savvattha had given Mittavati to her.

My father remarked, "You have not done good by accepting this girl, as Caru has only recently learnt the arts, and due to attachment to worldly pleasures his knowledge will slacken."

But my mother retorted, "Why do you disregard the girl thus obtained?"

All this was reported to me by the maid-servants.

Then on an auspicious day, and a time approved by an astrologer, the ceremony of holding hand was performed. Mittavati was subjected to ceremonies in accordance with her family customs. I enjoyed the music dance and painting. Once Mittavati went to her father's house. There her mother, my maternal aunt, gave her own ornaments. She gave her a bath, dressed her up, fed her and then sent her back. My aunt retained the ornaments which we had given Mittavati. When my uncle returned home in the evening, my aunt showed him the ornaments given by the parents-in-law, saying that she had given her own to her daughter.

The maternal uncle remarked, "Why did you not give these to her at the time of her marriage? Now they will say that you have exchanged them!"

She said, "I shall return them in the morning."

The next morning my maternal aunt called on us. I had gone to the teacher at that time. Mittavati got up and went to my mother. After returning the ornaments my maternal aunt saw that her daughter's unguent was undisturbed.

She asked her, "O daughter! Caru was not here tonight? Or is he angry with you? Why were you staying alone?" After keeping quiet for a long time, the daughter replied, "After giving me to a devil, now you ask me?"

Hearing this my mother said with annoyance, "Oh! Caru, expert in seventy-two arts, is your devil?"

Mittavati replied, "O aunty! don't get excited. One who is indifferent, dances alone, sings alone, greets anyone and laughs, how can he be called natural? If something is bad and it leads to unhappiness, no favour will ever be shown to me."

Hearing her words my mother-in-law tearfully told my mother, "Knowingly you have taken revenge on me, since you never told me the defects of your son."

My mother replied, "let it be. It is not proper that you should join your daughter in speaking badly of my son. I'll show you something you'll remember for a long time. You get away, do not stay before me."

Depressed in mind my aunt went away to her home.

At his wife's advice Savvattha, my uncle, came, and told my mother, "Why don't you do something for Caru? Why are you spoiling him?"

My mother scolded him, "You should look after your daughter and wife so that they are not seized by the devil! Having listened to your wife, you now want to inflame me! You get away from here, otherwise you will be outwitted." He went away.

This too was jokingly reported to me by the maid-servant in charge of the bed-chamber.

My mother got angry. She called for my friends Gomuha and others and told them, "Do me a favour and make Caru enter the house of a prostitute."

Gomuha replied, "Mother! father will be angry, and once fallen into an evil, it will be difficult to get him out. So enough of his entry into such a house."

She said, "If the merchant is angry he will be angry with me. Do what I tell you without opposition. You are talking of the evil, 'one who falls into bad habits will destroy his health', but my long-thought desire was 'how my son will be able to enjoy my wealth', and now the chance has come. If he destroys our wealth for a prostitute my desire will be fulfilled."

They agreed. This conversation was reported to me by the maid-servant, who said, "O noble one! Now you will stay in a prostitute's house and it will be difficult to see you."

After a few days, my friends requested me, "O Caru! Let us go to the garden. There we shall have our meals and play before returning."

I said, "If there is going to be a feast, why didn't you inform me beforehand?"

They replied, "We were occupied elsewhere. Anyway it's not your feast, so why should you be distinguished?"

I went with them. We reached the garden. Saying that I was feeling thirsty, I sat down to rest at a place sheltered by trees.

Harisiha went down to a nearby pond and after a short while he called out to me, "O come! See something wonderful!"

I went there and nearing the pond, I said, "Tell me, what wonder you have seen?"

Pointing out to the beautiful lotuses which seemed to have stolen the charm of a young lady he said, "Look, I have seen some extraordinary mead in the lotuses beautiful as rubies *(kamalraga)*. What could it be?"

After reflecting for a long time Gomuha remarked, "This must be the lotus mead *(pokkharamadhu)* enjoyed by the gods, which has somehow been produced here. Collect it in a lotus leaf without delay."

It was collected. Then a conversation ensued amongst them about what should be done with the lotus mead, so rare for human beings.

Harisiha came out with a suggestion: "Why should we not approach the king? He will be pleased and will provide us with livelihood."

"But kings are difficult to contact and even if contacted, are not pleased easily," remarked Varaha. "So let's give it to the minister; he can be useful to us."

"But what have we to do with the minister?" interjected Tamantaga.

"The ministers are always ready to add to the wealth of the royal treasury so they can be pleased with wealth and not with the rare things."

"Let us give it to the city-guards," suggested Marubhui. "Because of his untimely movements he could be useful to us and become our friend," he added.

"You are all ignorant," interjected Gomuha, "Caru is our king, our minister and our city-guard. He accomplishes all our works.

He deserves the rare thing which we have procured. It is by his favour and kindness that we exist."

"Then all of them addressed to me and said, "Please may your Honour drink it."

I said, "Don't you know that I have been born in a family to which the taste of honey, flesh and drink is unknown? You want me to drink honey?"

"We know that," replied Gomuha. "Why should we force you to an unworthy act? But this is not wine, it is nector which they say is meant for divine beings. You should drink it without opposition, in good conscience. This will not violate the rules of conduct."

Then, O Caru! directed by the words of my dear friends, I agreed to have it. I washed my hands and feet, rinsed my mouth facing the east and assuming it to be nector, I drank the mead in a lotus leaf cup. It refreshed my whole body and I felt satisfied.

When I finished drinking my friends told me, "You go ahead and take rest. In the meantime we shall pick up the flowers."

I set out. The drink was extraordinary and as it started producing intoxication I felt as if the trees were moving around. I reflected, "Is it the effect of nector or by some stratagem have they made me drink wine?"

As I was reflecting in this manner I saw a lady in the prime of her youth, decorated with valuable jewellery and dressed in pure silken garments. She was sitting under an *asoka* tree. She motioned me with her fingers and I went to her. I thought, "Who could this beautiful lady be?"

She said, "Welcome to you!"

I asked her, "Who are you, O fair lady?"

She replied, "I am a female divinity, I have been sent to you by the lord of gods in order to serve you."

"But the lord of gods doesn't even know me, how could he send you to me?" I asked.

"The merchant, your father, is well-known," She answered, "He has sent me to show his love towards your father."

She continued. "You don't have to worry, we don't show ourselves to everybody, and furthermore the people we don't favour are not able to see us. If you don't believe me, just look at your friends – they can't see me and because of my power are not able to see you as well. You simply remain quiet."

Although my friends were quite near me, they did not notice me, and after calling for me again and again, they went ahead. After going a little distance they returned, all saying that I had not gone ahead. They thought I might have returned and they went away crying, "O Caru! where are you?"

She said, "Look at my power, now they will see you."

They saw me and said, "Where were you?, We were calling you but you weren't to be seen."

I replied, "I was right here."

They said, "Let's go." I started, but was staggering with intoxication. The lady told me, "Your friends cannot see you, be at ease."

She held my arm and head with her right hand. With staggering feet I took support of her neck. At the touch of her body I thought that she must be a female divinity of Indra, and my whole body was a thrilled. Held by her and in the company of my friends I reached the dining place, where servants already awaited. We were seated and the food was served to us. She sat with me on the same seat. I was feeling drowsy and as if in the dream. I could hear their words, "We have offered him to you."

I was made to sit in a carriage and was taken to her house. She helped me down from the carriage. I was surrounded by young ladies of equal age. She said to me, "O merchant's son! you have been brought to my house *(vimana, a palace with seven stories)*, now you should enjoy pleasures with me at your ease."

Then the young ladies surrounded me like an elephant by she-elephants, speaking charming words and holding my hand. They sang songs and I was led to an inner chamber.

Now I was sure that she was a female divinity. Attached to sexual pleasures, I slept. After the effects of intoxication were over, I got up in the morning and noticed the house of Vasantatilaka.

Then I asked her, "Whose house is this?"

"It is mine," she answered.

"But it is like a house of human beings, and not of someone divine," I said.

She replied, "If it is, then listen, I am telling you the truth: "O merchant's son! I am Vasantatilaka, daughter of a prostitute. In my childhood I passed my time in learning the arts. I am not greedy of wealth, I love virtues. I had chosen you from my heart. With the advice of your mother, your friends Gomuha and others have entrusted you to me by means of a strategy."

Saying these words she got up and changed her clothes. Then she approached me and requested me with folded hands, "O merchant's son! I am at your service, accept me as your wife. These silken clothes of mine indicate my virginity. I shall be your life-long devotee."

Due to my close relations with her I replied, "O fair lady! whether you submit or not you are my wife."

I passed my time with her freely. She showed me the articles meant for sensual pleasures which my mother had sent. Her daily fees was one thousand and on festive occasions she charged one hundred thousand and eight.

Enjoying myself with her in this way, infatuated by the happiness of sexual pleasures, twelve years passed.

Once after having a drink I was sleeping with my beloved. Suddenly I got up, fanned by cool breezes, and did not see Vasantatilaka. I got up and as I was reflecting where I was, I noticed a ghost-house *(bhuya-graha)* built at the entrance of the road. I recognised the place having seen it before, I realised that I had been taken there and abandoned by the prostitute, and I knew that I should return home unnoticed by anyone.

It was morning. I set out for my home. While entering the house, I was stopped by the doorkeeper.

He said, "Don't enter, who are you?"

I asked, "O gentle sir, whose house is this?"

He replied, "It belongs to the merchant Ramadeva."

I said, "Doesn't it belong to the merchant Bhanu?"

He replied, "His son Charudatta has turned wicked, who dwells in the house of a prostitute. So overpowered with sorrow, Bhanu gave up the house and has joined the ascetic order. After the wealth was exhausted, his wife mortgaged *(adatta)* her house and has gone to her brother's to live."

This conversation was overheard by Ramadeva, who was inside the house. He asked the doorkeeper who it was outside.

The doorkeeper replied, "Somebody is inquiring after the house of the merchant Bhanu. Maybe he is his son."

Ramadeva replied, "Don't let this shameless person enter my house."

I felt ashamed and overwhelmed with sorrow, I quickly left that place and reached the house of my maternal uncle. I went inside, and there I saw my mother poorly dressed and with distressed and dejected face. I fell at her feet.

She asked me, "Who are you?"

"Carudatta," I replied.

Then she held me and started crying *(parunna sa)*. Hearing her cry arrived Savvattha and he too started crying. We were consoled by the relatives.

Mittavati appeared in unclean clothes. She appeared as graceless as a decayed wall painting. She fell to my feet and started crying.

I told her, "No more crying! You are tormented by your own actions," and I consoled her.

Then some chaff of rice was brought and food was prepared.

After having food I asked my mother, "O mother! what has happened to all the remaining wealth?"

She replied, "I do not know about the amount which was in the treasury *(nihanapautta)* or given on interest *(vaddhipautta)* or that which was given to the relatives. When the merchant joined the ascetic order, the money that was given to the servants was lost. Sixteen crores of gold was spent for your pleasures. We carried on somehow or other.

I said, "Mother! People are calling me worthless, and I am unable to live here, Therefore, I shall go far away and will return after earning money. I am sure by your good grace I shall be able to do so."

She said, "O child! You are ignorant of doing business. And how will you live in a foreign country? We both are here and will take care of you."

I replied, "Mother! Don't speak like this. I am the son of the merchant Bhanu, how can I just stay here like that? Do not think in this manner, allow me to go." "Alright my son!" she said, "Let me consult Savvattha."

SAMBA AND HIS LOVE FOR A COURTESAN'S DAUGHTER

Once when Kanha had gone to the house of Saccabhama she told him, "O Lord! The women who are not highly esteemed by their husbands give birth only to inactive and impotent children, whereas those who are loved by their husbands bear children similar to the husband in beauty and virtue. I am not liked by you, whereas Ruppini is highly esteemed; that is why you have given her a son, distinguished on the earth surrounded by three oceans."

Kanha Vasudeva replied, "O Queen! Do not speak like this. You are the eldest of all in my whole harem, why should you say such things?" Saccabhama answered, "If it is so, then give me a son like Pajjunna."

"If that is your desire," said Kanha, "I shall propitiate the god Harinegamesi Harinegamesi or Negamesi was one of the commanders-in-chief (*payattaniyahivai-Kalpa,*) of the celestial infantry of Indra who played an important role in the conception and birth legend of Mahavira by removing him from the womb of Devananda, a Brahman woman, and putting him in the womb of Trisala, a Ksatriya woman *(naigamesapahrta),* so that your desire will be fulfilled."

Having informed the elders, Kanha then entered the fasting-house (*posahasala*) for three days' fast (*atthamabhatta*). The god was set in motion. He appeared on the scene and asked what boon was wanted. Kanha replied, "The queen desires a son like Pajjunna, kindly favour her." Negamesi remarked, "Whoever concieves first by you will give birth to a son like him. Have her put on this necklace." Saying this the god went away.

This news reported to Pajjunna by *Pannatti,* (*Maharohini, Pannatti, Gori, Vijjumuhi, Mahajala, Tirikkhamani, Bahuruva* and others are mentined as chief *vidyas).* Pajjunna learned that after doing his penance Kanha had gone to the bedchamber. Pajjunna was worried, and said to himself, "Saccabhama is jealous of my mother, and if she gives birth to a son like me, I can never be friendly with him. What should I do?" Then he thought, "But Queen Jambavat's mother and my mother are sisters (co-wives). Let me go to her."

Pujjunna left for the house of Jambavati. He bowed to her and was offered a seat. Then he said, "Mother! would you like a son like me?"

"Are you not my son?" she answered. "For the sake of Saccabhama the Lord has practiced penance; how can I have a son like you?"

"I am your son already, but if you have one more it would only be better," said Pajjunna.

"How is that possible?" she asked.

"That's easy," he replied. "Towards evening you just assume the body and beauty of Saccabhama, and while she is engaged in decorating and ornamenting herself in worship of the deity, you approach the Master without a moment's delay. "With these words Pajjunna went home.

By means of *Pannatti* Pajjunna made the body of Jam-bavati look just like that of Saccabhama. Her maid-servant remarked, "O mistress! You look just like Saccabhama!" Jambavati was pleased, and carrying umbrella, flying-whisk and pitchers, approached her husband. Then having enjoyed the happiness of sexual pleasure (*paviyarasuha*), and shining with the necklace, she quickly returned home.

Then Saccabhama, decorated and ornamented and having performed auspicious rites (*kayakouyamangala*), approached Kanha too. He said, "O fair lady! How is it that after changing your dress you have simply come again?" Saccabhama was annoyed and replied, "You must have signalled out someone who is dearer to you, and she must have visited you already, and now you are taunting me!" Kanha said, "O lady! It was just a joke, do not be upset. Who would dare to come here?" Saccabhama was mollified and after staying with Kanha for some time, she too returned home.

Vasudeva reflected, "The poor woman must have been tricked by someone, but I shall find it out." He started searching his harem. In the course of time he came to Jamba-vati, and found her shining with the necklace like the Ganges in autumn with a row of swans. She bowed to him and said, "O Lord! Listen, I saw a dream last night."

"Tell me what it was," said Vasudeva.

"I dreamt that I went to you and afterwards you gave me a necklace. When I got up I found the necklace round my neck. Now you tell me the outcome of my dream."

Kanha thought that this must have been the doing of Pajjunna. He said to Jambavati, "O fair lady! You will give birth to a son who will be an ornament to the Jadava family." With folded hands Jambavati accepted what was uttered by Kanha.

After completing her period of pregnancy, Jambavati gave birth to a son whose hands and feet were marked with auspicious signs, whose eyes resembled a bloomed lotus and whose face was as beautiful as the newly risen moon. At the same time the births of sons to the ministers Maisayara, Ajiyasena and Daruga was reported to Kanha. After hearing the news of Jambavati's son he told the messengers, "Let all of them be friends to the son of Jambavati." After the birth ceremony (*jayakamma*) was performed, Jambavati's son was named Samba; the other sons were named Buddhisena, Jayasena and Sudaraga. Being fondled by Devaki, Ruppini, Jambavati and the graceful Pajjunna, Samba grew up happily. Once Samba was taken to Kanha in order to salute his feet; Kanha made him play. Kalindasena made her daughter Suhiranna fall on his feet too. Kanha asked kalindasena whether the girl was her daugh-ter. "Yes, she is, Your Majesty," she answered. She was ask-ed to leave her daughter near the prince, so she put Suhira-nna near the footstool. While playing together, the prince and Suhiranna embraced each other. Kanha looked at his minister, who motioned that it was all right.

At an opportune moment Kalindasena respectfully stated that the girl was the daughter of Hemangada of Kancanapura, and if His Majesty pleased, the girl might be allowed to remain in the service of the prince. Kanha answered, "Let it be so." And he informed the elders (*kodumbiya*): "Su-hiranna is now my daughter-in-law who should be given the same treatment as my son; she should be in no way neglected."

Then the girl was sent away. She grew up. Samba was taken along with his friends to Sumuha the master of arts, where he began to learn the arts.

Samba learned the arts in the company of his friends. He attained youth and looked like another Vasudeva Buddhisena, after asking the prince, took his scented crest of flowers, used garments and left-over sweetmeats (*modake ya bhuttasese*), saying that he would eat the sweetmeat in a solitary place.

The chamberlain reported that Suhiranna and Hiranna, the two courtesan-daughters, were to perform a dance in the Rayanakarandaya garden whi-ch they should witness. Samba was pleased. He got into the chariot with his friends and left for the garden. Sudaraa was his charioteer. An axle of the chariot had to be repaired on the way. There appeared a beautiful girl who saluted the prince. Buddhisena told the prince quietly to put up the loose fringes (*payaraga*) of his crown with both hands. Samba did so. The neighing of the horse was heard and was taken as a good omen. Samba inqui-red after the girl who was so noticeable. Buddhisena replied that she must be from noble family.

They reached the garden and occupied a seat in the assem-bly to witness the performance.

Hiranna showed all kinds of dances during the time it took for water to run through a vessel (*naliyagalaehim*). Then after the water was exhausted Suhiranna started her dance.

Buddhisena stood in front of Samba. Jayasena asked him to move aside (so that the prince could see the dance). Buddhisena replied that he was being pushed by the spe-ctators and could not move. Suhiranna performed dances. The teacher gave her a bath with the left-over water in the vessel. Now when Buddhisena moved away from Samba's side, the prince could get a look at Hiranna being spri-nkled with water like the goddess of wealth. She too looked at him with devotion, like Rati looking at Kama.

Samba got into the chariot and left for the city in the company of his friends.

Addressing the prince, Jayasena said, "O noble one! Buddhi-sena is poor and a weakling; he is only eloquent in talk. One who is unable to resist the pushing of a crowd is a bad man."

Buddhisena answered, "You are like a blind man who is unable to distinguish between different appearances."

"And you do!" exclai-med Jayasena. "If you are so clever, tell me how many kinds of men there are! Your know-ledge will be put to test."

Buddhisena replied, "A man can be divided in accor-dance with wealth (*attha*), reli-gion (*dhamma,*) and desire (*kama.*) One who enjoys himself and at the same time can add to the wealth earned by his forefathers is the best from the point of view of wealth. One who does not let his forefathers' wealth diminish is the middle, and one who exhausts all such wealth is the lowest. From the point of view of religion, a man is of two kinds: the best and the middle. One who achieves self-enlightenment himself is the best; the middle is one enlightened by others. From the point of view of desire a man is of three kinds: one who loves and is loved in return is the best; one who is loved but does not love in return is the middle; one who loves but is not loved in return is the lowest.

Jayasena asked, "And to which category does the noble one belong?"

"As far as wealth and religion are concerned there is no end," replied Buddisena, "but in the case of desire he is the middle."

"And what about you?" Jayasena asked.

"I am the best," said Buddisena.

"What! exclaimed Jayasena angrily." "Fancying yourself to be so learned! You overestimate yourself. You have some arrogance, putting the master in a lower category than yourself!"

"You understand nothing," replied Buddisena. "One who is loved but does not love in return belongs to the middle category."

"All right," said Jayasena, "then by whom is he loved?"

Buddhisena replied, "I shall tell only if the master asks."

Samba said, "All right, I am asking you."

And so Bhuddisena told the story:

Having waited upon the master, I was going along the road when I came across some persons with writing plate and inkpot in their hands (*patta-livasanahatthe?*). They were talking between themselves:

"We have been asked by His Excellency to register the fools and the wise in the city of Baravati, and then to report the matter to him. So if Buddisena gets into the chariot, I shall note his name down first in my list of the wise; if he does not get in, then among the fools."

Overhearing their talk I thought to myself, "This list will be read out in the presence of the king; if they write my name heading the fools, I shall be put to disgrace. Therefore, there is nothing wrong in getting into the chariot. "Thus contemplating, I was then addressed by the charioteer, "O noble one! Get into my chariot!"

I got inside, and we went along, enjoying the beautiful scenery. In front of us a mahout (*adhorana*), seated on an intoxicated elephant, asked the charioteer, "O noble one! Keep away, my elephant is in rut (*aviheo*)". Heeding his words, the charioteer turned his coach to one side and we went on through to the dwellings of the prostitutes.

We began to hear the envious, teasing, the original words are *Isita-khijjita isia* is acting the part of a woman; *khijj'a* is censuring and conciliatory talking of young people.

The coachman reached a house with an arched gateway (*bhavanam satoranam*) where the oblations were made.

There I saw a girl surrounded by maidens, as the goddess of learning (*Sarassati*) is surrounded by sacred arts (*vijja*).

She bowed to me and said, "Welcome to you!" Then she washed my feet and when I was seated she asked, "Where do you come from?" I replied, "From Prince Samba." She looked in that direction and folded her hands together and raised them to her head.

She asked me, "How do you entertain yourself?" and I replied, "By practicing the arts." There were several maidens sitting nearby, but they did not attract me.

Then another young maiden came, and she was suitable to me. She said, "Buddisena! Do not return to the elders. This Bhogamalini here will always think of you."

After she left, Bhogamalini said to me, "O noble one! You must be feeling tired after your trip in the coach. A bed is ready for you in the inner apartment, go rest yourself."

I entered the apartment and stretched out on the bed. After gently massaging my feet, she said, "O noble one! Now I want to massage your chest." I thought that the maiden must be skillful (*niuna*), since after massaging my feet she now wanted to press my chest. But she exclaimed, "I shall press your chest with my breasts! (*thanehim vo uram samvahissam*)." There was a wonderful difference between the touch of her breasts and the massaging of her hands. In this way she made me enjoy sexual pleasures as a female elephant makes a male elephant enjoy them.

In the course of time, I came out of the house, but because of my attachment there I started visiting it often.

One day, while speaking sweet and encouraging words, Bhogamalini said to me, "O noble one! Do you know the reason of my being here?" I replied, "No, I don't; tell me, 'O fair one!"

So she began her story:

My mistress Suhiranna was given to the prince from her childhood. She looked at the prince amorously. She grew up in the course of time. Then the prince said to Kalindasena, "O Kalindasena! Let your daughter visit my inner chamber."

Once Suhiranna wanted to go along with her mother to the royal palace. But her mother refused to give her permission to go.

When her mother had left she hung herself in her own house.

By chance I happened to see her, and I cut the noose and made her lie down on a bed. I tried to console her. She said, "O Bhogamalini! Where am I?" And I answered, "On the bed and in the hearts of good people."

Again she asked, "Who has brought me here?" And I replied, "The gods and myself." Then I asked her, "O mistress! How could you dare to think of committing suicide?"

She said to me, "Listen, O friend: From my childhood I was given to the prince. When I grew up, I was once in the king's assembly, where I saw the prince. But now it is impossible even to have a glimpse of him. This is why I have decided to take such a step."

Hearing her story, I said to her, "Enough of disappointment, O my mistress! Listen: is there any other girl who is more distinguished than you who could be dearer to the heart of the prince? Very soon your desire will be fulfilled."

After consoling her in this manner, I talked to her mother who sought consultation with her friends the mahaout (*hattharoha*) and the scribes (*lehaehim*). They said, "We are frightened of the prince, but Buddhisena is the prince's confidant, and it is in the fitness of things that he is told about the girl's virtues. We shall bring him here somehow, and he will do the job."

Then you, Buddhisena, were brought here by the charioteer (*rahina*), the scribes (*lehaehim*) and the mahaout (*mahamatta*).

You should not hesitate in this matter only because Suhiranna is the daughter of a prostitute. Listen, and I will tell you why:

In ancient times there ruled a sovereign king called Bharaha. He was devoted to one wife. The feudal lords presented him with some girls, who were sent all together to the palace.

The king, saw them coming as he was seated with the queen in the palace. "Whose contingent is that?" inquired the queen. The king replied, "They have been presented to, me by the feudal lords."

The queen reflected, "I should find out some remedy for this before it is too late. Perhaps one or more of them may become dearer to him."

She told the king, "O lord! I want to make myself free from fetters (*pasa*; it may also mean a palace. In that case the meaning would be: "I want to fall down from the palace)."

"My Lady!" exclaimed the king, "why do you even utter such words?"

"These maidens have come, and tormented by the fire of grief, I shall die," replied his wife.

"If that is what you have decided," said the king, "they will not even enter the house."

The queen exclaimed, "Then if that's true, let them stay in the outer chamber!"

The king consented. The young girls attended the king in the company of the female holders of the royal umbrella and flying-whisk. In the course of time they were all given off to different groups (*ganas*). This is the origin of courtesans (*ganika*).

After Amiyajasa gave birth to many children, Kalindasena was born to her.

This Suniranna is born to Kalindasena by Hemangada. You arrange the matter in such a way so that the prince comes to know about her great love for him. With this Bhogamalini ended her tale.

I (Buddhisena) consented to do what she said. In order to obtain Suhiranna's confidence I carried the flowers, perfume, clothes, and betels to her. The girl who you saw in the garden was she herself.

And listen why I obstructed the view of the noble one at the dancing contest: I did it purposely, so that Suhiranna might not be careless in her performance while looking at the prince. Buddhisena's tale ends.

Talking in this manner they reached their home.

In the evening Samba said to Buddhisena, "You go and fetch Suhiranna so that I shall be included in the first category of those who are loved and love in return." Buddhisena replied, "But they do not trust me, so let Jayasena come along as my helper."

Both went. Having reached their destination, Buddhisena told the maidens, "I have been deputed by the prince to say that the mistress should come to him." But they replied, "Who is going to trust you?" Buddhisena then pointed to Jayasena, who also reported the prince's message. This was conveyed to Kalindasena. She asked them to wait until the girl dressed herself.

Kalindasena went to Jambavati and reported the matter. She went to Kanha and conveyed to him Samba's desire. Kanha consented, saying that she would be honoured later along with the other princess-es, so Suhiranna could be at his service.

Kalindasena sent the girl in a coach. Buddhisena advised the prince, "O noble one! Be careful!" He replied, "How gratifying love is!"

Suhiranna came to the bed-chamber and got on the couch. Having closed the door of the chamber, Buddhisena went away.

Whatever hairstyle, kind of garments or ornaments she employed, Samba too followed it. She trained him as a *sarika* trains a parrot.

They passed the night enjoying excessive pleasures.

Then Buddhisena arrived. Samba told him, "Let her leave before this is known to the elders."

In the meantime female attendants sent by the queen arrived with cosmetics, clothes, and ornaments for both of them. Samba felt happy that Suhiranna's arrival was known by his mother.

Samba passed his time happily enjoying sensual pleasures with Suhiranna.

Sambo Hemangadanrpa-
Putrya vesyaprasutaya
Suhiranyakhyaya reme,
rupadatyapsarahsriya

Jinasena does not give the tale
of Samba in his Harivamsapurana.

The wedding takes place with Suhiranna, along with 108 girls from the royal families.

BRAHMAN'S COURTESAN LOVER

Story of Rupinika

There is in this country a city named Mathura, the birth-place of Krishna; in it there was a courtesan known by the name of Rupinika; she had for a mother an old bawd named Makaradanshtra, who seemed a lump of poison in the eyes of the young men attracted by her daughter's charms.

One day Rupinika went at the time of worship to the temple to perform her duty (Such people dance in temples, one of the oldest and most interesting customs of religion, that of sacred prostitution), and beheld from a distance a young man. When she saw that handsome young fellow, he made such an impression upon her heart that all her mother's instructions vanished from it. Then she said to her maid: "Go and tell this man from me that he is to come to my house to-day."

The maid said, "So I will," and immediately went and told him. Then the man thought a little and said to her: "I am a Brahman named Lohajangha; I have no wealth; then what business have I in the house of Rupinika, which is only, to be entered by the rich?"

The maid said: "My mistress does not desire wealth from you." Whereupon Lohajangha consented to do as she wished. When she heard that from the maid, Rupinika went home in a state of excitement, and remained with her eyes fixed on the path by which he would come. And soon Lohajangha came to her house, while the bawd Makaradanshtra looked at him, and wondered where he came from.

Rupinika for her part, when she saw him, rose up to meet him herself with the utmost respect, and clinging to his neck in her joy led him to her own private apartments.

Then she was captivated with Lohajangha's wealth of accomplishments, and considered that she had been only born to love him. So she avoided the society of other men, and that young fellow lived with her in her house in great comfort.

Rupinika's mother Makaradanshtra, who had trained up many courtesans, was annoyed when she saw this, and said to her in private: "My daughter, why do you associate with a poor man? Courtesans of good taste embrace a corpse in preference to a poor man. What business has a courtesan like you with affection? How have you come to forget that great principle? The light of a red (Ragini means "affection" and also "red") sunset lasts but a short time, and so does the splendour of a courtesan who gives way to affection. A courtesan, like an actress, should exhibit an assumed affection in order to get wealth; so forsake this pauper, do not ruin yourself."

When she heard this speech of her mother's, Rupinika said in a rage: "Do not talk in this way, for I love him more than my life. And as for wealth, I have plenty, what do I want with more? So you must not speak to me again, mother, in this way."

When she heard this, Makaradanshtra was in a rage, and she remained thinking over some device for getting rid of this Lohajangha. Then she saw coming along the road a certain Rajput, who had spent all his wealth, surrounded by retainers with swords in their hands. So she went up to him quickly and, taking him aside, said: "My house is beset by a certain poor lover. So come there yourself to-day, and take such order with him that he shall depart from my house, and do you possess my daughter."

"Agreed," said the Rajput, and entered that house.

At that precise moment Rupinika was in the temple, and Lohajangha meanwhile was absent somewhere, and, suspecting nothing, he returned to the house a moment afterwards. Immediately the retainers of the Rajput ran upon him, and gave him severe kicks and blows on all his limbs, and then they threw him into a ditch full of all kinds of impurities, and Lohajangha with difficulty escaped from it. Then Rupinika returned to the house, and when she heard what had taken place she was distracted with grief, so the Rajput, seeing that, returned as he came.

Lohajangha, after suffering this brutal outrage by the machinations of the bawd, set out for some holy place of pilgrimage, in order to leave his life there, now that he was separated from his beloved. As he was going along in the wild country (*Atavi* is generally translated "forest"), with his heart burning with anger against the bawd, and his skin with the heat of the summer, he longed for shade. Not being able to find a tree, he lighted on the body of an elephant which had been stripped of all its flesh (for the *vritam* of the text *kritam*) by jackals making their way into it by the hind-quarters; accordingly Lohajangha, being worn out, crept into this carcass, which was a mere shell, as only the skin remained, and went to sleep in it, as it was kept cool by the breeze which freely entered. Then suddenly clouds arose from all sides and began to pour down a pelting shower of rain; that rain made the elephant's skin contract so that no aperture was left, and immediately a copious inundation came that way, and carrying off the elephant's hide swept it into the Ganges, so that eventually the inundation bore it into the sea. And there a bird of the race of Garuda saw that hide and, supposing it to be carrion, took it to the other side of the sea; there it tore open the elephant's hide with its claws and, seeing that there was a man inside it, fled away.

But Lohajangha was awaked by the bird's pecking and scratching, and came out through the aperture made by its beak. And finding that he was on the other side of the sea, he was astonished, and looked upon the whole thing as a daydream; then he saw there to his terror two horrible Rakshasas, and those two for their part contemplated him from a distance with feelings of fear. Remembering how they were defeated by Rama, and seeing that Lohajangha was also a man who had crossed the sea, they were once more alarmed in their hearts. So, after they had deliberated together, one of them went off immediately and told the whole occurrence to King Vibhishana.

King Vibhishana, too, as he had seen the prowess of Rama, being terrified at the arrival of a man, said to that Rakshasa: "Go, my good friend, and tell that man from me, in a friendly manner, that he is to do me the favour of coming to my palace." The Rakshasa said, "I will do so," and timidly approached Lohajangha, and told him that request of his sovereign's. Lohajangha for his part accepted that invitation with unruffled calm, and went to Lanka, with that Rakshasa as his companion. And when he arrived in Lanka he was astonished at beholding numerous splendid edifices of gold, and entering the king's palace he saw Vibhishana.

The king welcomed the Brahman, who blessed him in return, and then Vibhishana said: "Brahman, how did you manage to reach this country?" Then the cunning Lohajangha said to Vibhishana: "I am a Brahman of the name of Lohajangha residing in Mathura; and I, Lohajangha, being afflicted at my poverty, went to the temple of the god, and remaining fasting, for a long time performed austerities in the presence of Narayana. Then the adorable Hari commanded me in a dream, saying: 'Go thou to Vibhishana, for he is a faithful worshipper of mine, and he will give thee wealth." Then I said: 'Vibhishana is where I cannot reach him.' But the lord continued: 'To-day shalt thou see that Vibhishana.' So the lord spake to me, and immediately I woke up and found myself upon this side of the sea. I know no more." When Vibhishana heard this from Lohajangha, reflecting that Lanka was a difficult place to reach, he thought to himself: "Of a truth this man possesses divine power." And he said to that Brahman: "Remain here; I will give you wealth."

Then he committed him to the care of the man-slaying Rakshasas as an inviolable deposit, and sent some of his subjects to a mountain in his kingdom called Swarnamula, who brought from it a young bird belonging to the race of Garuda; and he gave it to that Lohajangha (who had to take a long journey to Mathura) to ride upon, in order that he might in the meanwhile break it in. Lohajangha for his part mounted on its back, and riding about on it in Lanka, rested there for some time, being hospitably entertained by Vibhishana.

One day he asked the King of the Rakshasas, feeling-curiosity on the point, why the whole ground of Larika was made of wood; and Vibhishana, when he heard that, explained the circumstance to him, saying: "Brahman, if you take any interest in this matter, listen, I will explain it to you. Long ago Garuda, the son of Kasyapa, wishing to redeem his mother from her slavery to the snakes, to whom she had been subjected in accordance with an agreement (Kasyapa's two wives disputed about the colour of the sun's horses. They agreed that whichever was in the wrong should become a slave to the other. Kadru, the mother of the snakes, won by getting her children to darken the horses. So Garuda's mother, Vinata, became a slave), and preparing to obtain from the gods the nectar which was the price of her ransom, wanted to eat something which would increase his strength, and so he went, to his father, who, being importuned, said to him: 'My son, in the sea there is a huge elephant and a huge tortoise. They have assumed their present form in consequence of a curse: go and eat them.'

Then Garuda went and brought them both to eat, and then perched on a bough of the great wishing-tree of paradise. And when that bough suddenly broke with his weight, he held it up with his beak, out of regard to the Balakhilyas (Divine personages of the size of a thumb. Sixty thousand were produced from Brahma's body and surrounded the chariot of the sun. The legend of Garuda and the Balakhilyas is found in the *Mahabharata*), who were engaged in austerities underneath it.

Then Garuda, afraid that the bough would crush mankind if he let it fall at random, by the advice of his father brought the bough to this uninhabited part of the earth and let it drop. Lanka was built on the top of that bough, therefore the ground here is of wood." When he heard this from Vibhishana, Lohajangha was perfectly satisfied.

Then Vibhishana gave to Lohajangha many valuable jewels, as he desired to set out for Mathura. And out of his devotion to the god Vishnu, who dwells at Mathura, he entrusted to the care of Lohajangha a lotus, a club, a shell and a discus all of gold, to be offered to the god. Lohajangha took all these and mounted the bird given to him by Vibhishana, that could accomplish a hundred thousand *yojanas,* and rising up into the air in Lanka, he crossed the sea and without any difficulty arrived at Mathura.

And there he descended from the air into an empty convent outside the town, and deposited there his abundant treasure, and tied up that bird. And then he went into the market and sold one of his jewels, and bought garments and scented unguents, and also food. And he ate the food in that convent where he was, and gave some to his bird; and he adorned himself with the garments, unguents, flowers and other decorations. And when night came he mounted that same bird and went to the house of Rupinika, bearing in his hand the shell, discus and mace; then he hovered over it in the air, knowing the place well, and made a low, deep sound to attract the attention of his beloved, who was alone.

But Rupinika, as soon as she heard that sound, came out, and saw hovering in the air by night a being like Narayana, gleaming with jewels. He said to her: "I am Hari come hither for thy sake"; whereupon she bowed with her face to the earth and said: "May the god have mercy upon me!" Then Lohajangha descended and tied up his bird, and entered the private apartments of his beloved hand in hand with her. And after remaining there a short time he came out and, mounting the bird as before, went off through the air.

In the morning, Rupinika remained observing an obstinate silence, thinking to herself: "I am the wife of the god Vishnu, I must cease to converse with mortals." And then her mother Makaradanshtra said to her: "Why do you behave in this way, my daughter?" And after she had been perseveringly questioned by her mother, she caused to be put up a curtain between herself and her parent, and told her what had taken place in the night, which was the cause of her silence.

When the bawd heard that, she felt doubt on the subject, but soon after, at night, she saw that very Lohajangha mounted on the bird, and in the morning Makaradanshtra came secretly to Rupinika, who still remained behind the curtain, and inclining herself humbly, preferred to her this request: "Through the favour of the god, thou, my daughter, hast obtained here on earth the rank of a goddess, and I am thy mother in this world, therefore grant me a reward for giving thee birth: entreat the god that, old as I am, with this very body I may enter paradise. Do me this favour."

Rupinika consented, and requested that very boon from Lohajangha, who came again at night disguised as Vishnu. Then Lohajangha, who was personating the god, said to that beloved of his: "Thy mother is a wicked woman, it would not be fitting to take her openly to paradise; but on the morning of the eleventh day the door of heaven is opened, and many of the Ganas, Siva's companions, enter into it before anyone else is admitted. Among them I will introduce this mother of thine, if she assume their appearance.

So shave her head with a razor, in such a manner that five locks shall be left, put a necklace of skulls round her neck, and stripping off her clothes, paint one side of her body with lamp-black and the other with red lead (thus she represented the Ardhanarisvara, or Siva half-male and half-female, which compound figure is to be painted in this manner) for when she has in this way been made to resemble a Gana, I shall find it an easy matter to get her into heaven."

When he had said this, Lohajangha remained a short time and then departed. And in the morning Rupinika attired her mother as he had directed; and then she remained with her mind entirely fixed on paradise. So when night came Lohajangha appeared again, and Rupinika handed over her mother to him. Then he mounted, on the bird, and took the bawd with him naked, and transformed as he had directed, and he flew up rapidly with her into the air. While he was in the air, he beheld a lofty stone pillar in front of a temple, with a discus on its summit. So he placed her on the top of the pillar, with the discus as her only support (she held on to it by her hands), and there she hung like a banner to blazon forth his revenge for his ill usage.

He said to her: "Remain here a moment while I bless the earth with my approach," and vanished from her sight. Then beholding a number of people in front of the temple, who had come there to spend the night in devout vigils before the festive procession, he called aloud from the air: "Hear, ye people, this very day there shall fall upon you here the all-destroying Goddess of Pestilence, therefore fly to Hari for protection."

When they heard this voice from the air all the inhabitants of Mathura who were there, being terrified, implored the protection of the god, and remained devoutly muttering prayers to ward off the calamity. Lohajangha for his part descended from the air and encouraged them to pray, and after changing that dress of his came and stood among the people, without being observed.

The bawd thought as she sat upon the top of the pillar: "The god has not come as yet, and I have not reached heaven." At last, feeling it impossible to remain up there any longer, she cried out in her fear, so that the people below heard: "Alas! I am falling, I am falling." Hearing that, the people in front of the god's temple were beside themselves, fearing that the destroying goddess was falling upon them, even as had been foretold, and said: "O goddess, do not fall, do not fall." So those people of Mathura, young and old, spent that night in perpetual dread that the destroying goddess would fall upon them, but at last it came to an end; and then beholding that bawd upon the pillar in the state described, the citizens and the king recognised her at once.

All the people thereupon forgot their alarm and burst out laughing, and Rupinika herself at last arrived, having heard of the occurrence. And when she saw it she was abashed, and with the help of the people who were there she managed to get that mother of hers down from the top of the pillar immediately.

Then that bawd was asked by all the people there, who were filled with curiosity, to tell them the whole story, and she did so. Thereupon the king, the Brahmans and the merchants, thinking that that laughable incident must have been brought about by a sorcerer or some person of that description, made a proclamation, that whoever had made a fool of the bawd, who had deceived innumerable lovers, was to show himself, and he would receive a turban of honour on the spot.

When he heard that, Lohajangha made himself known to those present, and, being questioned, he related the whole story from its commencement. And he offered to the god the discus, shell, club and lotus of gold, the present which Vibhishana had sent, and which aroused the astonishment of the people.

Then all the people of Mathura, being pleased, immediately invested him with a turban of honour, and by the command of the king made that Rupinika a free woman. And then Lohajangha, having wreaked upon the bawd his wrath caused by her ill usage of him, lived in great comfort in Mathura with that beloved of his, being very well off by means of the large stock of jewels which he had brought from Lanka.

Hearing this tale from the mouth of the transformed Vasantaka, Vasavadatta, who was sitting at the side of the fettered King of Vatsa, felt extreme delight in her heart (Kathasaritsagara).

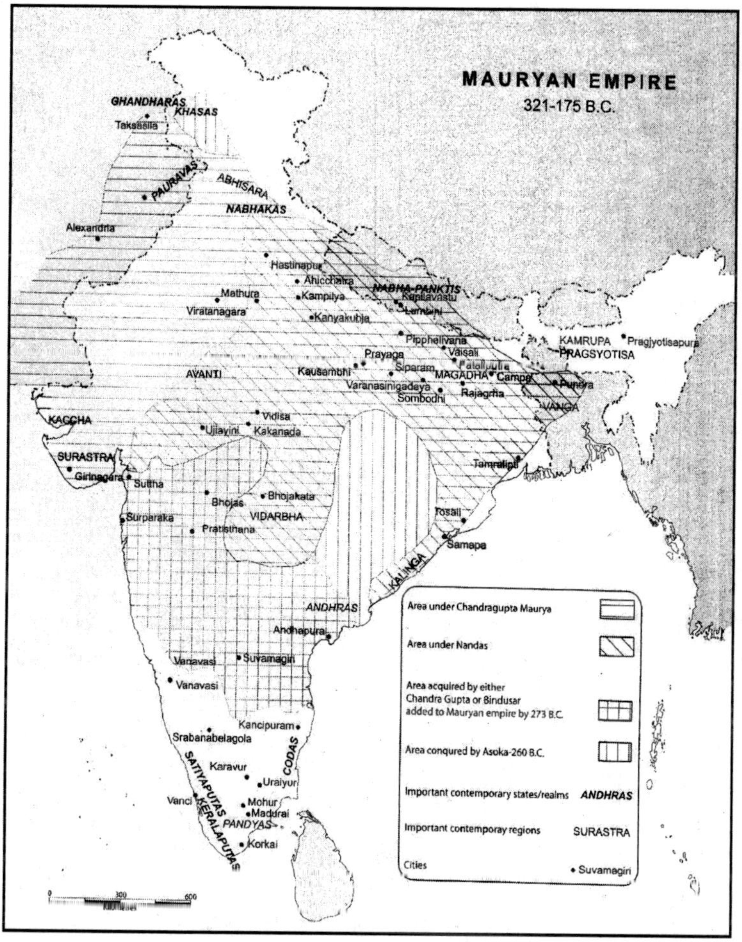

Mauryan Empire (321 – 175 B-C). Credits > Historical Atlas of India NAT (MO) Govt. of India (2007) Courtesy National Library, Kolkata.

Chapter Four

Caturbhani (Four Play)

Ubhayabhisarika

Vararuchi

(After invocation enter the Sutradhar (Director) of the Play)

Sutradhar: "What are you to me? What am I to you? Let go, let go my skirt, you cheat. Why are you staring at me? Well, great man, I am not pining for you, you know. Your lips show the marks of your new mistress's teeth. No, no, that angry woman is yours; I am nothing to you. Get out, you fickle creature, go and worship that queen of your heart." Gentlemen, this is how the cunning courtesans of Kusumapura tell you off in the heat of your quarrel. But I am just a reporter, sirs, a mere mouthpiece. Oh, what is all this noise, just as I have begun to address you! Well, let me find out.

(offs tage voice)

Ah, it is the Vita, all in a flurry! Poor man, he is weighed down by his friend's worries and looks like a *lodhra* tree lustreless in the withdrawing winter. *(Exit)*

(enter the Vita)

Vita (Rake): What an enchanting spring! The cuckoo, the mango, the *asoka* blossom, the hammock, the heady cup of wine and the moon in the sky, all piling sweetness upon sweetness! Such beauty can cast a spell upon Kama himself! Oh, how over-powering is this spring! On such a day as this lovers are ready to forgive each other—look, messenger girls are flitting around with messages from lover to lover. Girdles cunningly inlaid with gems, coral and pearl are adding to the gaiety; so are soft silks, delicate mantles, fragrant garlands and golden sandalwood paste. In this joyous season, in this pervading languor of the spring, desire is stirring in every heart. It is a pity that the merchant-prince Sagaradatta's son Kuberadatta *had* to quarrel with his Narayanadatta. Here is the message his servant Sahakaraka has brought: "In the courtyard of the temple of Narayana, Madanasena was singing in the opera, The Worship of Love. Suddenly, Narayanadatta turned towards me and said, 'So, she means more to you than I do;' and afraid and furious that I had lost my heart to Madanasena, she stormed home. She wouldn't even look at me, though I was at her feet. Consumed with longing, I passed one single night as if it were a thousand nights. So, now I beg you to bring us together—you who are the eternal Springtime of Kusumapura, the most trusted friend of the courtesans, you must help me."

The moment I received his message I left home, though it was already dusk. For, I know, I know from experience, how unbearable the tyranny of Love can be. My wife got very suspicious and wouldn't let me come out. She is fully aware of her own youth, but doesn't trust my grey hairs. Still, I had to come. I have promised to calm down Narayanadatta; and, once I have taken on this delicate task, I have to see it through.

The spring itself, with the sweet song of the cuckoo, with the freshly awakened tendrils of the mango is beseeching the angry woman. Besides, what need has a woman for any other man, when her own is so handsome, generous, courteous, soft-spoken and bursting with the vigour of youth.

(wandering about)

Oh, how lovely looks this main street of Kusumapura; sprayed and scrubbed, bright with masses of many-hued flowers, it invites one to come and live here! The shop-fronts filled with countless varieties of lovely things are gay with crowds, busy buying. The mansions, all in a row, resound, some with sacred chants, some with music and some with twanging of bow-strings. You can almost hear them talking to one another as if they are the ten faces of Ravana. They rise skyward into the clouds; and from that height, curious young women, peeping down through their half-open windows, look like so many dazzling flashes of lightening—so many Apsaras in the Kailasa mountain. The nobles and officers are all out on their horses, elephants and chariots. Coquetish messenger girls, gaily bejewelled are flitting about trying to catch the eye of young men. They certainly can put to shame all the beauties of paradise. The daughters of the courtesans, young and artful, are promenading, as if they are obliging the very streets they tread upon. Like bees, all eyes are drinking in the beauty of their lotus-faces.

There are so many happy people on the streets today—free from fear and care, all in a festive mood, gaily attired. bejewelled, perfumed, adorned with flowers and enjoying the public sports—many of them are celebrities. Heaven itself seems to be here in this lovely city of Pataliputra.

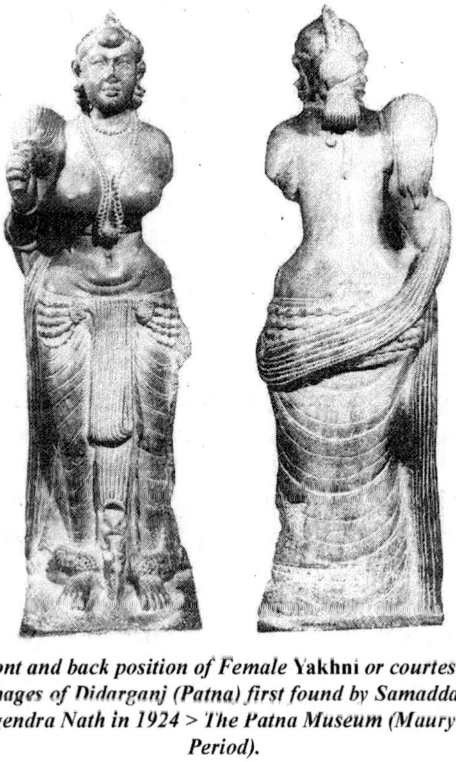

Front and back position of Female* Yakhni *or courtesan images of Didarganj (Patna) first found by Samaddar Jogendra Nath in 1924 > The Patna Museum (Mauryan Period).

(walking about)

Lo, this surely is Charanadasi's daughter Anangadatta! She looks as if she is returning after a night of love; so languid, yet her walk so graceful, her beauty so soothing to the eye. But her lover has obviously enjoyed her roughly. Her dancing eyes are, today, heavy with sleep; her lips show marks of her lover's teeth. The amorous play has disturbed the strings of pearls on her girdle and now they are all over her hips. The very sight of her is auspicious for me. But, there, she is going away without even looking at me. I think I'll call her. But, no, she has turned round of her own.

(approaching her)

Child, aren't you going to greet me? What? What are you saying?

"*You* took a long time to recognise me; anyway, I *am* greeting you now."

All right, all right, I am blessing you. May you win a lover, young, independent, generous, hand-some, wealthy, clever and amorous—now, young lady, that should be enough. He who could spend a night with you, the very *Lakshmi* among our courtesans, *he*, certainly, has made a success of life. Verily, he must be the master of Kama himself— What?

"I am just coming back from Nagadatta's house; Nagadatta, the chief minister's son."

Now, my dear girl, these people *used* to be rich. Yes, once upon a time. Obviously your mother could'nt be liking all this; but—well,— why is she looking down shyly and smiling! Yes, I have guessed rightly, haven't I? Don't do this. You are ruining your mother's hopes. And all because you are in-fatuated with him. You have given up your lucrative profession—so hard to get out of, once one is in it. Visiting your lover at his house, enjoying those amorous pleasures! You are kicking at your own sisters in the trade. Well, I am glad you are ashamed of yourself; you should be. What is the use of swearing that you won't do it again? All right, I myself will go and plead with your mother. But you, certainly, have gone against the whole code of conduct of the courtesans. Well, get along. What is it now?

"I am bowing to you."

Well, my girl, let me bless you again: whatever you have learnt has clung to you and has become a virtue. I need not praise it. Now, may your youth, so pleasing to the eye, be perennial! She is gone; I must go, too.

(walks about)

Oh, here comes Vishnudatta's daughter, Madhavasena. She is rushing along like a fawn chased by a tiger; she doesn't seem to care whether her servants catch up with her or not. It is only for her mother's greed that she has to suffer and submit to some lecherous ruffian. Poor thing, her face looks tired; but her hair and the flowers she is wearing are all in place; the delicate lips show no marks of her lover's teeth; the sandalwood dust on her breasts has not been rubbed off; obviously, the lout did not embrace her; even her girdle is not awry. But she has been so frightened by the crudeness of his love-making that she didn't even stop to look at me. Well, she is gone. I better follow her and find out why she looks so forlorn. Good, she has herself turned round. What are you saying, my dear?

"I didn't notice you."

Well, my girl, I don't blame you. When one is exhausted, and one's mind is not at ease, naturally, one is apt to be a bit confused. What are you saying?

"I am bowing to you."

I bless you, my child: may your lovers be wealthy; may the disagreeable ones be poor; and may your mother's greed never force you into a boor's arms! But, child, where are you coming from?

"From the house of Samudradatta, Dhanadatta Sarthavaha's son."

Well, you are a lucky girl: he is today's Kubera. — What deep sighs! Her lips like soft petals are quivering; she is knitting her eyebrows; poor thing, she has turned away her face. so, my guess was right. I can see, child, that you passed the night yearning for the sun to rise, unwilling to do what you were doing. You offered your *bimba*-red lips painfully; there was no loving whisper, no merry giggle; even the embraces were lifeless, loveless. Constantly you yawned and sighed; you lay on the bed, full of misery; mechanically you went through the act of love. Well, dear, don't be sad; a rich man, however ugly, is always acceptable—at least, that is what they say. The scriptures tell us that you should earn money making love to men whether they are delightfully attractive or disgustingly repulsive. What? What are you saying?

"So you and my mother think alike!"

Not at all. There is a reason for everything. All right, you may go now; someday, I will come to your house and explain to you the principles…

Oh, she has gone away without even a word of goodbye—just shows lack of breeding; but, well, the wretched girl has been so upset. I must be getting along.

(walking about)

Ho, ho, isn't that the wandering nun, Vilasakaundini? Such delicate grace in her walk! Just to see her is to feel a new life coursing through your veins! The heady perfume of her clothes has maddened the bees; they have deserted the sweet mango blossom and are hovering around her…I think I'll go up and talk to her. My eyes and ears are just tingling for her…

Dear lady, please accept the greetings of Vaisikachala, the best friend of the ladies of the town—What did you say?

"I have no use for a Vaisikachala, the master Vita. I would like to meet a Vaiseshikachala, the master philosopher."

True, true, there is something in what you say. Your large lovely eyes are restlessly flitting around. After a passionate night your face looks lovelier than ever; sweetly tired, with lips slightly swollen. Your slow, languorous walk makes no secret of the amorous hours you have spent. I can quite see that your lover has taught you that the Vaiseshika philosophy is based on love, sexual love. Did you say something?

"You are a slave of sex and are talking like a slave."

Sweet lady, the slaves of your lotus – feet are, indeed, blessed. But what hope has one like me—a sinner?

"My guru has forbidden me to talk to those who know nothing of the six categories (Substance, Quality, Generality, Action, Intimate union and particularity) of the Vaiseshika school."

Quite right, virtuous lady, quite right. Your body itself is the Substance, oh doe-eyed beauty.

There is Quality in your loveliness. Your youth is for the Generality—the community. Every young man praises you in Action. What other desire can one have than for Intimate Union with you? And as for Particularity, you take a young blade, if you like him; if you do'nt, you throw him out. Oh, you are laughing, you have no answer—so I have won the argument. What is that?

"In Sankhya philosophy Purusha, the Supreme Being is Stainless, devoid of all quality and knows his field of Action."

My God, we have been silenced! Though you, surely, do not look comfortable after such talk. I have, however, no desire to hold you back you, young people, from your carnal delights. Go ahead go ahead!

Oh, she has vanished ! Well, I think I should move on, too.

(wandering about)

What do I see now! Isn't that Charanadasi's old mother Ramasena? She is so very ancient; still, she must throw around coquettish glances and giggle and try to walk like a voluptuous young thing. She is coming this way. It's really amazing! She has had her day; she has enjoyed her lovers fully. She has used her own attractions to suck dry everyone who fell for her. In her own days she was the apple of discord among so many young men; and now she is going to fleece the paramour of her daughter. Well, let's have some fun out of this old hag. How many lovers has'nt she finished off, how many amorous young men hasn't she struck down! Ah, this veritable thunderbolt, I must greet her.

Where are you off to Ramasena? Now that you have passed on your looks and luck to your daughter—who is your next victim?

Her book of curses is always ready for you.

"Your vile manners will be your doom."

There, there, enough; just tell me where you are going.—What did you say?

"My daughter has been with Dhanika since yesterday. I am now going to fetch her on the pretext of taking her to the musical."

Oh, Charandasi has certainly made a terrible blunder. You were such an expert in squeezing the last drop out of your paramours. And then you would loss them aside like lemons sucked dry. And fancy, *your* daughter breaking the code of conduct laid down in the scriptures as if she were a nun.

This girl has enjoyed this man fully and has taken a lot of money out of him. She knows that he is a pauper now; still, she cannot tear herself away from him. She has fallen in love with him, that's all. What is the use of teaching her the scriptures of the courtesans?—Yes, what?

"I am fetching her home on the pretext of taking her to the musical. Could you also be there and explain to her the ancient lore of our profession?"

Sure, I will. But, first, I must go and help a friend of mine. After that I will be at your service. Go, now; I will be off too.

You can never trust these prostitutes! These cruel, greedy creatures, insidiously they caress and fondle their man, strip him to the skin and, then, no longer interested, quit him forever, as the soul quits the body. Then they pass on to another to gratify and ensnare him. To the lovers the real plague are the mothers of the young courtesans; and there is no escaping them. May God protect these bastards ; may these cunning old hags perish—these who cleverly rob lustful men, using their daughters as their fine tools.

(wandering about)

Lo, who is this coming up, there?—Yes, it is that curse of the streets, that God's own oddity, neither man nor woman, Sukumarika; the very sight of her brings one misfortune. Well, well, all one can do is to hide one's face and walk away, without stopping to greet her.

(does so)

Blast her! She is coming after me! There is no escape from death. Where shall I go now? I think I had better satisfy her with a few sweet words and then quickly get out of the tiger's jaws. What did you say?

"Greetings to you, sir."

Well, my dear girl, keep your man for ever! Be the mother of many sons! The way you make eyes, lift your eyebrows, move your lips, swing your arms, trip gracefully, smile invitingly,—you surpass all women in coquettishness.

But your girdle is in such disorder; it's hanging loose over your large lovely hips! Now, tell me who is this lucky man you are coming from? Though I must say that you don't look as if you got much satisfaction out of him. Yes?

"I am coming from the king's brother-in-law Ramasena's house."

Oh, lucky man! But why have you two love-birds parted?—What did you say?

"You know, Ratilatika, that mere servant of a prostitute, entered the royal court and smiled at him amorously with such cunning sweetness and made eyes at him, throwing honeyed glances, just oozing with love as if to spray his heart with longing; and then, her rapturous thrills proclaimed to the world that she was his for the taking. And he, too, quietly nods at her which, of course, means 'Yes'. I could not stand this; and when I got furious with him, he fell at my feet. Even then, I was so eaten up with jealousy that I would not forgive him. Then he just picked me up and carried me to his house and placed me on his bed and lay by me. But at night, when I was tired out after our passionate love-making and had fallen asleep, he was seized with a fit of lust and stole a way to her. He hasn't come back home for days. Oh, it is the same me who would not listen to his entreaties and now I am consumed with regret. I was coming to you for help, sir. It is lucky, I found you. Oh, sir, he means more to me than my life—please try and bring him back to me."

But, my dear girl, that fellow Ramasena has made a big mistake. He could make love to you holding you in a tight embrace—no breasts could come in the way; nor is there any monthly break in continuous enjoyment as in the case of other women; nor any chance of pregnancy to *mar* your youth and beauty. He who deserts such a wonderful girl as you, will surely have to give up all sexual enjoyment. Well, you proud girl, go to his house and wait there for me. I have a little urgent work to do for a friend of mine. I'll finish it and go there. That man is puffed up because of his sister's high position. He does not deserve the love of such a gentle girl as you. I will compel him to fall at your feet. All right, you go now.—She is gone; I must hurry away, too.—Phew, What a lot of trouble I had to get out of the clutches of this queer creature. Now I really must get going with my work.

(walking on)

Who is this one greeting me now? God be with you! We are meeting after a long long time; surely, you are Parthakasarthavaha's son Dhanamitra? How is it that Kusumapura's full moon is in eclipse? Oh, how many young girls hadn't you forced to flower! To how many servants, hangers-on, relatives and cronies sunk in the darkness of poverty hadn't you brought light! Were you going to some other country to make large profits there taking with you all the fortune your family had amassed? Were you robbed on the way? Or did the King confiscate every thing you had because you had displeased him? Or did you gamble? For, one single throw of the dice can turn Kubera himself into a pauper. Why are your nails and hair so long? Why are you so dirty? You look as if lost in thought. Your face is pale and pinched and you are wearing such coarse and foul rags. You look as if some divine sage has cursed you—Oh, what are you saying?

"I fell in love with Ramasena's daughter Ratisena and she with me; everyone knows this. She would not give me up even when her mother's greed became excessive. My friends warned me; but I wouldn't listen to them; I placed at her feet everything I had. Of course, she took it all. After a few days, pretending to go for a bathe, she made me change into my bathing dress, pushed me into the pool at the Asokavanika and shut the gate. Luckily, the guards of the park realised what had happened and let me out by the wicket gate. But how can I live in this utter poverty day after day in this city where once I used to live in such pomp? In desperation I was leaving for the forest when, suddenly, I have chanced upon you. I am telling you all this in confidence. I shall do whatever you think will be for my good.

Love scene terra-cotta art < Sungadynasty.

How greedy these prostitutes are! And how crafty!

Come, let me embrace you! It is fortunate that I am seeing you alive. There is an antidote even for the bite of the dreaded cobra; one can save oneself from a fierce elephant in rut in the depth of the forest; one can sometimes escape from the teeth of the cruel shark even in the middle of the ocean. But I have never seen anyone come out alive once he has fallen into the blazing volcano—a greedy prostitute. But tell me, my good man, was Ratisena the cause of this trouble or was it her mother? Eh?

"Why should I lie? Ratisena is in love with me. All this has happened because of her mother. If you, sir, could arrange that we two meet even for a short while behind her mother's back, then you will have saved my life."

Yes, I, too, have heard from others, how much she loves you Ah, he is in tears—Now don't be sad. I have some urgent work to do for a friend of mine. After I have finished, I'll come back and help you. Now, get along.

'Oh, these prostitutes, they are so cunning and depraved. They pass on their misdeeds to their mothers, exactly as crafty kings, pass on their wicked actions to their ministers.—So, here goes this wretch, this master-cheat. Let me also get going.

(wandering about)

Who is this calling me by my name in a voice sweet as a cuckoo's in the spring? (looking into the wings) Lo, it is Priyangusena—Priyangusena, here I am. Yes, my angel, what is it?

"My greetings to you."

Well, my dear girl, my blessings: You who in bed ward off your lover playfully, striking him with your soft hands and feet, you whose ample hips are squeezed by him in excess of passion, may you be always happy.

Now, tell me, my dear girl, who is this privileged man whom you have permitted to massage your tired hips and rub your body with fragrant oil of many scents?

Even when unadorned, you look lovely like the king's pet elephant without her bells, necklaces and silver hangings; one who hasn't seen your artless natural beauty has missed something in life. Seeing you smiling, adorned with pearls and gems, covered with the marks of a lover's nails, fragrant with unguents, your eyes lightly touched up with red eyeshadow, clad in soft silk reaching down to your thighs, your girdle slipping off revealing these lovely rounded hips, your breasts heaving with warm youth, seeing you thus Kama himself would go mad with longing and lose all self-control.

Yes? What did you say?

"Your words are sweet."

You think I am flattering you? Don't be shy. Tell me why you called out to me. What is it?

"Listen."

All right, my girl, I am listening.

"In the palace of our mighty King Purandara there is going to be staged an opera in the classical style called Purandaravijaya. Along with Devadatta, I have been engaged and paid in advance to play a role in it. I have to thank you for this good fortune of mine."

You mustn't talk like that. When the moon is full and the night bright, none needs a lamp: one who is strong does not need any help. You should thank yourself for all your good fortune.—Now I see why Ramasena who has been courting you, has of late, been especially nice to me.

Why! Her raised eyebrows, her narrowed eyes, her cheeks and her quivering tender lips, all show her secret joy. And now she has turned away her lovely face and seeing her relatives she is laughing. At long last Ramasena's efforts have borne fruit.

But surely Devadatta is a fool if she thinks that she can compete with you. You have everything, beauty, grace, youth, joie de vivre; you have mastered the four types of acting, the thirty two different gestures of the hands, the eighteen expressions of the eyes, the six stances, the three steps, the eight sentiments and the three movements in music, both vocal and instrumental. All forms of dance have found perfection in you. When you dance you surpass even the Apsaras who had conquered the hearts of all the gods, the demons and the sages. But, then, my lovely girl, why need you dance at all? Every natural movement of yours is a dance; and with your grace you make men's hearts and eyes dance all the time.

She is blushing—she has dismissed us with the parting gift of a lovely blush and has gone. Now I must go, too.

(walking on)

Oh, but this, surely, is Kanakalata, Narayanadatta's maid. I see, she has profusely dusted her two hard breasts with scented powder, and worn bunches of flowers round her hair and her wrists: she must be a little drunk the way she is walking, looking particularly merry. I must talk to her—but why is she coming so close to me to bow.

Yes, my woman, what are you saying?

"My salutations to you, sir."

May you always be your lover's sweetheart! Now, why have you honoured our streets with your lotus-feet?—What is that?

"You always say such nice things, sir."

No, no, I don't mean to flatter you.

"I am much obliged to you, sir."

That's all right. Tell me now, why have those two lovers—two chakravaka birds separated? Tell me, quickly.

"Consumed with jealousy my mistress had given up food, bath and sleep, had thrown off all her jewellery and was sitting on a rock under a small Asoka tree in the Asoka grove. The moon in the clear sky, the tremulous humming of the bees and the breeze heavy with the fragrance of a thousand spring-flowers, all these increased her longing and added to her misery. Her friends tried to comfort her with soothing words.

Just then, someone — as if he too was smitten by love-passed by the grove, humming some songs in *vaktra* and *apavaktra* metres to the soft liquid music of his *Vina.*

He sang

> What's Youth,
> Beauty, Wealth?
> Alas, alas!
> If you don't frolic
> With your young love,
> When spring is here!

and then another song:

> Life is sadder still,
> If the moon shines bright in the sky
> And the cuckoo-calls fill the air,
> Yet you don't court your love.

The song soothed her, cooled her anger and suddenly, she just couldn't wait; not even for you, sir. She called me and left on foot for the master's house. He too finding the spring tormenting was coming to my mistress to beg her for her love. And they came face to face at the door of the vina-player, Visvavasudatta. Coming out unexpectedly, Visvavasudatta found them there rather shy and embarrassed and took them inside. In the morning my mistress asked me to fetch you. Now, sir, will you please come with me?"

Excellent, excellent. Oh, I am so pleased. You certainly deserve a reward. Let me bless you first—may your youth last for ever; may your lover prize you all your life; and may you get whatever you wish for. Now, you lead the way.

(walks on)

What is Kanakalata saying?

"We go into this house."

All right we will, (enters) Don't worry, the love-birds are here all right.

The lovely spring has brought you two together. May every other season do the same and help lovers to end their quarrels.

The Spring with all its vaunted qualities has made me totally redundant; for, I had no part in bringing you two together. What shall I do now? But may be, I should not blame the Spring at all. May be, this reconciliation has nothing to do with the quiet beauty of the Asoka grove or the loveliness of the moonlit night or the impassioned notes of the *vina* or even the kindly ministrations of friends and messenger girls; may be, the manifold attractions of the season cannot take any credit for it at all. The real reason is that you two young people have at last come to appreciate the genuine qualities of each other and that has strengthened your love. Such love as this is very rare, indeed. It feeds and grows on your own goodness and mutual adoration! This is Kama's own law of true love.

Now everyone in Kusumapura knows the story of your love. So I shall go now. What? Did you say something?

"It is your constant care that has nurtured our love; and it is because of you that we have come together. How can poor lovers like us praise you enough when the whole of Kusumapura worships you for your delightful and endearing ways?"

Now, now, enough, enough. One should not prattle away and stand in the way of young lovers making love. So I go now, farewell.

(Bharata Says)

Just as you delight in your soft spoken young Love, ever graceful and beautiful as the full-blown lotus, so may our gracious king delight in protecting this lovely, sea-girt, hill-breasted corn-adorned land.

(exit the Vita)

Padmaprabhrtaka

Sudraka

Then, at the end of the benediction, enter the Sutradhara.

SUTRADHARA: Triumphant is the blessed Rudra, who in anger—nay as a kindly favour—gave Cupid a more dazzling body, the coquetry of women.

Moreover, The *kurabakas* gleam with blossoms, the cuckoo calls, a delicate shoot, laden with *ashoka* flowers beckons, the mango-perfumed breeze transports the humming of bees; now the God of love, bow in hand, roams the woodlands.

What's more, the flocks form an orchestra, the koel, thrilled with fresh tree-sap, sing the chorus, the vine, mistress of the forest-seraglio, dances, guided by the wind-professor, the trees, bristling with flowers, applaud her with shoot-fingers, illustrious spring arrives, and frost, pale as a pearl necklace, quickly slips away.

Flowers burst forth all around, even from the root, the trunk, the boughs, the twigs of the *ashoka* tree, like secrets entrusted to an informer. Ah! This is the time melodious with busy cuckoos, with chaste tree flowers, with mango trees supporting jasmine, intoxicated with bees, cooled by breezes, dear to the young. *(Exits. End of the Prologue)*

Then enter the Vita.

Good good! This truly is delightful. For the year-vita, withered by winter-senescence, returning spring-juvenility shows itself by virtue of the application of the *elixir vitae:* cool mist. For now, this grove acts like a youth, garlanded with blossoming vines, its trees dancing with agile hand-gestures — quivering shoots; the cuckoo acts like a hair-tuft on the head formed by the *tilaka* tree; the bee, resting in a jasmine flower, enacts the side-glances of a damsel; over here the lotus-pond with upright dark buds is as beautiful as a girl whose tender breasts have just recently grown; the spring breezes blow, misbehaving like rogues fondling the swollen breasts of exquisite women, glistening with the exhaustion of love-making.

To elucidate: mighty is this season, harsh with the torment of Cupid's arrows, since the passion-bee of Karniputra, who has partied away his youth enjoying Devadatta, flits over to Devasena, a mango-stalk swarming with passion-blossoms. She is delicate with the advent of adolescence that barely leaves behind childhood. But hold! Will Karniputra really go that far? Even an exquisite rice-pudding mixed with honey and ghee becomes more delectable when blended with condiments. So methinks he hankers after a different flavour: intimacy with a young beauty, embodied in a *chandala* girl, delightful with merrymaking, jokes, and the straightforward hospitality of youth — a flavour which is the condiment to reveling in the wine of making love to Devadatta. *(walks about).*

How strange! This malady of Love indeed is flighty yet serious. Whereby even Karni putra, who achieved intellectual brilliance by studying many sciences, is an expert in all the fine arts, and who is a professor of the *ars amatoria* with professionally trained girls, has been reduced to this state. For, his eyes bleary, utterly strained with insomnia, his face washed-out like a dawn-moon, his body enfeebled with brooding, ever yawning, all his senses aflame, the very pleasures that normally delight him—moon, spring, garlandry, music, perfumes etc.—now scorch him.

Rather, as far as Devasena is concerned this is to be expected. How so? For this girl is Cupid's worthy lustfield, the grace of her figure and her youth are easily able to drive Karni putra crazy. For, her face with darting eyes, radiant with unkissed lips, chubby-cheeked, her chest budding with freshly risen breasts, her arms, tender like vines, her belly with an indistinctly rising hair-line, her buttocks which have grown plump all of a sudden, her unrestrained temperament, naturally sweet—whom would these not drive crazy? *(walks about)* He now languishes with difficulty on a bed, love sick on account of Devasena enduring a fever brought on by excessive exertion, while he is supplied with remedies for inflammation—pearl necklaces, palm fans and sandal paste,—his vital breaths sustained by the hope of her arrival. But today in the morning an errand boy of Devadatta called Pushpanjalika approached politely, and said to Karni putra:

"Venerable sir, my mistress Devadatta informs you: 'Venerable sir, on no account must you believe that my esteem for you has lessened because I did not come yesterday. My sister, the *chandala* girl, was somewhat unwell, and I took pity on her and spent the night with her. But now I will come.' Then, after entrusting a reply to Pushpanjalika and dismissing him, Karni putra, seemingly improving, said to me: "My friend, Sasa you heard it yourself, 'I will come today.' Now is the proper occasion, approaching, with queries about her well-being, to fathom the reason for Devasena's affliction: she will confide it in private. I am folding my hands with respect: using every means possible, you, beloved of the Gods, must pull out the barb of Cupid's arrow that has darted from Devasena and buried itself in my heart up to the fletching."

Then I said to him smilingly: "Very well, master rogue, why are you lighting a lamp during the day? Am I not well aware of the meetings of your glances, the silent messengers of your desire? Moreover, I am none other than Sasa, the buddy of Muladeva. I shall not return until I have seduced her." After I said this I set off. Now I must proceed in such a manner that I waste time by telling tales and asking questions from my friends on the main street so that I come upon the *chandala* girl without Devadatta *(walks about)*.

Oh, the supreme glory of the city of Ujjayini, the belle of the land of Avanti, opulent with all kinds of accoutrements, the ornamental cosmetic painting on the cheek of the Jambu-continent face of the Earth!

For here, sanctifying Veda recitations, the sounds of elephants, chariots and horses, the hum of bow-strings, things worth seeing, things worth hearing, the debate of the learned, commerce involving the accumulated products of the four oceans, song, music, gambling, jests, here, what's more, the chatting of pimps, there all the arts, and these lines of houses, alive with pet birds, resounding with an abundance of bracelets and girdles. *(walks about)*

If only I perceived some sort of an omen indicating a successful completion of my desired undertaking! (Looking) Oho, here, in fact, is the son of Sharadvati, the honourable Sarasvata from the lineage of Katyayana, who is addicted to poetry. He is playing with a yo-yo in the porch of his house, his fingers busy with a piece of chalk, as if miming with the grimaces of his eyes and brows the poetic flavours he relishes when they present themselves after reflection. No doubt, in such moments poets do not tolerate even a dear friend to block the gushing torrent of inspiration, but it is impossible to pass by without adorning my ears with the flowers of his words blossoming on the vine of eloquence. I would feel myself cheated. I'll approach him. *(approaching)*

My friend, Katyayana, why are you chewing over the air? What are you saying? "The demon of poetry himself impels me." Not so fast, you cobbler who stitches together verse-patches from old poems, why are you now seeking new verses, as a cowherd who has lost his herd searches for fresh footprints? Well, my friend, what subject have you versified?

What are you saying? "But this is obvious: I have made a verse about this current, delightful spring season." May I hear it? What are you saying? "Surely, read it out, it's here on the wall." *(looking)* Where is it? Ah, here we go.

This time of year, when the laughter of flowers bursts forth and bees are drunken, bewildering with the chattering of koels, when breezes are graced with the descent of blessed sweat and desire is harsh and violent, will accomplish what a thousand go-betweens, skilled in reconciliation, would not: handing over even a young, shy girl of choice body helplessly to her lover.

Bravo! This augurs well. My friend, may this verse bring you fame, as does the birth of a good son. And what's more, may you never have a share in the resentment of Goddess Speech. Hey, who is laughing at this? *(looking)* Oho, the toady Dardaraka is also here. Hey Dardaraka, what is so funny about this?

What are you saying? "Sir, you are clearly besprinkling the ocean when you worship the Lord of Words with words." Don't say so, you ignoramus. Does not the spring season deserve an offering of flowers? And furthermore, haven't you heard before?

People offer lamps to the sun, water to the sea, and flowers to spring.

We, for our part, shall worship the Honourable Lord of Words with words. Fine. You have revealed yourself a parasite: this gentleman has been rendered a service. Or rather, this spring time is free from the prattle of cuckoos: conform yourself to this, sir. I am off. *(He walks about and looks).*

Oho, here is someone else Kamdeva's advisor in irregular meters: counsellor of Vipula the very foundation of Prakrit poetry. He has set out somewhere, with eyes downcast, as it is usual in the courtesans' quarter. I know! He thinks himself slighted because Vipula has been treated with disrespect when Muladeva was won over by the charms of Devadatta. This fellow is clearly jealous. All right, I shall drown him in a flood of jokes. *(He points.)* Hello, my friend, you are passing by, miming the grace of the daytime moon, without waking up the water-lilies. Let me ask you something.

Courtesan before King Love scene Kamasutra.

That extremely solid, broad intellect of yours: That extremely solid heart of your Vipula, endowed with the knowledge of the arts and devoted to pride alone, is surely not anguished? What are you saying? "I have grasped the meaning of your riddle. Don't you know Muladeva, the master of swindlers?" Oh no, don't say so. Even though he has gone over to the love-sports of Devadatta, his heart is Vipula alone.

What do you say? "This is also a lie typical of Muladeva." So be it. No doubt, you are genuinely sincere, sir. Why don't you scold now your pupil, Vipula who was approached by Karniputra in order to appease her love born anger? He came as autumn comes to settle the river troubled by the monsoon rains—he was deemed useless and thrown out like a fan in winter.

What are you saying? "When? How?" Listen, my friend. Surely, recently Karniputra, accompanied by myself, set off to conciliate Vipula. Then he, taking up his position in the porch, pushed me forward imploringly, in order to examine the abyss of her anger. And then I approached her, speaking kind words. But she, her beauty spoiled by the blemish of jealousy, as soon as she saw me, said: "Why this exertion?," and turned away. Then I told her jokingly:

> "Who told you what? To whose words is this a retort? So turn back your moon-like face, madam, and speak. For I shall be incomparably delighted as soon as I see that you are amicable. This knitting of your brows terrifies me as would an angry snake."

Right after that her friend, Avantisundari told her: "Your face is distorted with the waves of frowning and red with anger, your lips are scorched by your sighs—why don't you speak to your dear friend who has come to you? Expert with feminine guile, you fight against your good fortune. Give up your anger, you peevish woman. Everything breaks quickly when stretched too much."

Then, Karniputra showed up, saying, "What delightful company!" And she, shaking him off with anger as he bowed before her, said to him: "Without doubt you come because you have quarreled, or maybe because she threw you out. I am just here for you to while away your time when you cannot get your beloved. Why rekindle my heart that is indifferent with hopelessness? Why drink bitter medicine? Welcome. Please go."

What are you saying? "If that is so then I will go to rebuke that ill-behaved woman." As you please. May she heed your counsel. Let's go. *(walks about)*

Alas! Another embodied obstacle to our progress has arrived. For here is the son of Dandashuka, the eminent grammarian Dattakalashi, whose prefix is "Paninian," coming right towards me. I hope I can escape his net of words without complications. He seems distraught. Ah! He must have been crushed in a debate. Consequently his voice, itching for a fight, resonates like a temple bell, no matter how lightly touched. And this fellow is fond of courtesans. He has designs on Rashanavatika, the daughter of Nupursena. Oh dear, I pity poor Rashanavatika like a garland hung from a donkey's neck. He stretches forth his hand and accosts me.

What are you saying? "Art thou hale?" Good grief! Never mind, I will socialise with him. Welcome, O storehouse of words. My friend Datta kalashi, you seem distraught. Are you well?

What are you saying? "I have been assaulted by the crow-like Katantrika grammarians, who are strong in battle: compounds." Alas, a strife of crows and owls! My friend, luckily I see you with your wings unshorn: with your theses intact. What are you saying? "What now is my standing among the bastard Katantrika grammarians?" Just as is theirs for you. I'm off.

What are you saying? "Whither art thou desirous of precipitating thyself? Rest awhile. Why art thou put to flight?" Ah! Have mercy! Please do not strike me with such word-thunderbolts, harsh with painful blows. Speak to me in plain language. I am not *au fait* with the speech vice of you grammarians, a dose of poison for the ears, vile like the bellowing of a camel.

What are you saying? "How could I renounce now a style of speech, a hundred-killer war-machine with its countless verbal bases, which I mastered as a result of clashing with the bulls among garrulous disputants? And how could I make my diction as sweet and soft as a woman's body?" Ouch! I think I've been hit! Oh how helpless you are, Why?

In an uninhibited chat, when attending to women and friends, when a new task is begun, when talking to ordinary people what pertinence have hard words and syllables or what pertinence have thorns in a flower chaplet?

What are you saying? "Inappropriately that wanton woman spoke a rain of words in anger." Now who is this "wanton woman?" What are you saying? "Who would call her 'beloved'?" *(reflecting)* Aha! I know, Rasanavatika. And this is proper. Nothing is more distressing than this that she who is like a cuckoo who moves amidst bountiful bilva trees should resort to an inherently harsh tree.

What a pity! This is a great joke. Let me relish it. Friend Dattakalashi, I am eager to hear more about how your mistress lost interest in you who are so spontaneously courteous. Tell me in detail. What are you saying? "All right. Yesterday, on the ritual occasion as the moon passed through its node, the 'wanton woman' came to the wall of the courtesans' quarter, and, itching for sex, approached me as if to embrace me as I was about to make a ritual offering of ghee. Then I said to her: "Thou cinderwench, mayest thou not touch me as I am about to make an offering!" Alas! This is precisely that camel music. A passionate woman must be tenderly received. Is this affection or a quarrel? This will not do you ignoramus! It is not appropriate for you to alienate a passionate woman who comes to you affectionately. Moreover, you terrify women-folk with your speeches, sparking with grammar, intolerable with difficult words. Have you not heard this before?

He who in private touches his impassioned beloved who is intent on love, whose feelings are most tender, who needs to be engaged with inherently sweet syllables, with the flame of speech that desiccates the ear, he plays a lute with a firebrand.

Rashanavatika has really set herself a formidable task in hobnobbing with this man. Or rather he is her curse. My friend Dattakalashi, you have heard the ear-medicine. Good day to you, I'm off. *(walks about)*

Here comes another human jungle. For this son of the Lord Justice, Pavitraka by name, a secret whores-man, an impure fellow who is an adherent of the Pure Vaishnavas' doctrine, gathering up his wet clothes and contracting all his limbs as if avoiding the touch of strangers on the High Street, he leans against the base of a Shiva-pedestal at the crossroads, covering his nostrils with two fingers. This wretch is so ridiculous, since, to begin with, he is said to be in love with a harlot called Mattakasinya the daughter of Varunika Looking. So why is he now carrying a water-jar? Now the book of his wanton conduct will be opened. Hey, Pavitraka why are you standing there like a turtle on the hot ground?

What are you saying? "I am avoiding the touch of strangers who are easily met on the High Street." Oho, so you say you are avoiding the touch of strangers? But then the vessel of Varunika's buttocks is surely as extremely pure as a ghat of the Ganges. What are you saying? "It's not like that." My good fellow, why are you selling now butter-milk in a household of cowherds? Does one start cheating among cheaters? What are you saying? "All right, please forgive me, Sir, your spy is apparently clever." Whose spy? A spy: what for? The sun does not enter darkness with a lamp. I have no need of spies at all, since I have a thousand eyes for such purposes. So take off the cuirass of dishonest behaviour. You, sir, are a good man only from the outside, for you are well-trained in hypocrisy, O you fellow student of the virtuous, bastard of Vitas! Demonical purity and addiction to harlots: this contradictory conduct appears to me as eating ill-matched food. And what's more, when you approach her so constricted by pure demeanor, you are seizing a jasmine flower with a pair of tongs.

What are you saying? "I have completely renounced flirtation." It is like the fasting of crows: who will believe it? What are you saying? "If you are so sympathetic, sir, please admit me as your pupil." Congratulations, sir, you have entered the right path. And if you have decided to become a pimp, you must immediately peel off the cuirass of hypocrisy that seals you from the love of courtesans. Proclaim aloud your name: a Vita.

What are you saying? "I bow to you." Well, now you have given me a small present. Walk freely, without constraints. Here is my benediction: May you gather the first harvest of love's growth when you lay your powerless beloved on the bed, her clothes ripped off and strewn about, her girdle about to drop, the knot of her petticoat undone, her hands hiding by turns the hollow of her breasts, her belly-folds, her waist, and her navel, sitting down melted by shame, and crying 'No, don't, let me go.'

What are you saying? "My ultimate bliss is secured, I am cured." If so, now you should arrange the tuition fee. What are you saying? "But look, I am folding my hands with respect." Ha, this generosity is surely prodigal. Fine, now I have an accomplished pupil. Now you have become a master, sir, not a mere pupil. Walk freely, without constraints. I am going. *(walks about)*

Wow! Great! Now the wind in the market—nourished by the heaps of various flowers, blessed with the touch of sweat that appears at this spring midday, blowing from among the garland-shops and mansions standing shoulder to shoulder—has approached me in deed, coming forth and blocking my way, so to say. *(looking at the flower-market)* Vasanta Vadhu appears as if embodied: the collection of various flowers form her bigger and smaller limbs.

For she—Her beautiful face is a full-blown lotus, her teeth: buds of white blossoms, her eyes are fresh lilies, her trembling lips: red *ashokas*, her sweet voice is the hum of bees, her breasts: two exquisite bouquets, she is adorned with a chaplet and ornaments of flowers, her dress is made of bright blossoms strung together, her shining girdle: a garland—this flower-market, the wife of spring, has the form of a woman entrusted to flowers. Ah, I find it hard indeed to pass her by when my heart is completely enraptured by the fragrance of the multitude of flowers. *(walks about)*

Oho, here comes another market-town of ridicule. For here is a Vita of obsolete dramas called Mridangavasulaka, who was renamed by the courtesans as the Bhava Jarad (Venerable Old Bull). He is coming out of the house of the handsome young singer, Sir Nagadatta. Bravo! He has managed to hide the pudenda of old age by the trappings of hair-dye, bathing, and unguents. And this fellow is everybody's pal. One cannot pass by without speaking to him. I shall make fun of him. *(pointing)* Venerable Bhava Jarad, do you have abundant provisions in view of your digestion: could you beg enough in view of your decrepitude?

What do you say, Sir? "Due to your loathing: Since you fail to interest me, Sir, now I am sloughing off the skin of senescence as an old snake; old gallant." Along with your vital breaths, as I see. Your

Honour has indeed become young again. You have been truly successful in rejuvenescence through magic.

For the ugliness of your head has been concealed by a substitute for youth made by hair-dye, grey hair has been weeded out with a pair of pincers from your upper lip, your cheeks are close-shaven, with great effort you have achieved a clear complexion, and with these merits of your body you have made it young, as one rejuvenates an old, crumbling house by plastering.

What are you saying? "Old wine, as we know, is inebriating." That is your honour's wishful thinking. May you have abundant medicines of *tri-phala, go-kshura*, and iron filings. I'm moving on. *(walks about)*

Oho, this guy here has ducked on the terrace of the casino when I showed up unexpectedly, and now he is concealing himself behind a stone pillar. *(looking)* All right, I know. This is Shaishilaka. What can be his motivation for avoiding my sight? I see! The brutality of assaulting Malatika's confidante has filled him with alarm. All right, I shall inundate him with the flood of mockery. *(pointing)* Hello, brahmin's Kumaraka why do you avoid meeting with a friend by hiding yourself, as one might repel moonshine with a parasol? He steps forward and laughs.

What are you saying? "Welcome, pilot of pals." Good fellow, how could I be a pilot of pals when I've been excluded from the violent affection of a couple's love-making? What are you saying? "There's nothing like that!" Hey you sex-gleaner, do not say so! It's public knowledge that a Buddhist nun lives in Shaishilaka's house. She, as I've heard, was sent on a mission to you by Malatika, Malakara's daughter, who had fallen in love with you. And you, aiming at the no-frills but pleasing charms of the nun's figure and youth as if at a prey, cared only for the present, not the future.

What are you saying? "My friend, it is a recognised fact that giving up present happiness in the hope of future pleasure is not among the goals of human life. One does not search for fire with a lamp." Ah, very well done. You could clearly keep the secret if you did not give me a detailed account. Give me now the particulars.

What are you saying, sir? "Who would disclose now the details of his own brutishness? But listen, I give you a resume." When I assaulted her she said to me bravely: "With your rush you overstep the bounds. Hey, you rogue, I am a respectable woman! Foolhardy man, what you have undertaken against me who had come to you on a mission is not proper. I ran into trouble when I came to the home of another man, with no witnesses around. No, don't, compose yourself, my dear, let me go before somebody comes in!"

Bravo! An act in a play has taken place, without drums. The son of Vasishtha consolidated the word Vita with this sexual break-in. My friend, may women love you. I'm moving on. *(walks about)* By George! I have arrived at the Courtesans' Quarter, the gathering place of all the guests of love-making. Which is absorption in Love, instruction in imposture, the treasury of illusion, the headquarters of cheating, not to be entered by the penniless, where pains are sweet—may this quarter of the courtesans be easy of access! *(walks about)*

Who is this fellow stepping out hastily from the courtyard of a courtesan, his body wrapped in a dirty shawl, his limbs all drawn in? Oho! I can see the edge of his red robe slipped down in his hurry. Aha! He is that corrupt Buddhist monk called Sanghilaka, who lives in the Forest of Dharma. Lo and behold, the Buddha's teaching is indeed proof against damage: shows the signs of approaching death, since it is still being reverenced day after day, in spite of being defiled by such vainly shaved bogus monks. Or rather, the water of a sacred place does not become polluted because crows drink from it. This fellow has covered himself and set off as soon as he noticed me. All right, he will not leave the range of my word-arrows unhurt. Let's speak to him first. (pointing) Hey you, zombie of the monastery: enjoyments, where are you going now, afraid of as an owl?

What are you saying? "I have just come from the monastery: a bacchanalia." I know that your reverend's monastic discipline: fondness of revelry is a solid fact. You fool, why are you walking in the street of the courtesans so distrustfully as a crane in a pond? Surely the alms of sex are being distributed.

What are you saying? "I have come to raise the spirits of Samghadasika who is dejected because of her mother's death, with the

Buddha's teaching." Ah, in my eyes the Buddha's teaching from your mouth is as defiled as the ritual rinsing of the mouth when made with liquor by mistake. Fie, for shame!

A monk who enters the courtyard of a courtesan by error or, even worse, willfully, looses his luster just as does the OM when used to introduce Dattaka's manual on erotics. What are you saying? "Show mercy, sir. Surely one should be kindly disposed towards all beings." Truly, your reverend, you are constantly find, and so you will achieve final Nirvana through cutting your desires: you always drink booze and so, thanks to the quenching of your thirst, you will completely zonk out. Now he offers his cupped hands.

What are you saying? "OK, may I be released now?" All right, enough of this futile exertion. In any case, release is hard to get for you.

What are you saying? "I am going now. One should also avoid eating at the wrong time." Ha ha, that does it. That's all that is wanting: the scheduled mealtime of this monk, who has never transgressed the Buddha's five moral precepts, is about to run out. Scram, you useless shavelling, a leper is not ashamed of herpes. Go, you are indeed a Buddha: clever. At last, this profligate has buzzed off. So now where shall I rinse my eyes, defiled by the sight of a debauched Buddhist monk? *(walks about)*

Excellent! I've chanced upon an eye cleaner for Vita. For here comes Vasantavatya daughter, Vanarjika by name, comely as a forest alley, combining a configuration of flowers, so to say, into her body, descending from the Kama-temple after properly accomplishing the arrangements of the worship. Since she proudly exhibits the flower-ornaments put on with all her care. I presume she must have set off to visit her lover. Well then, I'll approach her saying some affable words, *(pointing)* My dear Vanarajika, by making this offering of the first flowers of spring have you not lost a guest?

What are you saying, miss? "Welcome sir. I am folding my hands with respect." I appreciate this bud of courtesy. Surely spring, not long since it has arrived has entered into your body. What are you saying, miss? "How so?" Listen then. Your hair is filled with *kuravaka* flowers mixed with spring jasmine, your topknot is crowned with *ashoka* blossoms, *sinduvdra* adorns the slopes of your breasts, you have made earrings from fresh mango-blossoms with dangling fronds, your fingers are preoccupied with flowers: fair-faced one, you bear the embodiment of spring.

What are you saying? "Here is a little gift for you." Very well. Let it remain in your custody. I will reclaim it in due time. I wish you happiness! I'm off. *(walks about)* Oho! This is the house of Tambulasen, Irima's beloved. And this fellow always hangs around. Shall I enter? *(musing)* One cannot pass by without speaking to her. Well, I'll enter then. (entering) Hey, is there anyone in the house of my friend to take care of Sasa?

Oho! Tambulasen has come to meet me already before the entrance, out of respect for me, with not leisurely but rapid steps, dragging behind her overgarment that has slipped down in her hurry. This is indeed an extreme case of courtesy. I suspect she does not want me to enter, that's why she came out, to settle things outside. As I see the signs of fresh love-making on her, she must just have been allowed to get up from her sexual delicacies. Irima is clearly enjoying a sexual gymnastics by daytime. Ah, that fellow is indeed a sex maniac. All right, I shall make fun of her. Tambulasen why are you lavishing your courtesy? What? She says with words faltering by her panting due to sexual sport: "Welcome, my dear friend." Impassioned girl, bring a fan first. Tambulasen was clearly doing exercises. My thief, are you regaining your strength?

Erotic Love Scene > Kamasutra.

What are you saying? "I don't quite follow you." Sandal powder has been smeared off from this pair of breasts of yours when you were embracing your lover. Let me ask you something. Insatiable woman, Irima was sporting all night, without rest: can't you leave him in peace at least by daytime? Surely sacrifice is performed in the morning and in the evening. What are you saying? "You've always been fond of joking at the expense of others." That's not true. Haven't you heard before, sly woman, that concealing one's features is nevertheless also a feature?

What are you saying? "How do you know?" My thief, how come could I not know it? Look, your face-painting is blurred, the yellow paint of your *bindu* is smudged, tresses stick to your cheeks, the lilies, your ear-ornaments, have been removed, your pale-red lips are wounded, your eyes are languid: your face reveals that your lover is covetous of daytime sex. What are you saying? "I've just woken up. Do you suspect something else?" Fine, I am convinced. For I don't see anything about you, however subtle it might be, that could not be fathomed.

Nevertheless, I guess your body was wounded by nails and teeth at the end of your sleep. May the ancestors be satisfied, blessed woman, let there be offering for them, for your garment covers your right shoulder. And another thing that you haven't noticed in your hurry: fie on that botcher who was so deranged as to make two left-foot sandals for you.

My thief, where are you going now once you've been caught with hot goods? Well, she's gone inside and burst out laughing with her lover, *(listening)* This is Irima speaking, "Why hello, master of rogues, come on in!" My friend, who would cut the rope that ties two horses to the carriage of love-making? May the uninterrupted festival of sex go on in the same way. Son of Gargi, I am moving on. *(walks about)*

Oho, who is this girl offering food to the deities at the porch of the outer door? She is languid with sadness, with motionless face and eyes without mascara, her clothes are dirty, her long, thick tresses lack hair-oil, her bracelets are loose and her ring has slipped off because of the strewing of flowers; this delicate, gracile maiden has become even more slender.

I see, she is the daughter of Bhandirasena, called Kumudvati. Oh my, this poor girl has become quite unrecognisable. So for whose sake is she observing this vow, suitable when a wife is separated from her husband, but inconsistent with life in the courtesans' quarter? I know! It is rumoured that she is in love with that Mourya prince Chandrodaya. And that fortunate man has risen up in arms to bring his vassals to heel. By George, it is proper that Kumudvati has lost her beauty separated from Prince Chandrodaya. I say, she clearly puts to shame the women of noble families. And what's more, she is greeting with welcoming words the crow that has come out of desire for the scattered offering and is now standing in a niche on the roof of her house: "Good luck to you, head-ornament of the gable-niche, guest for the Sraddha-offering. Will he return in my life, my love who is always on the road? If he comes back, go now to the arch above another door, for once I've come together with my lover and become free from sorrow I shall give you curd and rice."

Why, her passion is indeed immune from deceit. This royal dowry is not fit for mockery. May her head be veiled by the first queen. I shall take my leave discretely. *(walk about)*

Oho! I thought I heard a noise on the right side of the orchard, confused with the chirrup of birds startled by the jingling of jewels. Fine, the door of this orchard is open. Let's see now *(looking)*. Ha ha! There is a veritable feast for my eyes here. For the daughter of Panchaladasi, Priyanguyastika, by name, is enjoying a ball game surrounded by her friends. Her pride, aroused by the swelling of her hips and governing her fresh youth, entices her, and she is well supplied with skill in all kinds of conquetry, sport and dalliance. "Lifting up the ball of realgar with her hand with fingers like mobile coral, she is as beautiful as a winding *nipa* vine striking a single flower with its twigs."

Granted, her sight is a priceless gain, but even a satisfied person cannot drink his fill of nectar. Therefore, I will speak to her. *(approaches)* My dear Priyanguyastika why are you demonstrating your skill as a dancer to your friends under the pretext of playing with a ball? What? She answers merely by smiling and continues to play. Aha! Her friends are counting her ball throws, I fear there is a wager between her and her friends. Ah, the joy of betting! By all means, I have clearly chanced upon something worthy of watching, delightful with various movements of bowing, stretching, spinning, leaping, retreating and running. Why say more? I think even the wind, eager to enter into her garment blown up by her turning around, turning back, and leaping, runs after her infatuatedly. Truly, because of it's inherent weakness, I fear for her the false promise of her waist, that can be seized with a single hand, that is bowed down by the burden of her breasts which are the seat of her youth. I cannot ignore her. Let me talk to her. Hey, you who are drunk with youth, you are engaged in exertions opposed to your delicacy. Stop, please stop! Hey! I'm talking to you. What, this just increases her mirth. Ah! I will teach her.

Your earrings are swinging as you are carried away in your obsession with the ball, your two arms are astir, your locks shower fullblown flowers all around, the strings of your girdle spring when you turn, and thanks to the speed they glitter and swing—may your waist be unharmed, as it bends down with the burden of your bouncing breasts.

She has managed a full one hundred throws and now stops. My dear Priyanguyastika by great good luck you have won the wager with your friends. What are you saying? "Welcome sir. Please accept my welcome gift of victory." My dear, just seeing you is a priceless gain. I am to be remembered. I'm off. *(walks about)*

Oho! Another pleasurable sanctuary for a friend has appeared. For this is the house of Sonadasi, the daughter of Nagarika and the beloved of Chandradhara. I will enter. I cannot pass by without speaking to her. *(mimes entering and looks around)* Oho! Here is Sonadasi seated in the gate-chamber mulling something over. Now why is she here, the beauty of her body departed since she is without ornaments, her body half wrapped in a dirty cloak, her forehead smeared with red sandal paste, her head wrapped in a turban of fine white cloth, the moon of her face bent down, lightly plucking a lute on her lap with her fingernails, humming a *Kaishika* composition with blue notes that are sweet and slow? She must be longing for someone. For a *Kaishika* song is synonymous with crying. What could this be? I have never heard them being talked about because of a love-quarrel due to Chandradhara. She must be feeling remorse because she frustrated her lover. Very well. I will make fun of her. My dear Sonadasi, why are you wearing the garb of an ascetic of the brothel quarter? My dear, surely Chandradhara has not committed an offense? What? You release tears as my answer. Restrain your tears. Tell me about it.

What are you saying? "I am ruined by my confidante who is only skilled in haughtiness." Surely Sonadasi, your friend is more important to you than anyone else, yet she upsets you? What are you saying? "Because of her bad advice I bear this misfortune." You are naive. You should speak to her like this—When I mostly remained cold I offended him, but now I cannot bear haughtiness even for a moment, O go-between. Take satisfaction now, you ignoble woman, having placed me here on the terrible scales of love. With your advice to resort to haughtiness alone, avoiding conciliation, you have brought me to the state where I must lift up my unaccustomed slack girdle with my hands.

What are you saying? "Now pride is vanquished by love. But your friend, his haughtiness produced by amatory triumphs, is obstinate." Then why don't you go to him? Fair one, put aside your bashfulness. Why are you deliberating, your face turned down and sighing, your eyes filled with tears? Lovely woman, see for yourself the slackness of your ornaments. Conciliate your lover with agreeable words. Why bother with vainly steadying your hands? Haughtiness, O innocent woman, is contempt for a stable reunion.

What are you saying? "But surely it is effrontery if a man is conciliated by a woman?" Nonsense! Learned woman, does not the Ganges approach the ocean? Have done with your bashfulness. Or rather, may your wish be granted. I myself will conciliate Chandradhara. Why say more? This very day I will rekindle loves fire sacrifice that has been deposited in separation for a long time. What? She smiles without interrupting her tears. Verily an image of the moonlight of the rainy season. Fair one, enough of these tears. Good fortune is at hand. What are you saying? "You must now be true to your promise." You will know in the morning. What? The tears have ceased. I take my leave. *(walks about)*

Oho! Another living textbook of erotics approaches. Here is the courtesan Magadhasundari the daughter of Negarika, awaiting the arrival of some gallant. Her face resembles the clear autumnal moon;

her hair is black, soft, curled, glossy and fragrant; her flighty eyes are a pair of blooming lily petals; the rays shooting from her teeth are reddened by contact with her ruddy lips more exquisite than coral; her teeth are like buds of jasmine flowers: white, equal, dense and pointed; the curves of her cheeks, breasts, thighs and buttocks are generous, her body is half concealed by the panel of the exterior door, she holds with two fingers of the right hand one side of the curtain and beats a rhythm on the ground with a part of her left foot lotus as she coos a *Vallabha* quatrain in the Shadja scale, entrancing to the ear, adorned with clearly articulated musical ornaments, its syllable not slurred, in a most sweet register with impassioned notes, while she enacts the evoked sentiments with eye and brow movements. Wow! Who can it be that is summoned like great Indra to a love sacrifice? Very well. I will ask her. Madam, gracile lightning of the cloud-brothel, I ask—For the benefit of what lucky man, oh moon-faced girl, are you peeping outside with your eyes white, black and red at the ends, casting sidelong glances?

Oh dear! She looks at me fearfully like a startled young deer. She must have come back down to earth. What are you saying? "Nothing like that! As an ascetic I am honouring spring." A likely story. Now what does your lower lip, scarred with fresh bite marks tell me?

What are you saying? "These are the marks of the spring breeze, still somewhat harsh with ice." Never mind. I understand. Considering your lips scarred by teeth-marks and the fact that you say you are retrained, it is evident that you are observing a lunar kissing fast that does not impinge upon your vow. She laughs, averting her face behind the door panel. May your asceticism prosper. I take my leave. *(walks about)*

At last! I have burst the shackles of the courtesans' prattle and arrived at Devadatta's house. Perhaps she has gone out already. Whom shall I ask? *(look-ing)* Ah, here is the young son of a danseuse, Darduraka, pupil of the dance teacher Gandharvadatta passing through a private door in the enclosed grove, I will ask him. *(pointing)* Hey, Darduraka, where are you coming from? Do you know what Devadatta is up to? What are you saying, sir? Devadatta has gone to ask Muladeva how he is doing. I was sent by my teacher to see Devasena." For what reason?

What are you saying? I was told: "Bring her the letter with a play containing Kumudvati's part!" And you brought it and she took it? What are you saying? "Out of respect for the teacher she took the letter, but she handed it to a friend who stood beside her." Then she saluted Kumudvati and said: 'I am quite unwell.' Ah, my suspicions are confirmed. This betrays her single-minded devotion to love. Darduraka what was written in this letter.

What are you saying? "Read it." *(takes it and reads)* May tough women-fillies, overcome by love, carry the lovely flower of Cupid, the crescent upon their breast-mountain-slopes, the shoot of the tree of passion, the blow in the battle of the bed, the goad for the exhausted horse in the chariot battle of love, the unfolding of coquetry the mark of secret enjoyment consisting of nail-marks fallen upon their buttocks.

Exquisite! This magnificent benediction augurs success for me who have set forth to seduce a tough woman-filly. Darduraka do you know where Devasena is? What are you saying? "She has gone to the enclosed grove." Ah, she is in the grounds where matters of love are brought to completion. Good, please go. I will enter. *(enters)* Oho here is Devasena, emaciated, wan, lusterless and pale, like moonlight afflicted by the dawn she endures an uncommon secret anguish, a mental ailment requiring a mild medicine.

Aha, so that's why she is enjoying the breeze alone, only with a confidant called Priyavadikaya who knows all her secrets and whose friendship is heightened by affection. Indeed, this too betrays her single-mindedness. Those in love all love solitude. She is in my sphere. So let's approach her. *(approaches)* My dear Devasena you must bear me no malice for interrupting your private talk. What are you saying? "Welcome sir, I greet you." Very well, I accept your polite greeting. Please don't bother to get up.

What are you saying, miss? "Please sit, here is a seat." Sure I'll sit down. My dear, why are you causing pain to your friends: why are you aching for a friend? What is this self-inflicted, invisible ailment with hidden pain, which had no preliminary symptoms? What are you saying? "It is nothing." So! You fancy yourself clever! Don't try to brush me off! You were always fond of me when I was looking for your toys, for example. What's more, I am that very Sasa, Muladeva's friend.

Now tell me what is really the matter. What is the reason for this pain? For, your body is languid without disease, the side of your cheek rests in your palm-lotus, your eyes are steadily focussed in meditation, your heart seems inert, yawning, paleness—thief, what is this new, evil transformation of yours? It fatigues you with sighs, yet it does give you delight—an inflamer of the senses, that craves only one thing: that requires only one medicine.

What? She sighs. Alas! the fire of love has flared up. So be it. Now I will get to know her inner feelings. If you will not take me into your confidence, then may you rare well. I must take my leave. What are you saying? "You are indeed fickle, sir." Oho, she admitted it! Now she will tell me her weak spot. My dear, how could I show fortitude when your body is in such a condition? And, long-windedness brings to mind another business. Please tell me the cause of your affliction.

What are you saying? "I could clearly not hide anything from your honour. But such is the nature of spring that, even in my heart that is guarded by the restraints placed upon me by my elders, something evokes a spontaneous longing." Very well, that is not the name of a disease. You thief, you too know this well, Devasena has become a young woman. My dear, if this is how it is then enough of these symptoms. You will become well with a change of season. What? She is being coy. Dear Priyavadinika what is written on this palm-leaf?

What are you saying? "A role for a play." Let me see it. *(takes and reads)* "In the play Kumudavti: the nurse maid in private admonishes the princess who is infatuated with Surpaka: You crazy girl, your chest is not yet uneven with breasts, the down running to your navel has not yet appeared, you are not yet accomplished. Give up this craving of young maidens, you wrongheaded girl. You are always being made to study the book of misbehaviour by your accomplished friends. Why are you poised, barely ripe girl, to do what slaughters love?" What does Devasena say? "I had not heard that part yet." Ha! You have blurted out your true state. You might as well have said: "I too am in love."

What does Devasena say? "You tend to detect pretense, sir." My dear, please stop brushing me off. Though he be hidden by clouds the opening of the night-lily heralds the moon. Go, you misandrist. Now you are unlucky. More than once you have said, hiding your feelings: "I am not in love." Then tell me, you thief, why have you become even thinner than your usual slenderness? Your cheek is consigned into your hands, your bangles hang loose, your mouth is parted with sighs. This person is afflicted with an ailment, you rogue, how is this endured, you who have such steady hands?

What does Priyavadinika say? "Now that a play on erotics has been produced: an opportunity for the art of love has arisen, by great good fortune our mistress is attached to an exceptional man, not a yokel." Then for whom in Avanti's city is this term "exceptional man" in use? What are you saying, miss? "Who do you think?" Wh-it must be Karniputra. For he Born in a noble family, is learned, not arrogant, smiles when he speaks, is skilled, not envious, speaks kindly, is handsome, virtuous and in his prime, is like an embodiment of Cupid without his bow.

What? Devasena is staring at the ground. You are too shy, there is no need to hide yourself with the hem of your robe. Tell me about it. I wish I could win her confidence! She remains silent. Or rather, coyness in fact belongs to women's dowry of coquetry, and especially so in the case of immature passionate women. So how could she speak herself. Clearly the uncommon expression "exceptional man" befits Karniputra. Nevertheless, insignificant as I am, I shall brace myself and sound her out. My dear Devasena what will it profit me if I listen to someone else's secret? It's clearly none of my business. So I say goodbye to you, miss. As for Karniputra, he is homesick for Pataliputra and, yearning to see his own people, is seriously unwell. He may depart today or tomorrow. I will see you again. But you must get well. Don't forget me.

(stands up to go, turns back suddenly)

Oh no! Who just said: "Alas! Now I am dead!" Ah, Devasena weeps. My dear, why this? Enough tears. All right, I understand. Fortunately your longing has reached a fit receptacle. Karniputra's illness too is on your behalf. You can become each other's medicine.

What are you saying? "Why are you shouting? You truly are ready to cause pain." Stop holding back. Are the chief stars, fair one, though

Courtship Kamasutra > Love Scene.

born together as the daughters of Daksha, not all devoted to the moon? Is the mango tree not climbed by two vines from a single root?

What are you saying? "Now then it must be resolved to protect both." Why, certainly! It is resolved. Tomorrow in fact your sister, as usual, will go to the house of the teacher for her dance lesson. Then you, lovely girl, regaining your confidence, will go to him under the pretext of asking about his health, or he will come here. Why is her head spinning?

What does Dear Priyavadinika say? "I do not like the idea of the gentleman coming here as much as I do her going there. The caste of courtesans gives slander as gift. Therefore, I myself will arrange for her that mistress Devadatta, returning from her dance lesson, will herself lead my mistress to the noble Muladeva to ask about his health." Excellent Dear Priyavadnika now you bear your name rightly. It is appropriate for her to go there. But she must look healthy. What does Devasena say? "Surely I am already feeling better because I have seen you." Why thank you. The transaction of love is completed. You must please give me a souvenir to support the life of Karniputra. What are you saying? "What shall I give?" What is then to wonder about? It's clear! You are as unblemished as a lotus—send him this lotus,' lightly and playfully bitten, rubbed against your sloping breasts, inlaid with your body paint pattern, withered by your sighs, its filaments discoloured with the juice of sandal tree, a sacred offering remaining from the early morning, a gift for felicity in love, its stalk blemished by twirling it in your hands.

What? She assents with a side-glance. Ah, I have received the gift that is an earnest promise of love. With this medicine I will revive Karniputra. *(takes it and stands up)* I must go. Farewell, miss. Lovely girl, receive my blessing: May the Love God himself, with ardent passion as his weapon, grant the success of your temerity when, for the first time, you stealthily make love, flustered with fear and jealous, your girdle and anklets swinging, when fear makes embraces weak, when undergarments slip and give way.

Exit the Vita

The Padataditaka (The Kick)
Syamilaka

(After the pronouncement of the blessing, the Sutradhar appears.)

Sutradhar: May you be protected by Kama who has propitiated the anger of Siva by his death in the fire of Siva's eye. His command, the gods including Indra wear like a garland on their heads. His bow is formed by the outermost corners of the large eyes of women [and] his arrows, the objects of the senses, exhaust and break the spirit of ascetics.

And moreover – May Kama protect you, Kama whose outer organs of sense, but not his might, have been snatched away by Siva who, resting his forearm on Vrsapati's hump for support, worshipped by Nandin and the Ganapatis whose words are overwhelmed by fear, laughingly and with frowning eyebrows looks upon Devi, her hand laid upon her breast.

So with bowed head, I beg to inform you, honourable *sirs*, that we have decided to perform the *Bhana* which is called *Padataditaka*, a work of the noble Syamilaka.

And so it is our desire to bestow the gift of our attention upon the exertion of that poet's spirit, for it is the tearful joy of genial people which dispels the strain which arises in the spirit of the poet who undertakes to compose a poem [as he thinks to himself], "This word must not be used like this here, this must be said in another way, this is well done, here the text has expressed the meaning perfectly."

And so, they who behave like cats and cranes, the noble ministers of the king as well as they who are devoted to inner peace, let them be off! [But] let those remain who are proficient in the art of the banter of the *dindikas*. The company of rogues wishes to drink honey without flies.

For ascetics obtain release not by wailing, nor does a comic tale hinder hope of heaven and so the wise man should simply laugh with an exciting spirit having given up hypocrisy.

What sound do I hear while I am busy with my announcement? (Listening) Oh, I know! Here indeed is the baldheaded Syamilaka, that herald of the rogues, who, upon entering the temple of the *vitas*, issues a proclamation while he strikes upon the gong. It is he who breaks asunder the joy in the union of lovers. He is the messenger of the time of day, the priest of the drums, whose rowdiness prevents the donkeys who bray out to him imitating the soft sound of the doves in the early morning.

But what is this he's announcing? (Listening) (In the wings) The banner of love conquers: the foot of the coquettish woman, belacquered and (encircled by) anklets, which she has raised against her lover, must be woed aside with his head.

He exits (The prologue is ended then the *vita* appears.)

Vita Not at all – what is there in this to announce? That thus while she gives expression to the soft sounds of love, her foot, which gingles with ankle ornaments, has won a victory after it has been raised up in the love battle and while the furthest part of her thigh is revealed by the garment sliding from it.

Hey, who is laughing about this? (Looking around) Dadruna-madhava, too, is here. Well, Dadrunamadhava, what reason is there to laugh abiml this? What do you say? "It is because it stands clear before my eyes that yesterday the honourable lady Madanasenika, the prostitute from Surat, has in the frenzy of her passion, favoured the honourable Taundikoki Visnunaga, [putting] her lotus-like foot on his head."

It is, as you know, truly said, "Joy surely comes to a man in his life, even after one hundred years." Thus, even Visnunaga has certainly received the consecration on his head in the form of a kick which is common to all lovers. What do you say?

"Whence [comes] this luck to him that he is worthy of such a feast of love battles? He regarded this exceptional honour of the goddess of the prostitutes' quarter as nothing more than a humiliation. His anger was manifested in the redness of his eyes, he knit his brow with quivering, scowling eyebrows, he shook his head, he bit with his teeth into his lip, he beat the one hand on the other and, after sighing long, he said, "Oh shame upon you, you whore, you do not know yourself and have presumptuously and disrespectfully put your foot on my head, the locks of which my mother, with devoted hand, has bound up with care, and which my father kissed when it lay bowed at his feet, saying, "You are a virtuous son," and which the Brahmans have sprinkled with holy water in which there were pieces of flowers."

However, when he spoke in this way to her, she paled like the night when the red twilight dims. As she raised her face, lustreless as the moon in the early morning, the glow of her passion disappeared because of her ungracious treatment, her whole tender body perspired as she despaired [asking herself], "What is this?" and, as her beauty fled before her dread, she pressed her head from which the flowers fell to his feet saying, "This [shall] not [happen] again."

However, although she lay bowed at his feet, he pushed her off and said, "Faithless woman, do not touch me, you are not fit to come near me making a sound like intestinal rumblings." Alack-a-day, the female cuckoo indeed follows the owl! It surprises me that even Madanasenika follows the apparition of a man who is an unmanly skinflint. But, on the other hand, she does not take into consideration gifts and love because he is a minister responsible for [the framing of] the edicts of the king. Such women are truly crazy about titles. One certainly learns that motivation in love is many-sided. What is that you say? – "From her longing for a title she has indeed in the process of obtaining the highest title suffered verbal affliction. Indeed the unfortunate woman shrunk back, while her lip, breast and face were washed by streams of tears which poured from under the folds of her eyelashes which were from shame cast obliquely down, just as the female king-goose which has been startled by sudden thundering rain clouds which have arisen."

But this is certainly not remarkable, I have heard something in this that has been worth hearing. But on the other hand, although I am aware of the story, I haven't asked about the ending. Go on, go on! What do you say? "Then I blamed him and addressed him as follows, Well now, pitiful grammarian, don't pound flowers with a mortar, don't play the lute with a torch, don't cut a bewitching woman who is as tender as a twig with a razor of words." When he had been addressed by me in this fashion, he went without paying any attention to me, to the house of Bhattijimuta, the chief of the *vitas*. Then the unhappy woman began to weep, resting her face with the cheeck on her twig-like hand.

Then I raised her up and spoke to her as follows, "Beautiful woman, a monkey is not worthy of a turban, nor an ass of pulling a beautiful coach. Stop your crying! This wretched fellow is really ridiculous! He is not worthy of such great homage is he a lover whom women in their infatuation do not violently torment by pulling his hair, whom they do not bind with their girdles or whom they do not strike with the lotuses fastened to their ears as ornaments? Quite the contrary, Kama stands at his side, youth is a feast for that fortunate man with whom women secretly play as with a slave after they have given up their seemly behaviour."

After she had been addressed by me after this fashion, smiling out of the corners of her eyes, she agreed with what I said and decorated her bed from top to bottom, covering it with her garment. I, for my part, while 1 considered the bad behaviour of that base lover, was roused by the sound of the morning prayers for the king, for day had dawned. After I had performed my duties, I went to the gathering of the Brahmans to dispel the image of my nightmare, as it were.

And it was at the gathering of Brahmans that I saw Visnunaga with dishevelled hair and distressed appearance; he had already gone there earlier and told of his merits [*karman*] with the following words, "Now here I am, a man of such religious merit, that they who are learned in the three Vedas should protect me, whose head has been polluted by the foot of a woman of low birth!"

Addressed in this way, the Brahmans looked at each other while their quivering cheeks betrayed their laughter and, after they had thought for a moment, they spoke, "Well now, holy man, we have looked at the law-books of Manu, Yama, Vasistha, Gautama, Bharadvaja, Sankha, Likhita, Apastamba, Harita, Pracetas, Devala, Vrddhagargya and other great seers. [But] we know of no propitiation for such a great sin."

And when he was addressed in this way, he raised both arms and complained with a still more sorrowful countenance, "Oh you earthly gods, it is not proper that you should abandon me as though I was a member of the fourth caste. Indeed I am a noble man, pure in conduct, of noble family, I have worked hard at the study of grammar and the science of logic, it is I who frame the edicts of the king, I am no ordinary man. Protect me in my misfortune, I who can find no way out [of my difficulty]. I give myself into your protection."

And when the gathering was addressed after this fashion some nudged each other with their elbows, saying, "He is an ox." Others stood staring at him for a long time smiling and saying, "Perhaps he is mad." Some despised him deeply and cursed him, saying, "He has been possessed by Kama." But, on the other hand, some lamented that woman saying, "She has behaved badly."

Now while the gathering was in this state, while the Brahmans were perplexed about what procedure they should follow [in this matter], and while Visnunaga lamented because he was perplexed by their mocking at his [request for] reparation, one of them spoke, a Brahman called Sandilya Bhavasvamin, the son of a teacher, who was himself a teacher well-grounded in the administration of justice, philosophy and the other sciences, who had achieved the highest proficiency in all the arts, was well-spoken, surrounded by a multitude of students, and possessed a humorous character.

After he had raised his right hand he addressed the gathering with a voice which was enlivened by his smile, "O Visnunaga fear not, give up your despair. There exists the following rule of law: those laws which are founded upon an agreement between respectable persons of land, class and family have an authority if they are not in conflict with the holy tradition. You must therefore gather together the class of *vitas* and ask the leaders of the *vitas* for reparation. They shall certainly release you of this outrage."

When he had spoken in this fashion, in the gathering a round of raised fingers sprang to life, accompanied by cries of agreement. When he had heard this Visnunaga departed with the words, "I feel that I am in duty bound." "And you are charged with the task of collecting the *vitas* together." Agreed. What do you say? – "Who do you regard here as *vitas*?" In the first place you are certainly a *vita*. What do you say? – "Why am I in particular favoured with the title of *vita*?"

Undoubtedly, listen after being in discussion the whole day with people who are involved in a law suit, and after having enjoyed a meal some-where at the house of a friend at the end of the day, you enjoy yourself at night wenching and moreover throw a weapon, there is even no water in your house and yet you boast.

So how can you not be a *vita*? What do you say? – "If this is so, I feel that I am in duty bound. You will gather the *vitas* together. [But] first we want to be told the characteristics of a *vita*." A marvellous idea! Listen he must be regarded as a *vita* who, during the misfortunes of his dear ones, protects them against the enemy even with his own life, who in case of suffering can support himself with his own arm holding a sword, to whom the courtesans turn when they are love-sick as the result of a conflict and who always places his possessions at the disposal of those who are needy.

Moreover, those who know *vitas*, extol him as a *vita* who, full of contentment, carries his head which has been honoured by pairs of the lotus-like feet of beautiful women as if it bore a diadem, and whose possessions, they who are tormented by greed (thirst), take with both hands as if they were water.

What do you say? – "We have heard what the characteristics of a *vita* are, now you should list the *vitas*." Listen, the honourable Kamacara Bhanu, Lomasa Gupta, minister Visnudasa, Aryaraksita who comes from the land of the Sibis, the Daseraka Rudravarman, Skandasvamin from Avanti, the *vayda* (doctor) Hariscandra, the Abhira prince Mayiradatta, the drummer Sthanu Gandharvasenaka, Upaya Nirantakatha, Indravarman, the first King of Aparanta from the mountain (Trikuta), prince Makhavarman from Anandapura, Jayanandaka from Surat, Maudgalya Dayitavisnu and others must, if possible, be gathered together.

What do you say – "Be that as it may. [But] do you also consider Dayitavisnu as a *vita*?" Undoubtedly! What do you say? – "Do you mean that bastard poet who has been given charge of the king's army?" Certainly, that's right. What do you say? – "Not at all."

The man who shrivels up although the king has shown him affection, who sleeps and wakens to prayers, whose garment smells of bdellium, whose forehead and knees are hard because of a triade of bunions obtained through worship of the gods (And) in particular for whom the days are passed walking from the temple to the palace and from the palace to the temple, devoted as he is to both buildings.

How on earth could he be a *vita*? Aha, that's how it is. Certainly this is for him the opposite of the character of a *vita* as is the smell of old butter-oil. But he whose twig-like finger has been taken away in a quarrel in the prostitutes' district in Eastern Avanti, in whose two thighs the enemy in Padmanagara has shot two arrows during a fight, whose arms have been pierced in Vaidisa by a mechanically-fired arrow which then penetrated the ground, and who even now still surrenders riches to *vaidya* (doctor) to rouse his virility.

I picture him as the foremost amongst the best of the *vitas* because he grants riches to coquettish women and, although his senses have been weakened, he amuses himself in conversations about love. It is passion and not the capacity which grants satisfaction to those who are wealthy.

How can he not be a *vita*? What do you say? – "If that is the case, he is the first amongst the *vitas*." That is why I picture him as foremost among the *vitas*. You can go. May all go well with you. Let me be off now. (Walking around).

Now I am turning into the town thoroughfare. Honestly, how extraordinarily beautiful the town of Sarvabhauma is! Ruled by king Sarvabhauma and its magnificence revealed in all her jewels, it is the ornament on the forehead of Jambudvipa.

Here indeed the concerts, the noise of womens' trinkets, the sound of pleasure-birds, the sound of Vedic recitation, the noise of the knives in the abattoir, intermingled with the sound of the bows and the noise of crockery in the inner apartments answered by the tame cranes, give the impression that the white garlands of the mansions converse with each other.

In particular people see here the many-sidedness of the creator's creation, diverse, concentrated on one place, never before known and made complete by the presence of the kings who have come from the mountains, the woods, the ocean's shore and the desert and who, in their hundreds, have established themselves everywhere the Sakas, the Greeks, the Tocharas, the Persians, the Magadhas, the Kiratas, the Kalingas, the Vangas, the inhabitants of Kasi, the Mahisakas, the Colakas, the Pandyas and the Keralas have created great joy everywhere in the city (Looking about).

Hey, who's this coming over here, I would like to know, imitating the play of a rich man's widow with a white palanquin from which the cover has been removed? (Upon reflection) O, I know. This is of course minister Visnudasa, characterised by a cane staff and a water-jug and unbefouled by lowly people. Indeed, although he has been appointed to such an important post as that of judge, he is not all too diligent in the performance of the tasks given him by the king, like a monk who takes pleasure in indifference because he is entirely absorbed in meditation.

For even though he has entered a court of law, like a bull in the market place, he meditates and falls asleep, while some of those who lamenting plead their case, sit on one half of his seat and move his knees with their hands while others, with bowed heads, pull his feet towards them.

This appearance, it is true, is the exact opposite of that of the *vitas*, but nevertheless he must be approached since he gives instruction in the law. What else can one do? Let me go to him. He has already seen me from a distance, has had his palanquin put down and has step out. Ah, forgive me!

You must not embarrass me because you feel obliged to be polite What do you say? – "But who is treating you politely? In doing this I am following the established rules of behaviour." Nonsense – is it fitting that you who are so polite, make the honourable lady Anangasena who, like Kama's army, is inclined to love you, so averse?

What do you say? – "Have I not, as befits her love, received her in a friendly fashion? Look here! I have, of course, wished her well, and conferred honour upon her, and when she had sat down, I read her the Yogasastra and, when I saw that both her eyes rolled to and fro as if [she were afflicted] by the wind-sickness, I said to her, "Drink ghee, my daughter."

So how have I not received her in a friendly fashion?" Ah, he has prepared a charming reception for his lover! Beginning to laugh he makes me happy with a lemon, a pure gift! Well now, it isn't possible to deceive me, your pupil, with bribes in such matters. In any case remain as you are. Let me be off now. (Walking around).

O, I have now arrived at the market place in Sarvabhauma where the stalls are full of men and women who have come to buy and sell good and bad merchandise from the land and waters of various lands. Ah really, here the crowd of people in doing business is rowdy like birds crowded in their nests or cows crowded in the fields.

For the sound with its echo resounds in the smith's shop, copper put on a grinding stone produces the screaching of an osprey, a sword that is held in a shell sizzles, reproducing the snorting of a horse and everywhere people are buying and selling.

And especially now flowers are sold which seem in their splendour to be laughing. In the taverns the goblet is passed around and drunk dry. Here the town's birds fly to the slaughter house garlanded with knives, while they are watched out of the corners of their eyes by the meat-buyers holding grass in their hands.

In particular, these crowds of people who jostle each other with their shoulders, and argue buying now this and then that, undulate like sheaves of corn, and here go gamblers who have won money at the game, to the prostitutes' district, accompanied by servants bringing flowers and carrying cakes, meat and liqueur with them.

Let me now leave the market road which is difficult to pass along because of the crush of the crowd, and, keeping the taverns in the flower market on my right side, cross over the Purnabhadra crossroads and turn into the way of the prostitutes' district along the Makararathya. To be sure, entering the district of the prostitutes for a man who has no money, is like going to battle for an unarmed man; both are senseless and lead only to ignominy and uselessness. But still I must definitely carry out my friend's command. Namely a meeting of *vitas* should be held in the district of the prostitutes. (Walking around).

Hey, who is this here who is serenaded with Yodheyaka-songs by drummers from Rohitaka, who have copper instruments and flutes? His garland of yellow Amaranth flowers hangs over one ear, as he pulls together with a turning movement his loose upper garment which spreads outward to the right and the seams of which are disarranged. His one hip becomes visible again and again as he raises the wine goblet with his left hand and dancing brings the temple of carousing to laughter. (Looking).

Ah, I know now. This is certainly the rascal Baspa, the son of a Baktrian, the cock of the prostitutes' district who is a unique object of amusement for all rascals. Well really, I never see him unless he is drunk or has drunken, but at the same time his hand is not oiled with so much as half a *masaka*. How is it then possible for him? (Upon reflection) O, I know how. He is of course intrusive, shameless, and annoys everyone with his familiar behaviour. Baspa goes with a handful of spices in the midst of the dancers, danceresses, servants and hostlers who drinking have formed a circle.

Ah, how skilled he is in obtaining a drink! Enough, I will not speak to him. I'll leave this place. (Walking around) Here is another moving, neglected garden of the *vitas*. Here, indeed, an old prostitute, called Dharanigupta, [descends] from the temple of Kama, where she has made an offer to the god for the fulfilling of her prayers. She places on her shoulders her hair, white as a blooming *Kasa*-liana, which has fallen [over her back]. Wearing clothes which have just been washed, she puts her falling upper garment back on one shoulder. Watching out of the corners of her eyes a dancing peacock surrounded by crows which have settled down when the offer was thrown down, with her right side towards the *Makara* pillar, she walks around it. Well really, even now the remains of her coquetry are some indication of the coquettish game of her youth, already long passed.

Indeed both her breasts, flabby, are surrounded by white rows of nails, her lip formerly sucked (dry), is limp at the corners of the mouth and swollen in the middle, even now because of her experience she gives the right answer with the wrinkling of her eye-brows, certainly her age has struck her beauty violently but has not taken away her coquettish play.

And so it is not possible to pass on without speaking to her. She reveals that she takes curlew-elixir by calling our dear friend Sthanumitra, the drummer, her friend. And so how should I approach her? (Upon reflection) Ah, I know. It is, in fact, two days ago that the unfortunate Sthanumitra experienced something frightful through her because of a far too great an attachment to kissing.

Ah fie, passion knows no compassion! devoted to kissing, with a cough, he spat out her tooth which had lost its root and which, touched by the tip of his tongue, [had found its way] into his own mouth.

And so I would, in truth, be cheated in my desire to enter the district of prostitutes if I passed by this holy place. But, on the other hand, can the falling of her tooth into the mouth of Sthanumitra be revealed. Let me therefore not make her shame superfluous by going to her. I pay her homage in any case. Let me now be off. (Walking about).

I have arrived here in the district of prostitutes. Ah, how exceptionally beautiful is the district of prostitutes. Indeed here rise the splendid garlands of the prostitutes' houses from the surface of the earth towards the vault of the heavens, layed out separately, full of beautiful foundations, verandas, walls, spires, eaves decorated with doves, window decorations in the form of a lion's ear, rafters, lower eaves of the windows of the projecting pavilions, towers, balconies to look down from, gateways, cornices, and daises.

The arrangement of their inner appartments is roomy, and they are layed out in good proportions. They are furnished with hundreds of clear shapes which have been beautifully made, splendid, chiselled out and filled (with a layer of stucco) and sprayed, while the openings are blown through, and the stucco is roughened and smeared (with plaster) and spread thickly and thinly [with a layer of paint]. The doors, windows, platforms in the courtyard, the inner courts, the galleries and the balconies are fitted with wooden joints. The spaces between the orchard and the inner-court are ornamented with one, two or three trees.

The houses are decorated with groups of trees which have been planted for a particular purpose, grass, fruit and flowers. The spotless water in the ponds is speckled with lotus-flowers. The houses are decorated with artificial wooden pleasure-rocks which have been put beside the water, underground rooms, arbours and with galleries of paintings, and their decoration is characterised by costly pearls, coral, and nets of tiny bells, while the pennons of the flags of joy are held high.

Here where horse-carriage stand, with Kiratas who climbed on to the carrying-poles, and which have to be carried by people from Avanti who sit with closed eyes leaning against the rims of the wheels, and here where horses from Cambodja and elephants, on which the uppermost covering is folded up and whose mahouts are lazy with sleep, are an indication that their masters have gone in.

And here in the district of prostitutes, one man, who comes, is enticed and another is craftily sent home with the same ceaseless flow of tears. These girls are on the lookout for those who are very wealthy. However, when they have paid, they are followed by their mothers and violently rebuked (Walking about).

Here a woman conciliates her incensed lover. Here a woman is gracious after her lover has pacified her. There a woman who plays the seven strings of the *vina* with her nails, wails a melody full of desire which for the most part consists of the *kakalipan-cama*-note, on the pretext that it is a beautiful song.

Here a lover adorns his beloved while she holds a mirror in her hand. There a mistress binds up the head-dress of her lover. Over there a woman is teaching her Maina bird to speak clearly. Here a peacock flushed with passion dances threatened by a woman with a Mango flower.

How this woman here strains her slender waist during a too energetic ball-game. Here a woman seated, plays dice with her beloved and there a proud woman is intently painting and reads a story aloud.

Don't be so surprised. Go and sit down, fair maiden. I have not seen you for a long time. What do you say? – "Today you must ask the one who has deceived me, who am blameless, [the reason for this]." Forgive me, good luck to you, in any case I must be off (Walking about).

Here comes another town of a friend. Indeed here comes Hariscandra, the *vaidya* (doctor) from Baktria, the son of Isanacandra, a disciple of Karikayana, illuminating the district of prostitutes, like the moon illuminates a lotus-pond. What is his purpose here? (Upon reflection) Ah, I know. Of course, he loves Priyanguyastika, the sister of (my) former mistress Yasomati. He wrongs me with his secret. And so it is not possible for me to go away without having approached him. Let me approach him. (Having gone up to him).

Well now, lonely *Cakravaka* bird of the lotus-forest that is the district of prostitutes, where have you come from? What do you say? – "I am on my way back after having given a medicine to Priyanguyastika, the younger sister of your beloved girlfriend." The fire of love is certainly not extinguished by-her sickness in that girl who has a rich supply of delight in love, that you have had to prescribe her a remedy to improve her digestion.

What do you say? – "Forget the joking. She really has a terrible headache, you know." Friend, is that really true? What do you say? – "No doubt about it. She can only be cured with difficulty." That's the way it is. The headache is, in fact, the prostitute's private property, made up of simulated sicknesses.

You see: When she his applied sandel-juice which looks like blood to her forehead, the prostitute, whether she is in love or not, speaks of headache, as, at the same time, she accompanies the talks of the one who asks after her well-being by playing with the filaments and leaves of a flowering blue lotus and her knitted eyebrows.

What do you say? – "Your jokes are really always coarse. I am, you know, on my way back after having given her a medicine to drink." That is correct. Without any doubt at all – You drank her face, its eyes elongated because you held her by the hair, while she shook her twig-like braceletted hand, stamped on the floor and held up under her navel with her hand her girdled garment which had fallen down, or you have induced that young girl to drink the filthy medicine from your lips

What do you say? – "Friend, you would do precisely that." Thief, if you will only not taunt me again with a secret! But today all the *vitas* have to gather together for a particular purpose at the house of Bhattijimuta, the head of all *vitas*. And so, friend, you must also come on time.

What do you say? – "The *vitas* already know that they must gather together this afternoon in order to give reparation to Visnunaga. And so you must go. I am also coming." Agreed. Good luck to you. Let me be off now (Walking about).

How did all the *vitas* know about this? So I have only to go to a little trouble, and have only to spend my time meeting prostitutes and friends. Hey, who owns this Indian horse, which although it is decorated with ornaments of the Huns, is not a horse which belongs to the Huns, and which marks the door of Puspadasi who comes from Pataliputra? (After having looked).

Ah, I know. It must be Bhattimakhavarman that jewel of a son of General Scnaka whose presence is indicated by the *dindins* from Lata, who folding their hands answer repeatedly with an *anjali* that something is ready although it is not and whose cheeks laugh with the earrings of white wood which are attached to (their ears).

It is, therefore, impossible to pass by without speaking to him. I would indeed reveal an indifference towards my affection [for him] were I to overlook him. Therefore, let me approach him. (After having approached).

Hello, is there someone here at a friend's house? (Listening) Here Bhattimakhavarman is indeed calling me. What do you say? – "Friend, why do you confer upon me still now the status of a king – which has long since disappeared - by your unusual behaviour in approaching a gate-keeper (who does not exist)? Wait a moment. I'm coming." Friend, I am waiting. (Looking around) Over here, over here, sir. It is Bhatti who's coming over here, ornamenting the innercourt of his house with footsteps which "move like those of a bull who, finding himself in sand, lifts up his feet. Ah! What practice in playful movements is this for him! The saying that the district of prostitutes is made up of coquettish play is correct.

In particular, he performs a one-man show, without vim and without drum, as he enters the palace with slow strides, progressing with arms swinging to and fro, with beautiful, thick shoulders and breasts, with his eyebrows which are skillful in coquettish play, con-stantly looking about him out of the corners of his eyes.

Let me speak to him. Bhattimakhavarman, why do you fill your friends with feelings of melancholy with an all too extravagant delight during the day? Good, may I be favoured only for a moment by seeing you. It is he who approaches (me) laughing, his garment in disarray and spread out to the right (and) he welcomes (me) with hands folded in respect and with panted, stammering words. How on earth can he have enjoyed her pleasures when he has just told me that Puspadasi was mentruating? (Upon reflection).

These *dindins* from Lata are truly not very different from Pisacas. Why? Every Lata, of course, bathes naked openly in the water, he always washes his garment himself, he sets his hair in disarray, he gets into bed without washing his feet, he eats everything, even when he walks along the road he puts on a torn garment, and even when he has only once violently attacked a weak spot (of his enemy) he boasts for a long time that he is a Lata.

He has behaved in every respect in accordance with (what is customary) in his own country. O no! You haven't killed the flower without thinking of the fruit of the creeper, have you?

What do you say? – "What do you mean?" Just look at this filthy upper garment [of yours].

What do you say? – "I think that this [garment] when it hung at the end of the bed, was sprinkled with betel." Not at all. What will this forehead [of yours] dripping with drops of sweat like little pearls have to say?

While he looks away, he begins to laugh loudly. Now, base lover, how were you deceived by her? What do you say? – "Who in fact has been deceived? I have certainly been favoured. Listen. Just tell me, how is it possible that.

That flowering creeper-like woman could be inaccessible while her forehead is broadened by the binding of her foremost locks of hair, whose heavy hips are covered by a garment reaching to the middle of her thighs and whose figure is revealed because the heavy ornament on the front of her girdle has been removed?

In particular, you should hear that when she stood in the roofed portico of her own house, her eyes turned aside, lowering her face a little and looking at her nail wounds, as soon as she was seen by me, she clasped both her hard, trembling breasts in her two hands, and entered the innermost part of her house and shut the door with the bolt in her hand.

When I then entered after her I kissed that coquettish woman passionately while her eyes were elongated as I held her by her hair, and her breasts sprung up when they were violently rolled around, and she said, "What are you? No!"

Well, this is, you know, a remarkable story. Let me ask her (about it). Go on, go on. What do you say? – "Then, friend from shame she shut both my eyes with her hands when I came near her hips, the disc of which was clearly visible now that she had removed her girdle."

Ah, shame on you! You who are no braggart, you are indeed to be feared and are to be reprimanded by noble men. What do you say? – "Even so I feel that I am under an obligation. Have you never heard (what is Written) in the *Mahabharata*. The man who has not many enemies, and before whom people are not fearful, and whom people do not reprimand when they meet him, he, oh Partha, is the lowest of mankind."

Well, this, you know, is indeed characteristic of a *dindin*. Yet, well, I am delighted with you for having the characteristics of a *dindin*. You deserve in all respects to have dominion over the *vitas*. [Accept] now this benediction. What do you say? – "I am listening attentively." Listen:

> May your beloved, when she notices that it is morning, and has embraced your back while you sleep, and has boldly climbed onto your side with one thigh from which (her) garment has been removed and while in that position she turns your lotus-like face around, holding you by the hair, may she drink (your face) and likewise make you drink her own lip.

Away he goes, after he has said: "I feel myself duty bound." I greet you with respect. Let me be off now. (Walking about) Hey, who could this be who decorates the balcony of her house as an Apsaras would her aerial car? This is indeed the prostitute from *Kasi*, called Parakramika, who playing cheerfully with her fluit delights the eye with the coquettish play of her beautiful body. It is astonishing!

With her swollen breasts covered by a golden garment that hangs diagonally over her upper body and her hips clearly visible because of her garment which reaches to the middle of her thighs, she walks about, swaying to and fro just as the twig of the liana that is the district of the prostitutes moves to and fro [and] causes her lovers' hearts to faulter.

In particular, her face is covered by the glitter of jewels on an earring which hangs down over her cheek. Having brought the sweetly sounding flute to her lips she plays it by regular use of puffs of breath during which the palate is directed downwards, emitting the sound *hi*. Frightened by the croaking of the frog, the house-peacock walks about her with a drawn face.

What on earth has happened that Hiranyagarbhaka, Indrasvamin's minister of secret affairs, storms out of her house and comes here? What is so strange about that? In Indrasvamin, Hiranyagarbhaka and the district of the prostitutes, we have warm mixed with warm. He approaches me with hands respectfully folded. Well now, Hiranyagarbhaka, why do you try to ruin this temple of the district of prostitutes with Pisacas from Aparanta?

What do you say? – "You know, my master, who prefers to be abroad, has charged me with such a task. This woman charged a mere 500 gold pieces in the past. Now it is utterly impossible to get her to go to an honourable person even when she has been invited with 1000 [gold pieces], and not even when her mother requires it of her. And so in any case you for your part must urge her to go." You're too naive. One certainly wouldn't obtain life even with 100,000 [gold pieces].

What do you say? – "Do you see at all any reason why we are a danger to her life?" Indeed the honourable lady Kutangadasi, who bears a flyswatter before the lord, has revealed that she experienced such a disaster through contact with your master.

What do you say? – "Just touch my body here. Is this really true?" She would not speak thus an untruth about your master. What do you say? – "Such is our majesty, become habit long ago." For just this reason it is impossible to change it. But this is not so.

Scene of erotic love from ancient Indian Literature.

Look, sir what prostitute would not desire the lord of the Konkanas who knows the rules of poetry, music and dance, and is capable, mild, courtly, and a *Daksinatya* if he is honest in his dealings with women?

In particular, the prostitutes look at Indradatta like female deer at the tiger with their lotus-like hands on their breasts, when he, like Bhagadatta, leads a young elephant or an elephant trained to dance about in the courtyards in front of the prostitutes' houses.

And in particular, she shames all lovers with her discouraging attitude, indicating that the bastard Kausika Simhavarman, the brother-in-law of our sovereign lord, is her friend. What do you say? – "She scorns him particularly because of his inordinate amorousness." A continuing inordinate amorousness, according to what people say, becomes your land perfectly. What do you say? – "I do not know what does or doesn't suit my country. Speak clearly." Why shouldn't I recount it if I am so favoured?

Listen marked by nail welts about his ears as if he has had to be tamed like a wild elephant with a goad, he like a bull [approaching] a young cow, approaches her here, her hips' ornament revealed, now she is without garment.

What do you say? – "And so I will go to him with this gift." If that is so, then respectfully inform Indrasvamin the following:

For no-one else than you, even if she is singled out with hundreds of hundreds [of gold pieces] will she reveal the scene of her hips, where the hollows of her loins are multi-coloured with the round marks of teeth and where she has her lover's garland as a girdle.

Good fortune be with you. Let me be off now. (Walking about) Hey, who is this who comes careering from the house of Ramadasi who comes from Surparaka and, surrounded by a crowd of *dindins*, characterises the district of prostitutes? (Looking about) This moving holy place of the *vitas* is the *Mahapratihara* Bhadrayudha, the lord of the Baktrians who inhabit the north, and of the Karusas and Maladas.

He, with braided hair and his ears ornamented with great, white wooden jugs, mocks the Latas by addressing people with the letter *ja*. And indeed, what a good understanding he has of the Latas! Certainly every Lata.

Has both his arms entwined with an upper garment and his waist bound. With a garment, [twisted) like a cord, and bearing down upon whoever he meets with the letter *sa* he goes striding hastily on, with bowed shoulders.

In particular, with both his hands on his chest in the form of a dove, he says *jaja* loudly without the letter *ya* and, with a pair of similar garments wound about his waist, he goes on as if he is touching mud with his fingers.

In any case, without Pisacas there is no dominion. Or better, it is especially fitting that he wanders about in foreign parts. Indeed wandering about to his heart's content he has placed his feet on the heads of the kings of Aparanta, of the Sakas and the Malavas and as the time went by when he had come to his mother and mother Ganga, he revealed the splendour of the royal house of Magadha.

Indeed the lovely girls of Aparanta sing of his deeds, the soft coastal breezes ruffling their locks of hair, while filled with desire they embrace the lianas of the trees on the sea shore wreathed with date palms.

What is being sung here? Thinking, "Oh what a man!" none wishes to take up arms against Bhadrayudha. He has no peer, for the *vitas*, you know, enjoy his accomplishments like a success easily achieved (Walking about).

Here is someone writing on the banner of the temple of Pradyumna. This is indeed characteristic of a *dindin*. *Dindins* are, in fact, little different from monkeys. And moreover do the *dindins* not love him greatly!

The *dindins* really do ruin a painting with their drawings. They put the filthy ink of the brush on the whole houses. Behaving like woodworms they walk over the floors of houses with wrought iron the edges of which are very sharp.

But what is this he's writing? (Looking about) "Nirapeksa." Indeed this is deservedly his name. One says justifiably: "The name indicates the real nature of character." This rascal indeed allows our beloved friend to pine away with the vow of an ascetic in the district of prostitutes by not troubling himself about her.

Indeed that unfortunate girl bears her tears on her eyelashes, curled, thick, dark and long, while at the same time she bears her face on her hand with its armband washed in her tears and a heavy grief in her heart. These three things three-fold she bears, the line of her body hair bowed by the three folds above her navel.

And so I will rebuke him for this. Well now, exalted Nirapeksa, being compassionate by nature and living in friendship, is it correct that you find pleasure in indifference towards a woman who delights in you? What do you say? – "I understand the intention of your cunning comment. It has become my lot to be a lay disciple of the Buddha. Tathagata has said, "So is the law in the world." Not at all. The word of the exalted Tathagata is a standard just for her and not in any other respect.

What do you say? – "Wherever and whenever has the word of Tathagata not been an authority for me?" Do you acknowledge this? What do you say? – "Undoubtedly."

Listen, noble sir, when you see a deer with its tongue hanging out from exertion, its head lifted in expectation and an arrow unchecked through its heart, do you not remember that Tathagata [was once] a deer in the same condition?

He has began to laugh. What do you say? – "One must not doubt the law of Tathagata, you know. There is indeed a difference between the law and the nature of man. I am not an ascetic." If that is the case, you should free the honourable lady Radhika, who finds herself in such a position, from the ocean of her sorrow.

What do you say? – "What ever you command, O friend, I greet you respectfully, may I be delivered." Deliverance from any point of view, is difficult for you to attain, but accept this blessing when you have returned from your stay in foreign parts, take her who longs for you and is bowed down, on your lap, comfort her fondly whenever she cries, bringing her face closer and closer to your shoulder, then loose her plait which is bound up and rough like the horn of a buffalo cow, and yourself cut off your beloved's long locks drunk on her tears.

He has gone off laughing. I'm going in this direction. (Walking about) Hey! Who's this coming here? He comes eating a radish, the tatters of his ragged garment covering his genitals, his face looking like that of a buck, with brown, hairy, plump shoulders, with reddish-brown eyes which are like those of a monkey; if he is not a Daseraka then he is certainly a Pisaca.

Well I see now. I've seen him before at the residence of the honourable Guptakula, the jewel of a son of his Majesty the king of the Daserakas, my brother, better still, my friend. What then is his purpose in coming here? He approaches me with his hands folded respectfully. What do you say? Ah! That messenger of love from Guptakula, the crown prince, has an abundant capacity in land, clothing and language. Already in the district of prostitutes, he asks for the district of prostitutes with the word "market."

And so it's not possible to allow such a jewel to be lost by informing him. Let him be like that. Let me address him in the following way. Good friend, look for a prostitute in the salt shops on the king's road. Delighted he bows and goes off. I'll go in this direction. (Walking about) Where can I now wash my eye, defiled by the sight of a Daseraka? (Looking about him).

Well I see now. This is indeed the house of Surasenasundari, my former beloved. Why, the sidedoor is just standing open! I'll go in here. (With a gesture as if he enters) Wherever can I remove the tiredness from walking about? Well I see now. Here the Priyangu street with its stone seat invites me, like a beloved [inviting some-one] with her lap. I'll go and sit there. (Looking about) What's written here? (Reads).

Friend, at the first rendezvous no cause for argument arose and I did not hear that he was either dejected or sick. Why then have you, after going to the young man whom you have long desired, returned just as you went, without your make-up wiped off? (Upon reflection).

Here is declared the proclamation of the misfortune of one or other woman whose love someone has rejected. Whoever can I ask about this? (Listening) Hey, here comes Surasenasundaki, given away by the sound of the ornaments on her feet. She it is who comes leaning on the beautiful handle of her umbrella with one hand, as lovely as a twig, while with the other she holds together the cloth about her waist, its girdle inlaid with jewels moving to and fro, while the lower part of her garment falls open; she laughs at me as her figure glitters more and more because of the sparkling of her ornaments as if she were the Goddess of Night with the planets and stars, the moon and warbling of the birds.

Well, truly, it is as if her majesty obliges even me to stand up. She comes to me with the hand gesture of a dove. Do not embarrass me with your mark of honour. What do you say? – "Allow me at least to bless myself by paying homage to you, sir, who has come to me even if it is after such a long time." Do not rebuke me too harshly. Favour this seat, fitting for your lap. She says, "I accept respectfully," and she sits down, shaming half of the stone seat with her round hips.

Ah, don't sit here. What do you say? – "Why?" Because here I saw that in the form of a *sloka* the shame has been spread abroad of a woman whose love someone has rejected. Why, she wipes it out with her hands! Thief, it is not possible to wipe it out. It is truly engraved on my heart! Why is she trying to hide this? What do you say? – "Sir, you know of course that my friend Kusumavatika is madly in love with your beloved friend Sivasvamin, the painting teacher."

Indeed I know. Moreover the honourable gentleman has been favoured by a visit from the honourable lady Kusumavatika. What do you say? – "This is the nature of a woman's heart, desperate with love. She has acted rashly just as women are wont to do."

This is indeed a remarkable story. I'll ask her. Madam, it is my trust, not curiosity about the secrets of another, that asks. How did the feast of their mutual union, long desired, turn out? What do you say? – "Listen." I am all ears. What do you say? – "It is told that when she had favoured that honourable friend of yours by pretending to be under the influence of drink, for him.

The first watch of the night slipped by with a story about wrestlers not nice to listen to, the second went by with the external exchange of delicacies of confectionary and mollasses, the third passed with talk about prospering limbs, [I wonder] if I can tell even you what happened after that."

Beautiful woman, from whom have you heard this? What do you say? – "I heard this story from the doorkeeper Padmapala, who came out of your friend's house and then I sent this *sloka* to her through someone who enquired about her well-being. Then, together with that servant, she came to me and laughing shyly because of her shame she spoke to me, "I ought not to insult you by not telling you a secret. Listen to this unheard [story]."

Then she told me truthfully about everything. And so you ought also to be party to this nectar to the ears. Bursting into laughter and clapping her hands, she recounts it. Beautiful woman, what do you say? – "Listen now to what my dear friend told me." She spoke to me, "Dear friend, when, despite the fact that I embraced him and repeatedly kissed him and when despite the fact that I took him onto my lap and urged him on with my nails, he, as though he was a lump of wood, did not strive to possess me, then I became tired and fell asleep embracing the side of the bed."

Then I spoke to her, "You have indeed experienced a painful situation. I don't understand what this means." Then sighing she spoke to me:

"When he, though he tried, conceived no amorous desire for me, although I approached him with every resource and with coaxing words, then I suddenly burst into sobs, the curves of my breasts quivering, as I realised my misfortune because all my ploys in respect of him had been in vain.

Then he tormented himself greatly by taking me weeping, onto his lap and doing all he could to comfort me again and again with futile kisses and embraces. But I said, "What is the use of your touching me with your hands?" Then he said with a dry mouth, as his embarrassment gave rise to bewilderment, perspiration and trembling, and his words were not over-bold. "Irreproachable girl, do not chide your own fortune, for when I beheld your riches, in every respect this eye of mine was at fault, but the nectar comprised of sexual union with you is counteracted by the bdellium which I drank beforehand in order to get rid of my fat."

Then I reflected, "If bdellium drunk to remove fat annihilates the senses, a lover with bdellium should not even bring about the effect of perfume."

While we both desired the long-awaited, futile sexual union for which the proper moment had come, the bard, the king's drummer, announcing the passing of the night, recited panegyrics and benedictions in loud tones, beating the gong.

Then I was rescued from that plight by him as if by an able friend and dismissed by my lover, as ashamed he accompanied me for a while. And I had scarcely reached my own home when you taunted me with the words of the person enquiring after my well-being.

Now I've told you the whole story. After saying, "I shall now make up for my vain watch by sleeping during the day," she went, having been given leave by me. You, too, sir, who came here immediately after that, have heard this." For isn't that why, I shall enter the deep ocean of the fame of men's deception, that is, Sivasvamin, the honourable Sivadatta's son, with this very ship of jest.

You see, madam, whoever drinks bdellium because he has put on weight, his fat, impetuous woman, soon dissolves and then to women in possession of youth he, like a Yaksa in a painting, becomes only pleasing to the eye.

Bursting into laughter she rises with the words, "I shall be off." Enough of saluting me with respectfully folded hands. I am leaving here. (Walking about).

What is it these throngs of prostitutes are looking at in the shade of every house on the road of the prostitutes' district? They are imitating the splendour of clusters of lotuses with raised stems by lifting their lotus-like faces which are flecked with the garlands of their eyes, wide open with astonishment. They have placed their twig-like hands on their breasts mutually exchanging signals, after abandoning their playthings such as the ball, the flute, and male and female dolls. Hey, whatever is this?

Here a water-jug is rolling, here a water-bag is being drawn along, here an upright barrel is moving forward. What sort of a double store room is this? What kind of a strange thing could this be? Well, I have now seen, this is a belly called Upagupta gliding towards me.

Well, it is rightly said in gatherings of rogues, "Harikrsna is a black forest buffalo whose throat is secretly in possession of the delights of taxes. Haribhuti is a buffalo, and Upagupta is a water-bag inflated by the wind."

How on earth is it possible that this unfortunate Madayanti, who carries Ganga's and Yamuna's fly-swat and who is a reciter of books, is enamoured of Upagupta, after leaving our dear friend, the honourable reciter of books who is well versed in the three Vedas, in the lurch? And accordingly she is embraced by both his delicate arms. Or rather, there is no point in embracing her. For this unfortunate girl has given up love-making because she is menstruating and only makes love verbally for the sake of the support of her family. Nevertheless he is accessible to her.

Dattaka's followers teach that love which consists only in words is unmanly. (Looking about) But why does he look so distressed? Ah, I know. I have heard in the district of prostitutes that her mother has hauled him up before the courts in order to extract! payment. Then he must have quarrelled with his mother-in-law. This is an important butt for jokes. It is impossible to deceive oneself by passing him by. I shall go up to him. (After approaching him) Well, Yaksa of the road of the district of prostitutes, where did you come from?

He halts, saying, "I respectfully salute you here," his words confused as a result of his fast respiration like that of a crow because of his fatigue from walking. Good luck to you. What do you say? – "Here I am back from the office of the minister of the crown-prince after going there for a lawsuit with that old harlot." Can I congratulate you on a victory? Or must I help you with your fine? What is that you say? – "Victory and fines! Why must I be concerned with them? It is all a lot of bother."

How do you mean? What do you say? "Visnudasa was deep in thought. As you know I was threatened by his brother from Konkana. Immediately thereupon he beat me. Visnu moaned and slept there. Moreover, his officials chased me, those who took notes and the clerks pursued me, the court-attendants also chased me and detained me for a long time. What is more, I then realised that on comparison of clerks with prostitutes and prostitutes with clerks you should pay the prostitute, for in her at least there is delight."

Fortunately, I see that you have escaped the traps of the clerks unscathed. You are wise in every respect. Now [receive] this benediction.

May the prostitute whose voice is soft, sweet and lovely, while she is languid with drink and filled with passion, approach you on the bed with [verses in] the *vaktra* and *aparavaktra* metres.

He goes off, laughingly clapping his hands. I shall leave here. (Walking about) Hey, who is this other man? He approaches drunkenly with limp limbs, adorned with fine scented earth like a Lata, as his eyes roll and his laughter is halted in his cheeks. Why has he entered the heaven of the district of prostitutes?

Well, I know, this is Trnapisaca, begotten by a Kira leather-worker with a slave girl of the Konkanas, a female Pisaca, in the house of the king of the Sarkaras.

What is more, he calls the king of the Sarkaras his father and Nirapeksa his brother. Generally those of lowly descent are born deceitful (Walking about) Well, what should I now ask him? "What in fact is his purpose in entering the district of prostitutes?" Hey, here is that old *vita* Bhattiravidatta coming along. Let me ask him. Well, Bhattiravidatta, do you happen to know why this spectre of a man enters the district of the prostitutes? What do you say? – "You are the very person who knows." Then you must go. (Walking about) Where can I refresh my spirit which is fatigued from penetrating the wilderness consisting of this man?

Well, I have seen it is to my dear friend Rama that this other home belongs, which he has bolted out of fear for his friends because he had put no stop to his love-battles with prostitutes.

So how can I enter now? (Listening) In view of the fact that the sound of the girdle, confused by the sounds of ankle ornaments, spreads far and wide, in view of the fact that a fist blow is descending, which betrays beating with the bangle, and in view of the hissing and gasping in the innermost part of the house, Rama is surely satisfying Rama in a way contrary to [the nature of] a young girl.

So let me not enter here. Who would break the wheel of the chariot of the delight of love? I shall go from here. (Walking about) Hey, who is this other scorched Salmali tree on whose thin branches there are but a few offshoots of twigs left, a *vita* in the district of prostitutes like a crane in a lotus pond, a desert demon?

Well I know. For isn't this Taundikoki Suryanaga from Supara? What is he looking for here? What, no sooner has he clapped eyes on me than he covers his face with the veil of his upper garment and runs away, walking around the Kama temple to the right. Well, seeing that my friend Visnu told me that two days ago, when in the company of pennant-prostitutes, who dwell in huts in the district outside the southern gate [of the town], and when he was being taken to court for a lawsuit by barbarian hostlers who were bringing an action through witnessess, he was rescued with difficulty [from his predicament] by General Skandakirti on the consideration, "He is the husband of my master Visnu's wife's sister," why then is he now hiding, as though he were ashamed of this contact with the district of prostitutes? (Upon reflection)

His contact with the king's son is making him feel ashamed of this behaviour. It is marvelous. Contact with virtuous persons, you know, possesses virtue. Since even he is so virtuously disposed, it is impossible to satisfy him without recognition.

Come, by walking around the temple to the right I shall assail him with a barrage of jokes when he confronts me. (Walking around) He begins to laugh now that he sees me directly opposite him. Well, Suryanaga, why are you making this new descent into the prostitutes' district as futile as a dance in the dark by insulting a friend? What do you say? – "What is my purpose here? Haven't I been sent by that bastard of a maternal uncle of mine, Maudgalya Haridatta, who is locked up in jail, in order to ask for news from his former mistress who is now ill? But you hardly understand me."

Isn't this truly marvellous, your constancy in matters of friendship and that prostitute's loyalty towards her former lovers, even when they are in dire straits. And that is why she is loved by her lovers, even if she is ugly or deformed, because she is full of love for her lovers, as though she were Laksmi depicted in a painting, her attire resplendent and lovely matching her beauty.

Moreover, I understand she is doing something which is extraordinarily difficult to accomplish. Why? Well, doubtless she licks his face, which is pale for want of a change [of air] as a result of his being locked up in jail, on whose brow scars have appeared as a result of his worship of the gods, which is covered with a large, full beard and is as it were distorted between its dark bones.

What do you say? – "That is precisely why I respect her." So be it. I shall announce that you are devoted to your friend. He embraces the soles of my feet, saying, "Pardon me, sir." What do you say? – "Sir, you mustn't disclose my visit to the district of prostitutes anywhere like that." Well, friend, who announces the rising of the moon? If you have in fact conceived a loving affection for the hunch-backed servant of that honourable *rupadasi*, your fame will already have spread in this place like drops of oil in water. Not at all!

How will you delight that hunch-backed girl, whose lotus-like face is bent down, whose bosom palpitates when she is embraced, who cannot use her hips when she is in passion because her back is bent by her exceptionally big hump, and who lies on her bed like a *tittibhi* bird?

What do you say? – "Heaven forbid, may that disaster be averted! Here a detailed explanation is welcome. You see, sir, what man of sense will touch the woman who looks like a liana in which insects have caused disease, who with her deceptive gait represents the grace of a camel, who with her arms constantly stretched out looks as though she is swimming in the water, and who by lifting up her face seems to be counting the stars in the sky?"

Ah, for shame, it is terrible. It is not fitting that you, who are so well versed in the law, should rebuke a woman whose pleasures you have enjoyed. Moreover, friend, though she be a hunch-back, thin as a lotus stem and bent, she is still suitable for enjoyment with the mouth, as it were the delight of wicked men.

But she is nonetheless no worse than those pennant-prostitutes who live in the forest. What do you say? – "Then who?" What, don't you know? To what passionate mistresses you go in the forest as a result of your inordinate passion, while you yearn passionately for a love which is hidden to man, while those women are to be had for but a small coin, accessible to lowly fellows and amenable to courteous men.

What do you say? – "Who told you that?" Don't I have a thousand eyes in such matters? Moreover, you will go further and further, you, my friend, who love a hunch-backed girl after abandoning a prostitute who lives by her beauty, you, having also left the hunch-backed girl in the lurch, will surely go to her mistress.

Bursting into laughter he goes off. Come, I shall leave here. (Walking about) Hey, who is that other man coming this way, after rushing out of the house of the Ceylonese girl Mayurasena? He has placed a cloth on his shoulders and is surrounded by southerners holding immaculate, crooked swords in their hands. He draws his loose, beautifully decorated upper garment together and is dressed in an iron coat of mail from Andhra.

His face is coloured with saffron and his hand is busy in taking betel. Well, I have seen. For surely it is the police officer Harisudra who lives in Vidarbha. Well, seeing that, although he begged her forgiveness before my very eyes by embracing her feet, she, thinking, "He is in love with Kaverika," addressed him as follows "Go to her, what am I to you? Of what possible use is the flame of a lamp by moonlight? Stop holding two Bilva trees with one hand at the same time."

How then can she be conciliated by him? Has she pardoned him of her own accord, thinking that her own misfortune brings disgrace in the eyes of the district of prostitutes because, though she was in love with him, he has left her in the lurch and openly loves another woman? Or can she have aroused jealousy because it is in the nature of women to love a man who is already loved? Or could it be that she has been put up to it by her mother, who had been reduced to poverty by her expenses? In any case, I shall ask him. (With a gesture signalling that he is approaching and with his hands respectfully folded).

Is it fitting that you, Oh lion of a man, out of desire for the delights of love with a Dravidian woman, should leave this beautiful Ceylonese woman in the lurch as the lion abandons his den?

What do you say? – "I have conciliated Mayurasena. I have just come from her house." Do tell of how the peace, which had for the greater part been broken, has been restored. What do you say? – "Two days ago I was invited to a performance at the house of the *pratihara* Draunilaka, the superintendent of prostitutes. And there I heard that it had been prearranged that Mayurasena should perform a dance. When the musical instruments had been tuned and a song begun after prior completion of a benediction for the deity, and when the dancer had begun to dance, you know, faults could be noticed in the performance of Mayurasena's dance in the very first figure."

Surely it is impossible for errors to be found in the performance of Mayurasena's dance! Whose is that deep fall then? What do you say? – "The exalted Varunois." That's right, the exalted goddess of wine is always present in the *pratihara's* house. Whom did that confusion from drink concern, then? What do you say? – "Your friend the dancer Upacandraka." Then is he a suitable person for something of this kind? But this happens to be his special delight. Go on, go on. What do you say? – "Then all the spectators were on Upacandra's side. But I took sides with Mayurasena."

Bravo, friend, you acted in accordance with the place and the moment. Go on, go on. What do you say? – "Then I could not refute their opinion. (However, although) I did not refute the spectators, my opinion was approved by the referee because rules comes first." Bravo, friend, you have purchased the honourable lady at an exceptional price. Go on, go on. What do you say? – "When I rewarded her before the eyes of all the prostitutes it seemed as if I was favoured by Mayurasena with a side-long glance out of the corners of her eyes and a smile.

But I was seriously reproved by the expression on Kaverika's face who, showing her annoyance, got up and left. And I only reached home with difficulty from that unpleasant situation, swept along as I was by a flood of doubts as though I had fallen in from both banks, because I was visualizing the anger and favour of both. And when I sat down I let the swing of doubt swing to and fro over the question as to what they would both do.

Then my beloved suddenly came to me and closed my eyes. Then laughingly I said to her "Oh you thief who are adept in closing people's eyes, what is the use of your furtive laughter; for does not the unique touch of your hands give you away?"

Thus, addressed by me and stammering with passion, which was evident from her sweet-smelling breath she said, "Tell me who I am." Then I said to her; "Do not my cheeks, rough with quivering hairs, give you the answer, charming maid? However, you yourself must answer your own question, saying that it is I."

Then she opened my eyes and said, "It is this very deception called the quivering of hairs that attracts me," and after saying these words she kissed me on the cheek and left. Then I said to her, "Where are you going, taking this heart away with you because of your kisses, you thief? I bear both of your feet on my head, do stay."

As soon as she had been addressed in this way she proceeded to a bed and seated herself on it. Then I personally washed her feet. And she said to me, "I have received the water of the feet. Come here now, you really are a cheat." Then, while holding up her girded garment with one hand, she became even more beautiful to the eye as she sat cross-legged, her waist doubled over, her arms as delicate as lotus-fibres and her back all turned to the side. Because at that time her waist was twisted around, the fold of her skin was irregular and her circular navel disappeared in it so that the line of her abdominal hair was uneven. Her necklace having down on one breast supported her other jar-like breast against which her cheek rested. Her earring in the form of a *makara* hanging down beside (that cheek) and dominating the adornment of her brow enhanced the beauty of her posture which was already beautiful because of the turn of her shoulder and cheerful like a Jasmine creeper with its clusters of expanding buds.

The bashful [girl], who [in this posture] was as beautiful as Rati, seemed to be pouring out water flecked with lotusses as she cast glances at me with her unique liana-like eyebrow raised. She said to me, "Whatever pleases you." Then I approached to paint her lotus-like feet after taking a pot of paint standing nearby from out by the window.

Then, my friend, when I directed my eyes on the application of the lacquer and she lifted her heel and her ankle so that part of her shin was covered by her ankle ornaments, I saw her vulva which was like the interior of the lips of a young elephant [or] like the pith of the banana tree, because her silken garment, rustling because of its newness, was undone and so did not encompass her thighs as it followed the twists and turnings [of her body] as she tried to hold it together. Pushing me away as I looked, saying, "You have impudent eyes," she "placed her foot on my breast and kicked me. Then, with my skin rough with the coat of mail of the hairs of my body, I said to her, "Beautiful woman, it is not fitting that you should reject me before I have finished painting."

Then she said to me, "Alright, finish it with your eyes closed, then." Then, [when] I applied the resin of the lacquer to both her feet with my eyes closed she kissed me on the lips holding me by my hair. Then when she saw me, my hair visibly quivering, she embraced me, saying, "You are like an Asoka tree in your passionate desire [to come into contact with a beautiful female foot], I honour your deceit."

Then she went to her bed. You who are loved by the gods, will know what happened after that. "If that is so, you should also join the *vitas* who are come together for the purpose of Taundikoki Visnunaga's conciliation. What do you say? – "Heaven forbid!"

On the other hand, this is a conciliation for me if my head were favoured with a kick from her lotus-like foot." If that is so, you are as invulnerable to all the *vitas*, as the snake Kaliya who dwells in the waters of the Yamuna and whose brow is marked by Krishna's feet, is to Garuda. Saying, "Here I respectfully fold my hands," he goes off laughing. Come, I for my part shall go to the gathering of the *vitas*.

Oh, what do you know? Absorbed in conversation with my friends I did not notice that the day had already passed, For now the sun is setting, gazed after by the lotus flowers, which seem to be mourning his departure and are closing, as after mounting the pinnacles of the houses his heat is removed by deep shadows, while for a long while yet he touches the lifted branches [of the trees] of the park with his rays and his glow is challenged by the eyes of the doves on the balconies of the houses.

Moreover, now the cat, betrayed by the cries of birds, leaps from the window onto the wall; the peacock, returning from the houses, proceeds to his usual sleeping-perch; the deer, eager to sleep on the ground, leaves the floral sacrifice of the dusk and here the goose is ascending from the water and goes to the railing surrounding the lotus pond of the house (Walking about).

Here the vapour of incense on the balconies grows dense rising like the clouds of dust from the cat's-eye gems through the windows, and on the roads bees are swarming, flying high and low, around this stream of bath water.

Ah, how exquisitely beautiful is the main road of the district of prostitutes here, where the courtyards in front of the doors [of the houses] have been cleansed, sprinkled and strewn with flowers, where servants are occupied, at their evening tasks, where the prostitutes are engaged in adorning themselves in accordance with land, age and property.

It is beautiful because of the movement of the female love messengers proceeding about their business, while intoxicated *vitas* are engaged in making all kinds of clever jokes and the road-junctions and cross-roads are thronged with freshly bathed and anointed young men who have been drinking and are merry.

For here an elephant cow cries who, after being made to squat, is slowly mounted. Here a woman is entering a car covered with a blanket and drawn up by the door. Here a horse is changing to a canter, carrying a prostitute with jingling ankle ornaments and girdle and bobbing earrings, being as it were unable to carry the heavy burden of her hips.

Moreover, here the walls of the houses are looking splendid, with their lovely windows wreathed with the lianas of the rays of the lamps, while here and there they are accompanied by the dark which is as dark-blue as blue vitriol, the interstices being white with fresh white-wash, as though they had been adorned with *pattra-lekha* decorations with Xanthochymus Pictorius paint and yellow arsenic sulfide (Walking about).

To be sure this cosmic feast called evening accompanied by the rising moon is lovely from every point of view. For now the exalted moon is rising here, which is a universal elixir of life for lotus ponds just as laughter is for the eyes.

This moon is rising in the goblets of intoxicated women as it were "to overhear their roguish, insignificant conversations, its rays broken by the tips of their earrings, [conversations such as,] "Tell me, why are you approaching to kiss me through the holes formed by the round leaves of the blue lotuses, Rohini can't see you, cast your fear to the winds" (Walking about).

Here a girl is singing in sweet tones, accompanied by her lover; here someone is strumming the melodious lute; here people are forming a party and taking a drink, while the moon has reached the gables of the houses in its ascent.

Moreover, now this exalted moon is making a bridge across the waters of the ponds with its beams, it is casting its staff-like shafts of light across the banana trees and, moreover, while painting the rows of white houses with its nectar it seems to be causing pearls to pour forth from the branches (Walking about).

Ah, you know, the world is as it were favoured with flowing milk called moonlight, the host of waves of which, spilling over the banks as they flow along, seem to be poured forth by the ocean of milk.

For now young men, tightly embraced by young girls, are riding horses or elephants or driving about in carriage and blanket-covered chariots here, as though they were couples of Gandharvas and Siddhas in heaven (Walking about).

Here a man, his gestures playful with passion is embraced by a woman who sits behind him (on a horse), pressing her breasts tightly against his back. Although as he proceeds he turns around and kisses his beloved, his horse continues from habit to follow the road home, without deviating from its path.

Scene of Painting a group of Sex Specialise hunt art.

But whoever is this who even in this moonlight is acting shamelessly, as though he were in the dark, enjoying the delights of the bed chamber in the street of the district of prostitutes? Ah, I know. It is Jayanandaka, the Saka prince from Surat, who is in love with the water-carrier from Barbary. But how on earth did he notice that that woman from Barbary has better qualities with regard to the district of prostitutes than the whole of that town of prostitutes?

Moreover, it is true a barbarian woman shines as the night of which the line of the moon is incomplete, as though she were the supreme goddess of the darkness, dark in respect of her eyes and white with regard to her teeth.

Or rather, people from Surat, apes and Barbary people are all of one category, so that this is not surprising. For is it not in this way that to him whose eye becomes attached to a Barbary girl, be she like a wild buffalo, even this moonlight is as the darkness because his glance is languid and dominated by passion.

Enough of him now, let him go his own way. I shall go from here. (Walking about) Who is this other Lata woman, from both of whose ears golden ornaments in the shape of a rolled palm-leaf are suspended, from the tip of whose plait a cluster of jewels, pearls and gold drops down, whose breasts and armpits are covered with a bodice and whose skirt is tied around the waist with the tips of the hem? (Upon reflection).

Well, I know, for this is Raka who is showing her happiness up in her attic in the street of the district of prostitutes by embracing Mayurakumara, the Abhiraka and brother-in-law of the king, who dances like a peacock. She has as it were purchased the wretched man through her sincerity.

Furthermore she holds that dark weakling of a Mayurakumara, whereas she herself is fair and sturdy, clasped to her breast as though he were the tip of her own shadow (Walking about).

Who is this other woman? (Upon reflection) Isn't this the Greek girl called Karpuraturistha who is deeply loved by our dear friend Varahadasa, the son of the honourable Sardulavarman, whose name is blessed? She holds a goblet with three fingers which is turned to the mock moon (her face), and, by holding up her earring, its reflection dancing across the surface of her cheek, she is, as it were, carrying on her shoulder the moon swinging to and fro with its beams.

After spreading out the long liana of her tresses with her nails that Greek girl contemplates her face in the drink, her eyes glancing sideways, resembling those of the Cakora bird. As though it were lacquer she tries to remove the colour of love, which had risen to both her cheeks, which are white and very delicate, like the blooms of the Bassia Latifolia.

Moreover, as regards to their qualities, I consider a Greek prostitute to be the same as a lover from Malava and a dancing female ape to be the same as a singing ass. Prajapati, you know, is in every respect adept in suitable combinations. For similarly the *Atmagupta* plant is attached to the *Khadira* tree, the *Patola* liana to the *Nimba*; the bond is truly strong when a Greek girl is attached to a Malava.

So though she be my friend I shall even so not address her. For who will listen of his own accord to the conversation of a Greek girl from the district of prostitutes? For it sounds like the screeching of a female ape, consisting for the greater part of the Sit sound. Its consonants are unrecognisable, yet is pregnant with some meaning as it is only indicated by a caress with the index finger. So enough of her! (Walking about).

Who is this other man, carrying his beloved off with him on an elephant as Udayana did Vasavadatta, while the tips of her tresses and the hem of her upper garment are quickly lifted by the winds blowing her face? (Upon reflection).

I know. This is that rich Vitapravala, as he is usually called by the *dindins*, the sovereign of those who wear a hip garment in the battle of love. Overcome with passion as he is, he is in love with that beautiful girl from the district of prostitutes, my daughter, and pays no heed to his parents' injunctions. To be sure he is an extraordinary *dindin*, but even so I am invested with the title of father-in-law. Enough, I shall not speak to him, but respectfully greet him with folded hands and go from here (Walking about).

Come, I shall now go to the gathering of the *vitas*. Here I am, after following the main road of the district of prostitutes in a most pleasant fashion, arrived at the house of the head of the *vitas* Bhattijimuta. Here servants stand in the gateway holding silver jars filled with water for washing the feet. The courtyard in front of the door is filled with thousands of chariots of the *vitas* who have assembled from everywhere.

It is truly said with justification, "The ventures of great men are truly grandiose." For now here flowers of five colours are thrown loosely in the air and are tied in bunches. Incense is passed around. Lamps are lit. A word of welcome is spoken. A chariot is unfastened. Coquettish gestures can be seen. Songs are sung. Musical instruments are played. A hand is offered [for support]. Friendly words are spoken. Some warmly embrace one another. Others affectionately lend each other support. Some bow respectfully. Others touch the back of those who are bowed. Some move about with a frown. Others kiss one another on the head. Some stand around with coquettish gestures. Others sit down playfully. Some pass sandal around. Some rub on make-up. Some apply ointment. Others sprinkle themselves with powder. Coquettish women join in the joking of the *vitas*.

What is the use of many words? With difficulty dwarves lift their feet which reach down in flowers as tall as their knees. Rolling their eyes and producing the sound *sit* [women] are taking the Ketaki leaves which are at their feet.

Moreover, these distinguished *vitas* look magnificent seated next to their mistresses who adorn one half of their seats. Cleverly they make harmless jokes. Simultaneously approached from all sides by prostitutes, they resemble bulls surrounded by cows in the cowshed.

Moreover, for them this gathering is like the sky with a hundred moons because of the moon-like faces of the women, with the horizon flecked with the encountering sidelong glances and as it were bolted by the arms of the young men in combat and covered with stones because of the breasts moist with sandal.

Moreover, these heroes here resemble trees of plenty for the prostitutes, as forthwith they spend their earnings and squander their fortunes. Even during their youth their club-fights are recounted in loud tones by the old people like those of Suyodhana and Vrkodara.

So straightway I shall honour the exalted Cittesvara, folding my hands before my head adorned as with a turban by my friend's commission. Bringing forward this matter in accordance with my friend's request I shall declare to the *vitas* the suit for the reparation of the honourable Visnunaga Taundikoki (Walking about).

Well, noble gentlemen rogues, you who have come together from the surface of the entire earth, who are fond of and announce disputes, hear ye, hear ye Kama, desirous of power as he is, dominates the ascetics. He is the lord of everyone's spirit, the master of the horses of the senses. Even powerful people bear on their heads his command which pales the flashing of the jewels of their topknots (Walking about).

Then triumphs the passionate ecstacy of coquettish women, their ear ornaments swinging to and fro as they laugh heartily. Their gait is uncertain and their glances are inconstant. And so it is that the coquettish gestures of youth triumph.

Hence I announce the following to you, noble gentlemen rascals, after bowing my head that is purified by the dust of prostitutes' feet: "But whatever is there to be said about this?"

Hear ye, that fellow Visnunaga fastens himself like a snake with its breast to the earth. So it is fitting that you should protect him, who is bewildered because of his conciliation.

What is that you are asking me? – "Whose misconduct [is that]?" Listen, his mistress in the ecstacy of her passion placed her foot adorned with ankle ornaments on his head. She threw up her face, tossing back her tresses. Arching the ends of her eyebrows in her fury the outer corners of her eyes disappeared. Biting her lips, her teeth flashing, her ankle ornaments jingled as with her hand she drew up her red garment which had slipped down.

What, are you all saying? – "But of which woman who is ignorant of the heart of a man are you spreading this disgrace which is called neglect?" The honourable lady Madanasenika from Surat, to be sure! The *vitas* are seemingly perplexed at the thought, "Fortunately it is no-one here."

For these Rascals are reflecting as though they have been moved to pity, while they are shaking their hands, furtively laughing, speaking words of reproval, making serious faces and looking at one another especially Bhattijimuta, appointed chief of the *vitas* seated here, has been reduced to a state of the greatest bewilderment by his compassion.

For this Jimuta, like a tired elephant, sighs, "Alack-a-day, alack-a-day!", and, like a cloud, pours water from his eyes.

Here he's calling me. Here I am. What do you command, sir? – "You are recounting anew what I have already heard before, that

[Visnunaga] went to the Brahmans for a conciliation. That is after all why I am seated here, and so you must appeal under oath to the honourable *vitas.*" Whatever you command, sir. Well, sirs, lend me your ears, lend me your ears.

He who says anything out of place here ought never to win the stakes at gambling. He should obey his mother and demurely go to his father. In his stupidity he should drink boiled milk or eat sweetmeats and must become the spouse of a married woman.

Moreover, anyone sitting here who says anything improper must leave the meeting, serve his preceptors, and being a prudish youth he skill resemble an old man, and when he sees grey hair he must did to the world (Turning around and looking about).

Here is Dharayaki Anantakatha calling me, after suddenly rising to his feet. What do you say? – "It is not this honourable gentleman's transgression but her's because she is ignorant of love."

Listen, sir, "That inconsiderate girl who placed her foot, whose touch causes the Asoka tree to bloom prematurely and in which Kama himself resides with bent bow and arrow, on that brute's head as it were out of foolishnesss, must surely do penance for an exceedingly long time" you have spoken well.

For similarly an ass has sung here, accompanied on the *vina*, here an ape has sung songs of praise, here the juice of the mango had been poured into boiled buffalo milk.

But the insulted man is pursued by conciliation. And here the offended man has come, and so you must favour him. Wherever is that grandson of Gogla's among them, who with one hand is readjusting his head-dress which has been disarranged by the impetuosity of passion, who with his index-finger is wiping his brow, strewn with pearl-like beads of perspiration, and is calling to me, saying, "Listen to his conciliation!"? Come, I shall go to him. These *vitas* here are angry, saying, "Who-ever is it who stands up as chief *vita* in the gathering of *vitas* and indicates the conciliation while his appearance is disfigured as a result of his way of life as a *vita*?"

Well, Mallasvamin, have you heard? Thus, speak the honourable gentlemen. What do you say? – "On no account, tell them, five days after my father's death, when my friends were distressed and my relatives agitated, and when I had set aside a screaming baby boy, I drank wine with a slave girl how could I not be a *vita*?"

If that is so you will be recognised even as a distinguished *vita*. Go and sit down. What do you say? – "He should be given his conciliation." Alright, I shall repeat it. Then why is the Sibi poet Aryaraksita forbidding it by saying, "Truly not, truly not, 'this is no conciliation," as he addresses me wheezing as he is troubled by his flatulency? This rascal is indeed an extraordinary *vita*.

For after all, he who is by birth one of the line of the Sibis and has grown old in Bhartrsthana sells his poetry for a goblet of wine in the houses of Brahmans.

What is more should that be so, poets now sell their art for a goblet [of wine] among the inhabitants of Kasi, the Kosalas, the Bhargas and in the towns of the Nisadas.

I shall go to him. Here I am, friend. What do you say? – "How will that small mouthful of rum reach that brute's head, [that small mouthful of rum] that is attached to the curve of her cheek like a bee is attached to a lotus, which after being surrendered by a coquettish woman, causes the Mimusops-Elengi tree to flower and which, having the fresh juice of the mango for a dear friend, is a joy to the eye?"

Here is another, Bhavakirti, who addresses me with folded hands with a view to the conciliation. This youth is indeed an extraordinary *vita*. For it is he who flung an old beggar-woman, whose red garment was in tatters and who had boldly entered for alms, to the floor so that she hurt herself and trembled, and as a lover did as he pleased with her.

I shall go to him. What do you say? – "This is a conciliation for her while dragging him by the hair she must bind him with her girdle; after that he has to massage her feet, when she has gone to sleep."

Well, that is also prohibited. Here's that rich Gandharvasenaka, whose name is ever being talked about by his servants, calling me with raised hand. It is hand of his which is cast like a shower of red lotus leaves over the strings [of the lute], his finger-tips guided around in three methods of lute-playing with different *karana* strokes, [and it is this same hand] which, placing the lute in her lap while following the lute case, enjoys the nail scratches of beautiful women in a wealthy man's harem.

I shall go to him. (Having approached) What do you say? "How great is the difference between the feet of an ugly ass and the girdles, inlaid with gems, of beautiful women, which are the banner of the hip, the chariot of the pudenda, and the magic lute of the encounter in the battle of love?" (Changing the subject).

Now here the poet Aryaka from the south is indicating a conciliation. What do you say? "Let her in her passion beat his head over and over again with the lotus fastened to her ear as an ornament, while [casting] glances stimulated by her playfulness [at him]."

This is also prohibited by this fellow Hastimurkha from Gandhara. What is that you're saying now? – "Shall there be a conciliation for him if that woman causes this [lotus], marked with nail scratches, fastened to her ear by its stem, inlaid and multicoloured by the glances out of the corners of her eyes, to descend with its sweet-smelling pollen on the head of that brute?"

The leading *vitas* are voicing their approval with the words, "Agreed, so he it." (Changing the subject). Here are two others addressing me, Gupta and Mahesvaradatta, these two friends seated together on the one chair, whose poetry is inspired by the *Vararucikavya*.

I shall go to them. (After approaching them) Well, Guptaromasa, what do you say? "His head must be washed with the water from her feet."

'What, this is also prohibited by Mahesvaradatta whose name is blessed his excellent friends who are versed in the three Vedas [saying], "He mustn't even drink the water from her feet."

Here my other friend Sauviraka, an old *vita*, is speaking in a voice enlivened by his spontaneous smile. What are you saying? — "I shall bring her, her delicate body even lovelier because her limbs are unadorned and the tuft of hair of her loins loose and moist from bathing, but he must hold the mirror, whose disc is spotted with the sparkle of her eyes, up to her."

"This, too, is prohibited by that Daseraka poet Rudravarman. What are you saying?" – "That scholar who was born into the noble family of the Kokis, that minister charged with the meetings of the council of the best of kings, ought not to wear his hair which has been defiled by the dust of the feet of a prostitute. He must be shorn."

Here Visnunaga is saying, "I feel in duty bound," and states, "Alas, I would rather my head, which is eternally blessed and has been desecrated by a kick from a slave, were cut off than my hair." What, this is also prohibited to him by that *vita* leader Bhattijimuta.

What do you say? – "He must wear his hair for a very long time without being touched by the hands of beautiful women, with the lianas of their eyebrows arched, their hands as delicate as twigs, sparkling with rings, inlaid with the beams of their nails, with the sound of bracelets sounding irregularly on them.

Moreover, listen to this conciliation for him. He must see me, my head favoured by her lacquered foot covered with ankle ornaments, while her eyes are languid and rolling with love and she claps her girdle with one hand lying in her lap."

Here the *vitas* are praising the *vita* chief Bhattijimuta, saying amid shouts of approval, "This is the conciliation." At this, Taundikoki Visnunaga leaves, after saying, "I feel obliged in every respect." Here is the *vita* chief Bhattijimuta addressing me. Here I am. What do you say? – "It is accomplished. What further service can I render you?"

Listen, may the procuresses, adroit in their conversation, be free of disease, may there be over a hundred *panas* for the rogues, may in this town the evenings on which *vita* gatherings are popular be great love feasts for the prostitutes.

(The *vita* goes off) Here ends the *bhana* named *Padataditaka*, the work of the noble poet Syamilaka, the son of Visvesvaradatta, who lives in the north.

DHURTA-VITA-SAMVADA
Ishvaradatta

Then, at the end of the benediction, enter the SUTRADHAR.

SUTRADHAR: Fame is spread through erudition, wealth is the propitiating of worthy persons, when they are pleased religious merit accrues: this is our mission.

Therefore, in order to delight the hearts of these gentlefolk, we shall stage some play. Madam, we need a song that will delight the heart in this season of rains that is made beautiful with clusters of white and blue water-lilies, white and pink lotuses, *nichulas, ketakis, kakubhas* and plantains, that brings joy to the wealthy and increase the sorrow of the wretched, those hapless individuals oppressed by youth and engrossed in anxiety. Now, this above all is the time —

Darkened by the hair-dye of rain-clouds, limbs shining with the unguent of lightning, decked out in finery of full-blown *kutaja* flowers — this rainy season presents itself just like a pimp. (*Exits*).

End of the Prologue. Then enter the VITA.

VITA: Well said, clouds, deft at drumming upon the mansions of the wealthy, pour forth torrents; a lightning streak, rippling like a wave in the brows of angry women, flashes forth; cold wet winds, coercing tight embraces, blow; Kama lets fly his unfailing arrows, drawn right back to his ear, into the hearts of lovers.

Moreover, the impassioned who depart abroad or who cannot return from abroad, are scorched; those who do not conciliate angry women or who carry anger to far, are simpletons; those who are enthralled by their lovers or who hold their lovers in thrall, are indeed fortunate." In this way the season seems to make a public proclamation announced by cloud-drums.

Ah! The rainy season's bustling excitement, thrilling the hearts of jovial people! For now *the rays of the sun are occluded by clouds laden with water, patches of the ground are wet: the hands of Divakara (Sun) are overwhelmed by perspiring breasts, the sides of Kumari* Maiden *Earth are moist with sweat,* the days seem lovely with the bustle of many days rolled into one. The forests are ready for recreation, with bees lured by the scent of *kutajas*, with dancing peacocks, with cool waters. The forest soil, astir with fire-flies, with fresh tawny grass shoots, invites the lac-reddened feet of maidens to tread upon it. The rivers, *flowing with turbid water,* their fords imperceptible, are as difficult to cross as cheating women *who are menstruating* are impossible to catch out. What's more, A breeze draws near, laden with the fragrance of *kadambas*, coming from deep inside the forest, cooled by showers, as if it carried gifts.

That is why this time is so delightful. It is inconceivable that there should be no yearning in it. For — Now in these days, turbid with clouds, when forests are scented with *kadamaba* flowers and breezes roam, even the heart of a happy person is filled with longing.

And that longing is of two kinds — that arising from a cause and that which has no cause. Of these two, that which arises from a cause is amenable to a cure. But that which arises without a cause, is as incurable as are the fake tears of a harlot. These last few days I have become bored to death, and the blame lies with the bad weather and the hindrances to my constitutional. Although my heart is satiated by the sweet cadences of my dear wife, I would prefer to make my escape. *(Looks about)*

Excellent! At least for now, the weather has cleared. For now, the clouds, their thunder stilled, resemble drums at the end of a concert. The tame peacock, alarmed through the fault of the bad weather, mounts the terrace, spreads its wings and cries. A lute, its slack strings detached and its bindings pinched, warms itself in the morning sunlight, like an impassioned woman shivering in the cool wind. The palace-terraces seem to sputter forth the remaining water, resembling immaculate pearl necklaces, through the mouths of the spouts. The mirrors, dimmed by the damp weather, are being polished.

Moreover, women, listless with the weariness of being confined in their fine houses, go to the windows. The golden girdle, a tight fit after the tribulations of the rainy season, is put on again. Arch-courtesans are hurried to the groves by their lovers. Lac-juice, which arouses passion, is applied to lotus-feet — friends to tender grass.

So where now can I quell this saudade? In the casino or in the brothel quarter? *(after some reflection)* With all due respect to gambling, but I'm down to this last piece of cloth to cover me. And dice, like parvenus, are not always benign. So off to the bordello! For there—

The captivating half-glances, the sweet chatter spiced with giggles, the shared seat—incomparable to the touch—half taken up by her full thighs, hands intertwined, betraying affection, and all those delicious pleasures can be won from courtesans by a man with *savoir faire*, even if he is not their favourite. *(Looking)*

Please close the door. What is it my wife is saying? "Your house has as many holes as an anthill." Even if there are other ways for tax collectors to get in, still, since they're familiar with other houses, they will target the door. And anyway, that's really enough back-talk. Phew, I'm finished, *(walks about)* It is fitting indeed that the name of *Kusumpura* should be established throughout the world simply as 'The City,' a distinction not shared by any other city. Many indeed are its lofty houses. People are amazed beholding all manner of prosperity stemming from masses of chattels and thronging crowds. What is astonishing about this? There are other prosperous cities, too. But let me proclaim its unique virtues.

For — *Sponsors are easily found, art is respected, women can be won over by courtesy, the rich are not arrogant, the uneducated are not jealous. all are versed in polite conversation, all are appreciative of the merits of others, and affable. Even gods, upon my word, can find joy in the City, abandoning heaven: You bump into creditors everywhere. interest is extortionate. women can be bought for a trifle, the rich are very arrogant, the uneducated are jealous, everyone is a gossip. all consider each other unimportant, the people are busybodies. Even demons. upon my word, can find joy in the City. abandoning the quest for heaven, (Walks about).*

Aha! That merchant boy Krsnilakah hastens this way. Indeed he has lost his virginity by frequenting the bordello. He is a worthy vessel for the attentions of a person such as me. He is being scrupulously watched by his father who fears that his family will go down the drain. Somehow he has made it to the bordello, and now his body glows, taken pleasure in by his beloved. I absolutely must congratulate him.

I will go up to him. *(approaches)* Master Krnilaka! May you ever enjoy a fruitful youth. Surely you are coming from the house of Madhavasenya.

What are you saying? "How do you know?" What is there to be known here? For lord Spring makes a match of equals. And I am not unfamiliar with your affairs. By the way, where are you running away to, leaving behind your beloved who craves incessant love-making?

What are you saying? "Now how can you know this?" This too is no mystery. How? On your hand which you have rubbed around on her tearful face one can see eye-liner. Your coiffure is even now disheveled from falling at her feet. It's obvious that you've abandoned her in body, leaving behind your heart. You are cleaving a path with difficulty like a boat tossed about by the wind.

What are you saying? "Well. I have to see papa." What? In this outfit? He'll kill you.

What are you saying? "If my father sees me in such a condition he may perchance drop dead..."

What has he not done to try to make you leave this lusty woman who is addicted to incessant love-making? A father surely is an embodied headache for a man in his prime. It is truly impossible for someone who has a father to even get a glimpse of swagger-adorned gambling, the touchstone of spirited men, where the tension of betting is heightened by mutual rivalry.

It is even less possible to get even a whiff of wine-goblets shaped like dancing peacocks, scattered with a trace of lotus petals, with moonlike circles produced by the sprinkling of mango-oil, rippling with the heaving breath of lovely women. Nor indeed is it possible to be a critic of cock-fights, where the spectators are divided into two camps, where courtesans are sharing seats with their companions, where, because of the proximity of their lovers, the stakes are not checked, in which there are intimate groups of enthusiasts. Nor is it possible for a man who is gazed upon admiringly by the wives of the citizens, whose lovely fingertips quiver with excitement and who put forward their large breasts through the openings of the windows, to tread the path of a lordly elephant who is violent with rut. Nor is it possible to haunt the high street on heroic nights red with blazing torches, girt in mail shirt, with a drawn sword for a sole companion, on the lookout for a major fracas, or ready to cut the fetters for a friend. Nor can some-one give up everything for a friend, his heart tormented with concern to return a favour, free from the blemish of self-exaltation, obliged by debt. All this may be endured. But that those son-of-slave fathers ward off their sons from the women of the bordello for the sake of wealth which is just base metal, as if they had themselves never experienced youth: I have a mind to take up a sharp axe to defather the world, just like the son of Jamadagni, Rama, who was poised to exterminate the warriors. Or have these wretched elders perhaps simply missed out youth? The simpletons have no idea how the taste of a courtesans mouth, fragrant like the water inside a full-blown lotus, with a flavour comparable to ambrosia, can reanimate even a dead man.

Moreover, the tinkle of the girdle, wide open plump thighs, lips bitten without hesitation, sloping breasts made to dance by the tremor of sighs, side-glances with knitted brows, horripilation caused by love cries, eventually accompanied by anger — who in this world could forget the imperious love-making with delirious courtesans?

What are you saying? "My friend, let me report you another disaster." What is it? Tell me, sir.

What are you saying? "It seems that papa has arranged a marriage for me." I'm doomed! Anything but that! Must I listen to such horrors? I could flail my arms and wail: straying from the highway of the courtesan he will take the dirt track of the wife of a good family.

Observe, sir: The heart really ought no to be condemned to the prison of a chaste wife, who is born blind in matters erotic, has a dour visage, habitually mumbles, inflicts dejection even upon the cheerful, who is shrouded in a veil of modesty, who plainly has never seen even her own pudenda, a dumb animal appearing in the guise of a woman.

What are you saying? "That is precisely my resolution." If that truly is your resolution, sir, then I'm glad. This befits our friendship. Go for now. I'll come to your house and instruct you again. *(walks about)* So here is the High Street of Kusumpura, delightful to plunge into even though it is terrifying to behold with its thronging crowds, like the ocean ringed with scattered waves for here:

Whoever sees me, even if in hurry, does not walk away interrupting his story. Even in a congestion everybody happily gives way. Nobody detains me for long, fearing that they may obstruct my affairs. Widely travelled men declare the fame of this best of cities to be well-deserved: Whoever sees me flees elsewhere, even if he is no hurry, interrupting his chat. Everybody rushes on, their hair standing on end, even if there is a danger of injury. Within no time someone harasses me, regardless of transgressing decorum. Those who are familiar with its inhabitants point out that the alleged fame of this worst of cities is a mystery. (*Walks about*)

Oho! This road, like the mind of a Vita, leads to the Courtesans' Quarter. I'm off. For, here I started a quarrel, here I've "had" a courtesan, here I was suddenly startled hearing something improper. Remembering all that I enjoyed here in the flush of my youth, I wander overcome with nostalgia. *(Walk about)*

Yes! I breathe again. I've entered the brothel quarter. *(miming a touch)* Here comes the breeze, caressing the ruffled hair and faces of courtesans their eyes half-closed, suffused with the fragrance of garlands and wine, like a sigh of the Courtesans' Quarter.

Behold the supreme splendor of the Courtesans' Quarter, where the turrets of the palaces resemble the peaks of Mount Kailasa, where the windowsills are leaned on by the sloping breasts of the hetaeras, which is cloudy with the diffused smoke of *agaru* incense, whose side-doors laugh with flower-strings, where amorous men hope to hear the chimes of sounded girdles and musical instruments, whose halting speech is the sound of anklets, and which is the head office of Kama. For here the courtesans' maids parade up and down like Kama's triumphal banners, with readied glance-missiles, the rows of their stainless teeth displayed in open laughter, speaking words in consonance with provocative eye-brow movements; their flimsy blouses are uncontrollable because of their swelling breasts and they are un-clothed as soon as they assume a pose; their delightful gait is unsteady with playful coquetry. One can see exquisite beauties, *petites dames* who are treasuries of coquetry, whose faces are adorned with perpetual smiles; their eyes are wide without wonder; their long, dark hair is smooth, soft, curly, and fine, they saunter slowly with the burden of the orb of their buttocks and carry themselves as rutting majestic elephants do; they are water fountains of carnal passion as it were, ranging hither and thither and their attractive gestures are uninhibitedly sweet.

Furthermore, the rows of the mansions, thundering as it were with incessant drum-beats, alarm the pigeon couples. The gates of the mansions vie with each other, marshalling hosts of craftsmen, with their flower ornaments tossed about by bustling servants. Fragrant oils which allay the fatigue of the battle of love are being applied. Coloured powders, to be spread on the slopes of swelling breasts, are being ground, Garland accoutrements, tender as the hearts of virtuous women, are being put on. The music of lutes, which engages the ear as much as the words of one's beloved, is audible. Wine, intimate friend of the lips of lovers and chutneys, flows.

Moreover, Courtesans make the heart-born God of Love perpetually draw his bow — with half closed eyes, with sloping breasts flashed under any pretext, with laughter adorned with bashfulness, with measured words, delighting the ear, with inherently sweet, deep sighs, with songs perfectly in time. *(Walk about)*

Oho! Here comes Varunika, the maid servant of Madanasenayah! With her youthful exuberance she cares not for her breast coverlet; her garments are made of transparent fine muslin, and she has made a miniskirt out of her hip-ornament. Her face lacks one earring because of her haste, her eyes are as flighty as those of a startled doe, her lower lip, bumpy because it has been severely enjoyed, is capable of shaking even the hearts of seers, and is quick to laughter. She is sticking a lily behind her ear, using the two fingers of her left hand as pincers, slightly raises one eyebrow as soon as she spots me, laughs, and strides on.

For, the ear-lotus displays goose pimples on the cheek of this wide-hipped lady, as though it had silently kissed her.

What strength do I have to pass her by without talking to her? So I will greet her. My dear Varunika! Detain yourself! What! She ignores my words and just carries on. My beauty! I am pleased by your insult. What? She has stopped, laughing. *(approaches)* You need not pay you respects. Let me ask you something. Who is it that happily enjoys this first swell of your pair of breasts, *golden like an autumn lotus with masses of cosmetic powder, pointing heavenwards,* as though they were a pair of sheldrakes, *yellowed with a mass of pollen of autumnal lotuses, flying up to the sky?*

What? Squealing just the single syllable "hee" she bashfully averts her eyes and hastens away, muttering to herself under her breath. That indeed is the essence of love! *(walks about)*

Erotic group love scene from ancient Indian Literature.

Oho, here is Bandhumatika in the doorway of her house, in conference with her maid Caturika seated at her side. Casting a glance unsteady with the dance of her vine-like eyebrows and as tender as an evening lily, she adjusts her girdle unaided. O what a task befitting her youth! O how delicate her dexterity! O how lovely her industry! O her effort betrays her tenacity! O what insolent words will she not say, trying to affix the fillets of her girdle! I definitely must worship her skill at wasting her free time. So I approach her. *(approaching)* Darling, may your enterprise succeed. Madam! Don't bother offering me a seat. But let me ask you something:

O irascible woman! How did this girdle of yours break, the dear friend of the fingers of your lovers, the stream of you navel-pond, a lightning-flash bright upon the cloud of your silken garment, a handhold suitable for manhandling, the string of Kama's bow, the sweet voice of the circumference of your buttocks a rosary to count repeated orgasms?

Rather, why should this be unclear? When, on the bed, the skirt was intimately removed from your buttocks and your lover fondly gazed upon them as, eager to be fondled, they rose up playfully, like the temples of a rutting elephant — O red-eyed girl, the breaking of your girdle surely must have made them uninspiring, just like the snapping of a lutes wire.

What! She lowers her head. No reply? I better leave. What are you saying? "Don't leave." Here I stand, immobilised like a snake transfixed by a spell. What! I can walk! I'm off now. *(walks around and listens)* Oho! It seems a woman is crying in the house of Ramadasi. In this case we may postulate many causes. Which among these is the specific reason for her crying?

For, if sobbing is caused by anger it swells to a *crescendo*, if by misery it fades in a *diminuendo*, if by affection it breaks in a *staccato*, if by fear it is discordant, if by the arising of joy it is vibrato. I believe her to be under the sway of anger, for she is in love, and also miserable: her weeping is crescendo at its onset, much interrupted, and then fades away.

My heart suspects it to be Ramadasi herself. Let's enter now. *(mimes entering)* Oh dear! It really is her. What! Seeing me, she wails all the more. Her tear-drops, tumbling from the corners of her eyes, brimming with the quintessence of wrath, seem to count the offences of her lover. *(approaches)*

Angry woman! What's this all about? Your teardrop sent forth by grief wells in your eyes that steal the beauty of a fresh lotus, rolls down to your lip, falls from that, reaches the firm slopes of your breasts, there too it finds no rest, shivers along the fine line of hair, and fills your navel, which deserves to be fondled by the fingertips of your lover.

Surely Jumbo has not committed something that befits him? What are you saying? "That man came to me, his lip marked by another woman, and as I reproached him, ran off feigning anger. For many days he has not returned." Dear me! What a way to add insult to injury! He absolutely deserves the severe punishment of those who destroy their own clan for committing just a single one of these offences, how much more for such an aggravation of insults.

But even if this is how the matter stands, considering that it is the time when banks of clouds throng together, we may endure the insult of this wretch. For now even kings who hold each other in hostile contempt set aside their quarrels, how much more lovers with hearts tender like *shirisha* flowers? If my words mean anything to you, take heed of the season and hasten to your lover at once.

At night descend from the tower of your mansion wreathed in hanging clouds, to the street, echoing with the sound of water gushing from the spouts on the houses, O timid girl, and when you reach your lover, your body shivering with cloud-born wind, speak your mind to him, clearly, in between bouts of love-making, the tremor of your lip allayed by the heat of his mouth.

What? The down on her cheeks standing on end reveals that she pays heed to my words. So I'm off *(walks about).*

Here indeed is Ratisena, her face speckled with droplets of perspiration because of her confinement to the inner chambers, squinting with her half-closed, lovely eyes, her tresses clinging to the sides of her cheeks. She must have just woken up, for, still somewhat groggy, she exposes herself to the wind entering through the open window. How lovely she is to behold! So I'll speak to her. *(approaches)* My dear, enjoy yourself! Seeing you, slightly tipsy, like western quarter flushed with the redness of twilight, even Kama would be bewildered and drop his flower-bow, how much more someone else?

Your personality is not impaired, the sweetness of your voice is the same, passion does not leave your eyes, and you've lost none of your modesty, recollection has returned and your mouth is still smiling. Intoxication, setting aside its defects, transformed, attends you with virtues.

O Ratisena! Please permit me to take my leave. Madam, I dare not leave without your inchoation. What! She slammed the window. Well! I am dismissed. *(walks about)*

Damn! Absent-minded as I am, I almost passed her by. For here is Pradumnadasi, adorning the street in the red-light district, betraying her fatigue brought on by love-making, which seems cling to her face, its cheeks wan from her addiction to sex, her large eyes rolling, her forehead yellowed with her *tilak* rubbed all over it, beautiful with disheveled locks. She has rows of fresh nail-wounds, visible through the transparent skirt covering the circumference of her buttocks, appearing like blossoming *ashoka* flowers fallen him into clear water. With her ornaments broken in love-sport, she looks like a female elephant with her accoutrements hanging loose at the end of battle. She covers her lower lip with her hand as if it were a lamp flickering in the wind, and moves with a hundred tiny steps as if trailed by a child. This passionate woman is to my liking! So lets have a joke with her. *(approaches)* My dear! Why do you conceal the *outstanding beauty* of your lip, which, invested with the marks of your lover's teeth, resembles the *glorious body* of a wounded hero? What! She smiles! Dear me! I have hurt her with my impertinence. For though she smiles but slightly, her bite-wounds cause her pain.

For her breasts swell as she draws a deep breath, her belly much deepened by the upward thrust of her breasts, her eyes elongated by her raised eye-brows, the fingers of her lotus-hands shaken with the agony of her bite-marks — if just any woman can enchant the hearts of men smiling in this way, a passionate woman surely is obliged to smile, when her lower lip is bitten.

What are you saying? "Long time no see." I have been confined to the prison of my house by this criminal weather. But who has enjoyed your attentions madam?

What are you saying, miss? "I am coming from Ramilaka's house." May such a good match be long lasting. I say! Ramilaka is the sole inheritor of the Love God's estates. Why?

O slender-waisted lady, the youth of him has borne fruit, who drinks deeply your mouth opened somewhat in a smile, resembling a goblet reflecting the half-moon.

Darling! Please guard your lip from naughty birds. Off you go, I'm also moving on. *(walks about)*

At last! Here is the door of the hovel where the rogue-couple Visvalakah and Sunanda live, ever-shut in fear of unbidden guests like the demon Kumbhakarna's mouth. For Visvalakah, who squandered all he owns, stripped bare to his body like a naked mendicant, sticks to Sunanda even though her hair is about to fall out only because he is addicted to prostitutes, just as a crow will hover about the outskirts of a village. As for her, well beyond her prime, whom it is pointless to approach, like a dried up river in the wilderness, she now, it seems, attends upon Visvalakah. So it would not be right to pass this couple without paying my respects. I'll start shouting. Who lives here? *(listens)* I hear the clattering of wooden platform shoes in time with approaching footsteps, which is like the thundering of the hooves of a galloping horse. Visvalakah must be close. Hark! It is he who bellows!

Hullo, what are you saying? "Who is it who is observing the donkey-vow?" I'm Death's messenger come for Sunanda. What! Recognising my voice he has fallen silent. Well, won't you open the door? Then stand firm. Behold, I spew forth the fire of a curse.

May your head be far removed from the left foot of a dallying woman, playfully lifted up in a love-quarrel, jingling with the sound of a shaking anklet.

The door is open. So I enter. *(mimes entering)* What are you saying, sir? "Aren't we dear to you? It is indeed not proper to cast such a curse." Well said. For such a curse could make even Brahma's world quake, how much more you? So now then the propitiation to countermand this curse. How?

Some liquor, *on which floats a new-blown lily, rippling with waves when lifted too quickly,* must be given to her who keeps the household of your heart, *who has a vast forehead-mark patterned on a fresh lily and who saunters about sportively with graceful swfti movements.*

With this I take a seat, *(sits down)* Don't trouble yourself to offer me water to lave my feet, for the high street of Kusumpura is by nature spotlessly clean, even more than palatial terraces. My feet do not need to be cosseted.

What are you saying, sir? "Connoisseurs such as Vishnudasa gathered in Ramilakas salon and some difficulties, delightful due to the clash of opinions, have arisen a propos the topic of *ars amatoria*. And when they found themselves incapable of fully unraveling these, then it was I who was solicited to put forth my hypotheses. And so I advanced my hypotheses. May I request now the honourable Devilaka also to expound on this matter? Whatever you say on this topic we shall take as authority. I was on the verge calling upon you at home to hear you elaborate on this matter. Now you yourself have put in an appearance. So if you have a moment to spare, let me explain."

At your service, sir! I'm all ears. I'll hold forth to my ability. But wind refuses to leave my *backside* like a spoilt brat that clings to the *hip*. So I cannot remain seated for long. If it please you, then let us converse while perambulating; this salon is spacious.

What are you saying? "Sure, no problem." *(They stand up)* Please speak, sir. What are you saying? "If it is money alone that binds courtesans to men, then how can they be classified into superior, inferior or middling types?" Sir! Gifts are in fact a universal means of winning over people, but especially so in the case of courtesans. Nevertheless there is difference. In all cases those who understand esoteric and exoteric matters teach that:

> A young prostitute of the inferior type falls in love as a consequence of gifts, or without a cause; the middling type becomes infatuated by seeing beauty in consort with youth, or due to gifts; a lady of the superior type shows affection to a benefactor of a ripe age, free from craving, who is more than just handsome, but instead, sir!, is a man whose ornament is appreciation.

What are you saying? "How is one to detect that a courtesan is in love?" I'll explain, listen: Lovely, sly side-glances, dancing eye-brows with smiles enlivening her face, innuendoes, fleeting giggles punctuated with claps, flashing the navel, arm-pits, and breasts, fiddling with the girdle, and deep, drawn out sighs reveal a passionate woman struck by Kama's arrows.

What are you saying? "Many such signs of passion are taught. But because courtesans are generally deceptive and because these are the signs of their trade, who would place his trust in them? So how is one to detect that she is in love?" Listen.

Tearful sighs, an affectionate gaze, emaciation, paleness, a mist of droplets of perspiration, showing an interest in a man even when his money is gone betray the sincerity of a passionate woman in love. *(walks about)*

What are you saying? "What is the logical reason that the first date is so confusing?" Listen. For young men—not for passionate woman, though—the first encounter is clearly not a suitable occasion to enact the theory. It is natural that the poor men are so confused. Why?

It's difficult strike up a conversation, and hard to get an answer, and even if a lively conversation should ensue it's difficult to win her confidence, and even if confidence be won it's nearly impossible to have her at will, and even if she is enjoyed to one's heart's content—the young courtesan may or may not show interest.

Furthermore, before the king, among scholars, and during the first encounter with a beautiful girl, even a smart man, his heart spoiled by fear, becomes afflicted with stammering. *(walks about)*

What are you saying? "For what reason do men fall in love at first sight even with worthless women? And what line of action should we take when they cheat on us?" When something is directly perceived, there is no use in stating a reason for it. Kama has great latitude in these matters. But the cheaters among the worthless women with whom men fall in love must be ditched instantaneously. Why?

A man of strong character can endure the bitterness of separation from his beloved. The grievously wounded heart of those scorned by their loved ones will never mend.

What are you saying, sir? "What if a woman falls in love with a man, but for him she is not the beloved whom he really appreciates:

should he leave her?" No, not at all! While maintaining his affairs with his other sweethearts too, and not slacking in his gallant behaviour, he should act towards her from time to time as if he were a man in love. Why?

Those men who have no respect for a lovely, passionate woman who is young and is in love, should, upon my word, be yoked to broad-shared ploughs with oxen whose hearts have been scorched by the plowmen's words. *(walks about)*

What are you saying? "What if someone has committed an offence: how should he appease his beloved?" Your uncertainty is indeed appropriate, for the anger of women in love is as resistant to remedies as is a remittent fever. Nevertheless there must be a cure for her anger. Today's youth hold that falling at the feet is the only medicine in this case. I don't have a high opinion of that. Just as the feet of aged priests are also touched—feet with hard and blunt nails, feet which look like old crabs, which are rough with corns caused by sandals, and smell foul because they are rubbed with rancid ghee—how can this be a way of showing our respect towards the feet of lovely women which are as tender as flowers-buds? Furthermore, it is also not free from defers. Why?

When a man grasps his beloved's feet she will necessarily shed tears. Flowing tears mean misery. When spirits become low, how could there be love?

Others, however, say the following: "She should be conciliated by repeated swearing of oaths." That, too, is an uneducated view. First, even women of good families do not believe the promises of their lovers, how much less courtesans? On the other hand, what point is there in conciliating a woman who might actually believe it? And it is taught:

"Living in a village, the prattling of priests, dependence on others, poverty, and an unsophisticated woman: these are the factors that kill a man's passion."

Some say: "She must be made laugh by any means whatsoever. Once laughter has removed her obduracy, she will become easy to enter into, like a river in which a ford has been discovered." In my opinion, although this is correct, nevertheless one cannot obtain the fruit of anger in this way. Why?

Pulling up slightly her very thin, draped garment, making her lower lip dance, saying something lewd with refined diction which is, at that moment, pleasing to the ears, when, enraged, a woman lets fall her left foot, which resembles a fresh lotus, on her lover's head: those who have mastered love say that this fruit of a love-quarrel a desirable offering to youth.

Therefore, female anger can be assuaged by the employment of humor, too. But having thus investigated the methods to allay women's anger, I propound nothing but "aggressive kissing," because its efficacy is immediately perceived. Why?

Grabbing her abundantly perfumed hair with the left hand, with the right clutching both of her hands for a while—due to the joy that falls to his share when forcibly kissing the moon-face of his beloved even an old man, having gratified Kama, will not wither.

What are you saying? "Do you know of a remedy for accidentally calling the beloved by another's name to her face?" Ah! Using another woman's name is a catastrophe for a lover! A cure for this is as difficult as a cure for someone bitten, by a venomous serpent, so I must immerse myself in meditation for a moment. Permit me a moment of concentration. *(ponders)* Yes! I have it!

One can boldly and dishonestly deny everything, or stay immobilised as if frightened because of what the woman says, or quickly pretend it to be a joke, or one should link it with another phrase and that one with yet another, or one might blurt out many other names—this is the remedy for the wound inflicted by a *lapsus linguae*.

What are you saying? "How can assault with nails and teeth, even though painful, arouse pleasure?" Ha ha ha! What a foolish remark! Look, sir: assault with nails and teeth, even though painful, arouses pleasure for those in love. How?

As the whip, wielded by the charioteer, makes a steed attentive to its speed, just so stimulation by teeth and nails in lovesport makes the heart focus one pointedly on touch. *(walks about)*

What are you saying? "How can one spot an indifferent courtesan feigning passion?" Now sir! What could be unclear in this matter? This is the teaching: one should substantiate passion in an infatuated woman. And it has been taught how. Consider Sir! Pro primo even the enlightened sages have no power to conceal their mien, how much less tenderhearted, dimwitted women? Therefore, it is the demeanor that must be carefully diagnosed.

What are you saying? "How?" She bursts out laughing for no reason, speaks without being addressed, jumps up with a start, does not understand what was said, does not display the coyness natural to womankind, when tightly embraced she lets go again and again, she is exhausted after indulging m love-play — a woman fallen out of love can be seen through, no matter how clever she may be: she is like a vine with barren flowers.

What are you saying? How is it possible to cure estrangement once arisen? Or is there perhaps no remedy for this condition?" Listen sir: love arises only in two ways: because of a cause or without a cause. Of these, love that arises from a cause can only cease due to a cause. In the same way, that which arises without a cause can only cease without a cause. Thus, since neither infatuation nor estrangement is uniform, how could it be possible to effect a remedy? On the other hand, I shall expound the remedy for love which has become stale:

> Frequenting other women, or a change in love-sport, a serious quarrel, or forbearance at the right time, clever words delivered with a smile, worship of her relatives or their praise, staying away on the pretext of going to a courtesan, visiting a big city, or some rash adventure, or gifts can rekindle the beloved's affection when it has become dulled by familiarity.

Moreover, listen sir: Each woman must be courted as it suits her: a young girl with being childish, a greedy one with gifts, an intelligent woman with being intelligent, a short-tempered one with soothing words, a stiff woman with devoted service, a good-natured one with being affable. *(walks about).*

What are you saying? "How can one captivate a woman who shows the symptoms of love, does not say 'enough' but does not move close to you, who bides her time?"

You've made a very good point. First of all the lover must know the nature of the woman. It can happen that the nature of the woman is just like that. But without the right means you won't be able to captivate a conceited woman even if you devote your whole life to this task. As for the secret of women, I hereby reveal it:

> If he gets her down and ravishes her quickly at a solitary place, as an elephant ravishes a vine it has crushed, or, knowing that she is drunk, arouses her gradually with half-uttered sentences and then lays her down, or cheats her using some other trick, or conceals his own feelings: such a behavior of a man will never be fruitless, for women have a perverse nature. *(walks about).*

What are you saying? "Wormnisers say there are four kinds of love-making: when her anger has gone, when the lovers are together for the first time, when the man sets out on a journey, and when he returns. Which one do you consider the best, sir?"

Here is my opinion in this matter: To begin with, making love on the first date, and, what's more, to a lovely girl whose confidence you haven't yet won, is a dangerous enterprise to throw yourself into, just as jumping into a lake of unknown depth is dangerous. As for making love when the man sets out on a journey: for a woman whose passion has cooled off because she is overwhelmed by sadness it will entail, when her eyes are clouded with tears and her heart-ache intensifies, it will become joyless and pathetic: as such it does not please me, like the disk of the moon when it is eclipsed. As for making love when the man returns from the journey: It is mildly-exciting, like indistinct music on a rainy day, because your beloved has not made her toilette and is bashful. Quite a different matter is that love-making which comes when anger slips away: it surpasses that wonderful elixir called nectar witnessed by scripture, which arose from the Blessed Ocean—churned by the Mandara mountain wielded by the Gods and the Titans and its potency maximised by the admixture of every medical herb—, which strengthens health and vitality. Why?

> The impetuous love-making of a woman who, at the end of quarrel, does not release that emotion from her heart becomes rugged with unchecked scratches and bites. *(walks about).*

What are you saying? "Sly foxes ridicule a man fooled by courtesans. How can an amoroso escape the courtesans' snares?" Oh, courtesans and scribes, both arc equal in that they strike at one's vulnerable points. Of these two the scribe, having made entries into his ledger(?), gives you peace for a while. But a courtesan is like rheumatism: both drain you completely. But if someone were to follow my lead, he could enter the courtesans' quarter.

For I placed no trust in women whose youth was spent. Young girls stayed only after I vetted them. I gave wide berth to those who had a madam: they are like rivers full of crocodiles. I do not lose my temper when I am treated with disrespect, nor do I think much of it when someone asks me a favour. I have turned grey in the courtesans' quarter, yet I haven't wasted a penny if it was unnecessary. *(walks about).*

What are you saying? "If one manages to be involved with two women simultaneously, which one should be kept and which one dumped: the long-time girlfriend, or rather the new girlfriend? Please answer this question, sir." This is a tricky question indeed. I find it hard to answer. What is your opinion in this matter?

What are you saying, sir? "I see no way through. It remains a huge dilemma. You alone are able to unravel it." Well, listen then: Since she is deeply in love, it is unseemly to dump one's beloved for the sake of a new girlfriend. However, just for the sake of her pleasure we ought not to reject a lusty wench who has willingly fallen into our lap. One should simply ignore the old acquaintance until she flies into a temper and goes away. Having had the other girl in some lonely place agreed to with her, one should conciliate one's beloved. *(walks about)*

What are you saying? "When someone strolls in the courtesans' quarter, how can he gauge at a mere glance the amorous prowess of women?" Nothing remains hidden for an expert. As soon as he notices a woman, a man should first of all examine her eyes. For the eye is the seat of all emotions.

Observe, sir: Eyes that squint, close softly, cast side-glances, are affectionate, large and immodest with lively pupils proclaim the amorous prowess of women.

Furthermore, if her face is slightly screwed up, her cheek somewhat hollowed, with dancing eyebrows and darting side-glances, she is a rough lover. Or, if her corners of her lower lip are shrunken, her body is covered with tooth and nail-marks, and her mouth rarely flashes a smile, we may deduce that she is a champion of love making. Now then, if you notice a woman with her left hand put on her waist, her right arm hanging loose, and one side of her hips raised, you may approach her also with confidence. For she would not stand like that if she had no self-esteem. And if you see a girl who covers one of her breasts with the hem of her garment, keeps one dainty painted foot on the threshold of her house, her body hidden behind the door-panel: she is indeed a snare embodied as a woman. Everything indicates her bewitchingly coquettish nature.

On the other hand a woman who appears holding on to the cow-udder-shaped studs fastening the door-panels, revealing the noose of her arms, with the knot of her mini-skirt loosened and the pool of her navel visible: since her appearance is a prelude to love, there is nothing left in be conjectured. Much might be said on this matter.

To summarize: She who holds her hand, its palm and fingers painted red, its nails bright, close to her cheek, who accompanies her speech with graceful gestures, whose gait is elegant, whose lips quiver as she smiles, who has a roving eye, whose countenance knows no inhibition, who has tied her mini-skirt below her navel, one should identify her as a man-trap, a woman who has attained the non-plus ultra of valour in the war of lover. *(walks about)*.

What are you saying? "Women's love can be of two types only: open or secret. Of these two which is better?" Sir, only courtesans can love openly. And that love is also artificial. As for secret love, that is possible in the case of respectable women as well as courtesans. When it arises simply from inclination, and especially because its drawbacks are few, it is delightful only with courtesans. Furthermore, respectable women, because they find it hard to get hold of men, will make love to anybody whomsoever. But a courtesan will not love just anybody.

Someone may opine: "Why would courtesans love someone secretly if love for them is not a sin?" On this I answer: Old flames, favourites of the king, benefactors, and the devoted but vile: such men are pampered by a bawd. For them courtesans will perforce be compliant even if they feel no affection. For what reason? Because they are motivated. Therefore, a man loved by a courtesan seeking secret love will have reaped a double fruit of birth and life.

And what's more, he certainly will fully enjoy the words of women interceding on their own behalf, preceded by hands folded in supplication, tearfully stammering, suffering the pangs of separation. Or a beautiful woman whose thoughts are fixed on him, who becomes pale under the pretext of some disease, and weeps when the moon rises with eyes are blood-shot with sleeplessness and with her ornaments hanging loose—a man hearing these syllables interwoven with sighs: "Please, my love, I beg you, show mercy to my body," from that woman reprimanding him herself: "Congratulations! For your sake alone, O merciless man, my body is reduced to this condition. I hope you are happy," and pondering these words which outperform the application of an elixir: "I am in such a state, you must believe me, my lord, I made you to take an oath," of that woman scratching and biting while urging him "Hurry! No, no, not like that!," having learnt from evidence and from the words of the go-between that "Just because of me she has been reduced to this state"—the pleasure admixed with pity which arises for a man, if someone can tell me of another like it, I shall give up my status of a pimp and become like a Vedic priest.

I will bear this lotus-parasol won by my own arm for a man who, winning even a fleeting tryst at night, while still standing, kisses a woman as his beloved on the mouth, come to him with passion all alone, her eyes tremulous with fear, her girdle stilled by her hand, and her stomach curved as she creeps forward with soft foot-fall.

And, to whom a passionate woman, in secret love-making, fearfully whispers: "Hurry my love!" she has bought the life-breaths of this man, fixing the price as she wills. *(walks about)*

What are you saying? "A beautiful woman or a warmhearted woman: which one pleases you more?" Both of these adorn a woman. As for kindliness in an ugly woman, it is wasted like dancing in darkness. On the other hand, beauty without kindliness is like a moonrise in the forest: what kind of pleasure will it produce? For me, kindliness wins over beauty. Why? Kindliness is an ornament even for an ugly woman, discourtesy ruins even a beautiful woman. For we see men leaving even beautiful women and attaching themselves even to misshapen, but kindly women. A beauty will invariably be haughty. And haughtiness is the great foe of love, for compliance is the root of love, and that springs from kindliness. If bare beauty were the cause, then it could generate the effect even in the case of a woman represented in a painting. Kindliness in itself contains the totality of all virtues except the virtue of beauty. Why?

A kindly women is always mellifluous, dresses tastefully, is unassuming, grateful, affectionate, and what's more, is quickly reconciled, not greedy and obedient.

What are you saying, sir? "People say that courtesans must be shunned by the virtuous because their polite behaviour is feigned. What about that?" In fact, here polite behaviour means approaching with pleasing virtues, and it comes natural to women. And two kinds are found in the case of a courtesan, based on expedience. There might be a view that whatever service is rendered dishonestly is artificial. That is no crime either. Why? Even if service be rendered dishonestly it generates pleasure.

On the other hand, who will be pleased by honest service rendered clumsily? Dishonesty is in fact a specific mental state bringing about some result. That is no crime either. And a woman preoccupied with her own benefit will invariably seek an excellent man. And men prefer women who appreciate their excellences. What's more, *Humility servility, kind words flattery, forbearance intolerance, continuous prudence spying,* arise from dishonesty. Who in the world censures this?

What are you saying? "The essential quality of a dishonest woman is perfidiousness. Suffering is the lot of a lover betrayed by his beloved. It cannot be cured." Sir! Everybody is betrayed as a consequence of some cause. But someone who cannot avoid that cause is surely himself to be blamed. And the fault you found in perfidy is inconclusive. We see that many deceived men love the woman even more.

Having breast-slopes, sly side-glances intermingled with tears and crafty at expressing emotions, sentences with words indistinct and pretty: even though these arise from dishonesty, they accomplish something valuable.

What are you saying? Many say: 'What is given to courtesans is wasted.' Dattaka also has taught: 'Infatuation is the ruin of men's wealth.' What is the right honourable gentleman's view on this?' Sir, money has three uses: giving, spending, saving. Among these giving and spending take precedence, but saving is despised. Why?

When money is stashed away there accrues no gain. When it yields no profit, there results dissatisfaction. Therefore, saving is not proper. Income is as fleet as a racing horse.

Wealth and piety produce comfort. Here comfort is defined as the acquisition of words etc. that are agreeable. Am someone frequenting courtesans attains that squarely. Now, among all words, it is especially sweet words that make one happy. And courtesans speak these, while others do not to that extent. How is this so?

Courtesans articulate felicitously and at the right time agreeable words with a pleasant sense, or sharp words with a pleasant sense. Rich in courtesy, they never voice either agreeable or disagreeable words with an unpleasant sense.

Sensory delights arise for a man who boldly fondles her loins, with smooth thighs and buttocks, its petticoat pulled up, its girdles cast aside,—would men not even sacrifice their lives for such a woman, not to mention money? It is alleged that alcohol is the most contemptible, so to say, of all drinks, nevertheless, its consumption is a pleasure when transmuted by courtesans.

Look, sir: He who has drunk a cocktail in the courtesans' quarter, briskly swirled and tumbled, or that which remained after her sipping, or what slipped from her mouth, with her lips as a canape, truly knows what flavour is.

Whoever has beheld the faces of courtesans, with heavy-lidded eyes, with quivering lower lips, with long eyebrows, glistening cheeks, has reaped the ultimate goal of sight.

Furthermore, A man who has smelled the tips of a courtesan's hair, dry after bathing, or her rich locks of hair adorned with flowers, or her dress, shed after wearing, or her lower lip, scented with fragrant breath and pink like a lotus, or her intoxicated face with red eyes, or her body moist with sandal-paste, is at once sought out by Kama, by way of the nose.

Admittedly, I am no authority in religious matters. Nevertheless, I will extemporize on how religious merit might be secured. In this world, ingratitude is the most horrendous sin. A man who has received that incomparable, sought-after bliss from courtesans and does not requite them is the worst of ingrates. But if he becomes grateful, then heaven is in his hand. So, in order to attain heavenly bliss one must by all means, without hesitation, give money to courtesans.

What are you saying? "How is it that this does not apply to a respectable woman, even though she is kindly, in the same way as it does to a courtesan?" Listen: the concept of 'kindliness' is one thing for a respectable woman and another for a courtesan.

First of all, if a forthright respectable woman says something agreeable, she either says it at the wrong time or she says something acutely agreeable, and therefore what she speaks is disagreeable. It is like this in all contingencies. Love is a variety of desire and desire is entreaty. And entreaty arises from not getting what you want. And in the case of a courtesans, even though she is enjoyed at will, that arises from jealousy, because she is owned in Common. And jealousy produces covetousness. Therefore, desire for a courtesan will never diminish if given latitude. And desire is the root of passion.

Furthermore, what sentient man, ensconced in the chariot of a courtesan's hips, would approach a respectable woman? For no man can overtake a chariot a cow-drawn cart.

What are you saying? "A man addicted to prostitutes is not respected by the public, and his opinion is not valued. Why should one be banned from indulging in that where virtues are evident?" You have declared that you are a super-pimp. Permit me a moment of concentration. *(reflects)* In this world, respect is of two kinds: fruitful and fruitless. Of these, the fruitless one is as ridiculous as the frolicking of a naked man. What fruit can there be for a man not attached to courtesans? Some may opine: "Addiction to prostitutes is disreputable." This view is not acceptable.

The whole world resents a happy man. And while it is proclaimed with one voice that the wives of others should not be frequented, this does not apply to courtesans. Someone might opine: "Association with women is not salutary, and courtesans are women." On this I reply: Nevertheless people ought not to defame a man who keeps the company of women.

Moreover, how can people defame a man who by frequenting the brothel becomes bold, becomes valorous in standing his ground, skilled in innuendos, light-bodied, radiant with virility, perceives the intentions of others, becomes joyful, gains a storehouse of methods of love-making, beautitude with an impassioned woman, learns the crafts headed by painting and obtains supreme comfort? *(walks about).*

What are you saying? "How, sir, do you view the pronouncement of people like Brihaspati, Ushanas, and other scientific authors who teach that one should not become attached to women?" Well, this serves only for instruction. I can see nobody who is not attached to women. For scripture reveals that even the great Indra etc. became lovesick for Ahalya and others. Sensuality is superior even to piety and wealth, since it results in the appearance of the desired entity. And women are the best of all such entities. For I also consider as deluded someone who rejects a courtesan and then lusts after the enjoyment of heavenly love.

Now as regards actuality and future potentiality, actuality definitely outweighs because its result is directly perceptible. What is amusing about haphazardly taking on another body, laboriously won by ascetic torments? See here, sir. A man realising from the tinkling of anklets that he is hastened to by an eloping beautiful woman all by herself, wounded by Kama's arrow, on nights when the lamp of the moon is extinguished by clouds, terrifying to behold with darkness twice as intense, with freezing winds, when roaming is made difficult by water laden breezes, dark in the rainy season—such a man has obtained the fruit of his birth and life. What are you saying, sir? "Indeed, the wearing of anklets renders good service to an eloping woman." So it is. Why?

How could someone silent on the first date announce herself if her anklets did not tinkle intensely because of her shaking feet?

In this vein, if a man, informed by the sound of the anklets, drinks in the impassioned face, its make-up patterns washed off by could-bursts, with eyes replete with collyrium and with unsteady lower-lip, and then, his head hanging down, he experiences the hellish torments of many eons, nevertheless they are praiseworthy for him because he has assented to the love of a young woman. What use has a man for heaven if he plunges into the water of a pool with blossoming lotuses with his beloveds who have been taught affection by Brahminy ducks, their make-up patterns shining like *bandhuka* flowers, and the resounding of their girdles accompanied by the warbling of water-fowl, when *Lady Autumn* reigns, her cloud-veil slipping away, her forehead-mark furnished by the stainless moon, when the winds have subsided, and the forest depths are perfumed by the flowers of the *asana* tree?

Or rather, that bliss has no equal which arises for a man who, helped by love, softly drinks from the mouths of his beloveds, though, averse to kissing, they protect their lower lips, with lips trembling by tin-onset of the cold, when winter has arrived with the wind laden with the scent of blooming *lodhra*, flowers mingled with jasmine, and locks of hair are bound with bunches of *priyangu* flowers.

Or rather, what remains to be achieved for a man who falls asleep between bouts of love-making lying on an exquisite bed in bed-chambers cloudy with the smoke of black aloe, his body fragrant with droplets of perspiration produced by tight embraces, his chest being pressed by the swelling breasts of his impassioned beloved, on the dark nights of late winter that rain with pearls of hail, when harsh winds blow and *atimukta* flowers are scattered?

Furthermore, the thirsty should drink the sighing mouths of women protecting their lower lips, their eyes tremulous because of their hair is being pulled.

What is gained in heaven where there is no sleep? Or rather, a man should not long for any other day if he is conciliated by his impassioned beloved, herself deserving conciliation, who has arrived without arranging a rendezvous, after giving up her pride by herself, on days of spring when the tracings of the make-up patterns are obscured by droplets of sweat rolling over them, when there are meetings with messengers of love, jewelled girdles are put on, mango-sprouts appear, and the breezes are fragrant.

Or again, the man who passes the time of midday with his beloved, her hair tied up with jasmine flowers, her breasts moist with sandal-paste, reclining on a bed of flowers, being comforted by the breeze of palm fans in a airy pavilion, in summer time when the cheeks of women are darkened by *shirisha* flowers, which is delightful with the enjoyment of the breeze of fans, vetivert, sandal-paste, pearl necklaces, jewels, and water, when the rays of the sun are fierce.

Or a man who is detained by his beloved in her airy apartments, their floors sprinkled with perfumed water, scattered with petals of *bakula*, jasmine and lotus, spends well his evanescent youth!

Moreover, a woman's flavour in her lotus-face, its lower lip throbbing because it is bitten, and the delight of her buttocks released from the dress, resplendent with the radiance of the girdle, and the felicity of her swelling cheek, bearing the curved wounds of nails — the heart captivated by these cannot possibly grow weary even in the next life.

But these ascetics, each imitating the behaviour of the other in the manner of ants, their hearts seduced by some false doctrine which is like a *fata morgana*, shorting 'Heaven, heaven!' without having examined it themselves, devoting themselves to such lethal means as subsisting on air alone, leaping off precipices, and entering fire, and other horrors such as mumbling prayers, burnt offerings, vows, and costumes, they hanker after heaven. They have no interest to investigate the facts of the matter.

Scriptures reveal that women are at hand in heaven. And since they are not human, men cannot enjoy those women due to mutual incompatibility. And since they are always at hand, what pleasure can those women, from which one can never be separated, generate? And since none of them surpass the others, there is no chance to enjoy hidden qualities. And as for the scriptural revelation of golden mansions and golden trees, that clearly shows the essence of the gods' lack of consideration.

Firstly, if the houses are golden, and the trees are golden, with what are the women adorned? What would be special about it? How on earth could gold taken from a construction site beautify women? And the pleasure one takes in young trees in orchards which are cherished and raised like sons by beautiful women with their own hands, their bunches of flowers transferred to the locks of virgins, how could that be possible with golden trees which are inherently clunky?

And that joy which arises for lovers addicted to the study of love while still young, as they are eager to gaze at each other, thirsting for the words of a love-messenger, squabbling with each other, and striving for the rewards of union, how could that be possible in heaven where women are paranoid of curses? And the days that seem to grow long for a man who with his friends ponders upon the means of reconciliation, delightful and well suited to the yearning of the occasion, when passionate women feign anger—how could these days be possible in heaven which is devoid of jealousy?

And when women lull a man to happy sleep, their bodies suffused with emotion, lying on his chest, giving his nose a *raison d'etre* by their exhaled sighs fragrant like *bakula* flowers—how could that be possible in heaven where nobody ever sleeps? And as for women's words, their syllables slurred by intoxication with date-wine, a trifle bashful, pleasing and dear—how could these be possible in teetotal heaven?

How could there be in heaven sex with newly-married women, with hissing that comes easily, full of moans heralded by embraces? Ah! I'd rather bed down with senile bigots than with heavenly nymphs. Scriptures teach that they are ancient, speak Sanskrit, and are majestic. They gave birth to the great sages headed by Vasishtha and Agastya: who could let himself go in their company?

Look, sir: Slyness, dishonesty, intoxication, jealousy, contempt, feigned anger are said to be the sources of lust; they are non-existent in heaven.

Therefore, if you yearn for the experience of unobstructed love then, sir, you must enjoy yourself here in this world, and above all with courtesans.

For here, he whom the bawd gazes at with tears in her eyes, following him up to the door, whom she detains by the edge of his garment as he, her beloved, passes her by, feigning anger, who, when really annoyed and becoming obstinate when placated, has his path blocked by the passionate women, fells the God of love, crushing him on his chariot streaming with lofty banners.

O no, its Sunanda! What are you saying? "I've heard everything." Look, my wares are sold. No trick has been played, darling. What are you saying? "Darkness clearly does not *fall out of: fly away due* to tin moon." Sananda! These words undoubtedly portray you, that's why you speak like this. So let's join her inside. *(They enter)* Madam, I wish to be dismissed.

For now, O sulky woman, the sun is slowly setting, *its rays withdrawn*, as a golden turtle diving under, *its feet retracted.* repeatedly struck by the side-glances of women who have fastened their loose girdles after drinking heartily date-wine, adorning their hair, friend of the lover's grasp, with bunches of flowers, and resting their hands on their girdles.

What are you saying? "You are not allowed to take even as much as half a step away from here." I really must go, sir. Otherwise my wife will lay hand on my body. What are you saying, madam? "I'll mollify her." Because she is menstruating, she is like a wicked person who does not accept conciliation: she cannot be conciliated. I'm off. What? She falls at my feet with Visvalakena! Woe! I'm crippled. Sananda.

I will not offend you: I bow and take my leave as the sea *does not transgress its tides:* floods it shore. May the king protect this earth girdled by the sea! (*Exit the Pimp. Thus, ends the Causerie called "Dhurta-Vita-Samvada" by Ishvara-datta*).

Detail of Mithuna on South Wall in Lakshan Temple of Khajuraha 10th Century.

Erotic Scene of Love Khajuraha Visanath temple 11th Century A.D.

Chapter Five

Kuttanimahatmayam

Damodara Gupta

To Reader

Dear Ones, Overlooking all blemishes,
Receive light from wherever you can;

So seek wisdom from the teaching of
Damodar Gupta in this work
Kuttni Mahatmyam

Unique in the entire universe as the city of learning and love; studded with all ways to luxury exists the city of Varanasi. Man of the heart who live in Varanasi do not think it beyond their reach to attain oneness with the mighty Lord Shiva himself. With bodies as beautiful as the moon. Surrounded by money-minded relations, live in Varanasi the women of lust ringed by voluptuous pleasure – seeking men like snakes entwined round Lord Shiva's neck. Where the earth itself, reflecting the beauty of hennah-coloured feet of charming women, looks as enchanting as the lotus in bloom.

Varanasi, the city which is like poetry itself, where the sound are so musical that the atmosphere becomes alight, as if lit with twinkling candles; a city where saints and mahatmas chant the message of peace; a city which abounds with the most cherished women singers and dancers.

Like the poetic metre do the citizens like in orderliness, the air resounds with harmony, like notes of music without discord. In here Brahmins alone lead lives of austerity and restraint – all others live drunk with the joy of living. Here Poetry reflects life and the drama of life is portrayed in as sensitive words as in the voice of the playful women sweet. Tenderness of young leaves and brightness of the forehead mark make the faces of women as lovable as the music of the harp dexterously played.

Here is blossoming with the fragrant *Tulsi* and is haloed with gods and goddesses. So is Varanasi peopled with men of learning and beauteous women of charm and distinction. Perched on the holy banks of the Ganga this unique city.

The Ways of the Courtesan

In that city of Varanasi dwelt the embodiment of beauty – Malati, a Jewel among women of lust. Just as the dragon gets restless at the sight of the multi-coloured jay, flying in the air so are men dazed looking at Malati. Just as Parvati, the daughter of the Himalayas, had captured the heart of a god, so had Malati drawn the hearts of the Men of Love towards herself. So were the eyes of the voluptuous held by Malati's. just as the entire universe rests on the trident of Shiva so was Malati the Pinnacle of desire among all women of lust. She was the city of sweet speech, of playful sport, of love, laughter and clever talk.

One day, sitting in the seclusion of her house–top, she heard someone singing a heart-ravishing song:

Venal girlhood should not grow
Drunken with her beauty's glow,
But should consecrate each hour
To the study of her power
And acquisition of those arts
Which sage experience imparts
For snaring and for keeping hearts.

Now when Malati, that girl with the large region, heard these words, she reflected for a long time in her heart, and then cried: 'He is only too right, this giver of friendly counsel; and therefore I will rise up and go to Vikrala. All existence is her meditation, and her door is besieged by a packed wave of attentive lovers, both night and day'.

So she made her way to the house of worldly–wise Vikrala which had become the centre for love-hungry men seeking ways to success.

She coming down from the roof, unmindful of other relations in the house, she made her way to Vikrala's home. Her big breasts, drooping and dried, and looking like fens, its bore witness to her withered dreams. With eyes sunken and reddish, the lobes of the ears were long and without ornaments.

She was surrounded by sexy women and her eyes were fixed on the presents brought by pleasure-seeking men. Malati put her head on the floor, paying her respects to Vikrala, and she asked Malati about her well-being. Then Malati took her seat. Then Malati, after a while, bowing low, beseechingly, asked to Vikrala. "Truly, all get entrapped in the net of your wisdom"?

Here, Men of love and lust, losing all their belongings, wearing tattered clothes and eating in charity kitchens come to your exalted door to pay homage to your wisdom.

What going here? Dhan Varma, having left all labour and losing all he had, is now like a footstool for the attractive Narmada. And Sagar Dutt, middle son of Naya Dutta, having made the home of his father desolate. He now sits infatuated by Madanasena. And Bhatt, that son of Narsing, playfully rubs with tender love, the feet of beloved Manjari. Shubhdev is the son of Bhavadeva Dikshit, even after being subjected to untold insults does not leave the door of Kesar Sena. All those women of love who denude sex-hungry men, even of their meanest possession, all praise the mastery of your teachings.

Malati think, I was born in a low home and had made a show of serving the poor and the sick. O mother, such is the cruel play of the God of Destiny, that even after displaying the beauty of the body we command no respect.

Then Vikrala gently patted Malati on the back, assuringly, and said: "O beautiful one, the smoke that floats from the fires lit. Beauty of your hair, and makes all men on lust your slaves."

Vikrala adds; "O one with the body beautiful if you want to get immeasurable wealth then try to capture the heart of the son of Bhatt, the King's Minister.

Bhatt used to live always in the capital and now owns the neighbouring village. Dear Daughter, for sure his son, Chintamani, will be drawn by your charm. "O one with the beauty of smiles, pierced with arrows of Kamadeva, the lord of spring, unfailing the son of Bhatt will fall in love with you. And now to explain to you his ways and qualities.

He wears a necklace of fragrant flowers, and adorns himself with gold ornaments. In his bag he carries rare articles of wax made in the land of the Turks. In the company of merchants, money-lenders, brokers, procurers and pimps. He seats himself on high cushions. The servants artfully place cushions for him to recline. With chewing the tobacco his cheeks get bloated and he keeps rubbing his hands. Unmindful of company, soaked in pleasure, twisting his eyebrows. He recites poetry of his own liking. Shaking his head in disapproval he stops others from expressing themselves and even disturbs those who want to recite the sayings of holy men.

His father speaks about him to the King so he continues to enjoy the King's approbation and favour. Whether he does or does not know the art of decoration, yet he carries a pruning knife in hand to make people believe that he knows the garden craft.

The son of Bhatt surpasses in playing the music which, descended from Brahma, is expounded in Rishi Narada's Book of Music, *Gandharva Shashtra.* Heroes of the caliber of Vasunanda, the master of the Bow and Sword, and no less than Parsuram the valiant worrior, son of Bharat, both pay homage to the prowess of this young man. The exponent of *Kamashastra,* the Art of Love, places the king and his son both in the category of animals.

He knows which are the places famous for entertainment and which dancing girl is the best artiste, and who is the most praised for natural spontaneity judged by the highest standards of Bharat's art. He inquires from the masters about the most complex details. About the form or content of vocal and instrumental Music he wants to know. Taking off the necklace of precious jewels he throws it to the dancing girl, and even without the right moment he acclaims: 'How wonderful! How good!'

This dancing girl is the creator of many new forms of sex-exciting poses. The Music of her heat–bewitching poses, gesticulations, coquettish and suggestive movements far surpasses the seducing capacity of the well known dancer Rambha. As a man of emotion, shaking his head he shows appreciation of the enthralling movements of the dancer.

A Courtesan with a mirror, vaital temple, Bhuvanesvara. Kalinga, Late 8th Century A.D.

O worthy maiden, these are the traits and qualities of the son of Bhatt. The way you can entangle him in the game of passion, of that I speak now. A maid servant who is clever, without modesty, glib of tongue, and sensitive to the minds of others should be put in his service. O beautiful one, at an opportune moment she should present him Garlands of Tambool blossoms and say words which kindle the flame of passion. "The dreams of thousand births have been fulfilled today. O light of the eyes, that I have seen you." Like an expert seducer she should flatter him, Cajole him, annoy him, make him angry and then seek his pleasure and happiness.

In pursuit of wealth women who sell themselves look with eyes of greed even on the rags on a man's back. In these circumstances it is meaningless to talk of devices of lustful women to men who are hungering for the scent of sex.

She should tell the son of Bhatt: 'Disappointment, as my bosom friend, disregarding all nicety, casting off the ornament of patience, is forcing me to express myself. In the heart of Malati, first, Kamadeva the God of Love, took abode, then, O God of Joy, her eye fell on you. Since then in a moment emotion runs high in her body, in a moment passion overwhelms her; in a moment she starts shivering, and in a moment she is bathed in sweat. Sometimes she has not a smile; sometimes, casting off patience, she cried bitterly; then she bursts into song, and then is found sunk in silence!

Mostly good people do not give credence to things talked about other people. Therefore, with precision I talk now of the virtues of Malati.

Truthfully when the Lord of Love lifted his bow, a few flowers fell off on the ground. Lord Brahma moulded those flowers into the living form of Malati of the most beautiful limbs. The softness of Malati's body excels the smoothness of Goddess Parvatis skin, on which even the snakes round Lord Shiva's neck slip while crawling.

Before Malati's Face the glamour of the lotus fades and her countenance is like the abode of the moon, the seat of all pleasures. Then, O Dear one, with whom can the face of Malati be matched? The rosiness of her lips put into shade the hues of the colour she uses. Having had a glimpse of the curvature of Malati's breasts, which are so like those of the celestial Nymph, Rambha, Kamadeva, the God of Love, become a victim of his own arrow. Not having seen so far Malati, who has the most ravishing movement of the hips when she walks, Kartikeyes, till this day, continues to be celebrate.

Most women think to be a freak of creation otherwise how could even the Almighty create anything so superb in beauty as Malati? Whatever madness Deva the author of Vatsyayna has written of Lovers and Princes remains ever present in his mind.

Art of Drama – NATAK SHASTRA OF BHARAT. The Text of Arts – KALA SHASTRA OF SHILAKHIL Book of Music – SANGEET SHASTRA OF DANTIL. Inspite of all the knowledge in these texts only a thousand tongued wise dragon could fully expound the Art of Play in the violin, the harp, the flute or other subtle instruments.

He who is not worthy of giving, Malati, with her glittering garments, would never be induced to lie on his chest in the joy of solitude, without a miracle. The jingle of Malati's bangles sweetened by the passion exciting solitude of the night would never reach the ears of one who is not generous in giving'.

O Malati of the Slender Waist, if the son of Bhatt after hearing all this remains indifferent, then the maid-servant should make a show of temper. "Is it the pride of your great fortune that you do not accept Malati, who is yours in love"?

What more is to be said? 'If you wish to trample on the heads of all other young men; then lose no time in taking in your arms Malati, the Jewel, resplendent with love'.

Hearing the maid servant speak thus, the heart of the son of Bhatt will beat faster and he will come to visit you. Then, O beautiful one, receive him in this manner:

Seeing him from a distance, get up to receive him. Pay respect, offer your own seat, and with your head scarf wipe his feet. Then effortlessly cast a glance on him and give him just a glimpse of your beautiful breasts – and then turn away quickly. Then, O Maiden of the Beautiful Waist, lead him to the room where the bed is lighted with candles and the fragrance of flowers pervades. Your dear mother will welcome him with soft and happy words and talk to him of a few things of interest:

'Today our life has found fulfillment. Today the gods are happy that you have graced this home. After long have come together those destined to unite through the blessings of the arrows of Kamadeva, the Lord of Passion.

This fortunate daughter of mine will now put her feet on the heads of all young maidens and the fly the flag of her pride. It is a foolish world where people rejoice over the birth of sons – true rejoicing should be over the birth of daughters. Through whose auspicious birth one gets a son-in-law like your worthy self.

To a person of standing, status and qualities like yours – out of love for my daughter I wish to address a few words to you. Sweet-tempered and soft-hearted Malati, I consign to your care; pray let it not happen that due to separation she becomes a victim of grief; O Maiden of Delicate Body, wearing exquisite embroidered clothes – go to him and extend welcome. Lovingly, blushingly, sit by his side – then, exposing a part of your body, talk to him lightly, jocking.

When the mother leaves the room and no stranger is nearby and you discover the son of Bhatt becoming passionate – then excite him a little. When the desire for the battle of the night overwhelms him and he tries to draw you closer then withdraw your body a little away from him.

Dear daughter, when he gets quite mad with desire then display your excitement without reserve. Submit the seat of love to him. Whichever organ he wants to uncover, and look at, and scratch, without resistance expose it to him, and let him enjoy.

When he bites with the teeth then groan a little; when he wants to play and squeeze, make gentle noises. And if he starts to scratch then draw a sigh. And if he handles roughly, then moan loudly.

To arouse the passion more and more make the breath emotion – laden and keep the body seductively moving that the body may feel drowned in perspiration.

O Maiden of the sweet voice, in the high moments of passion, make sounds like a lark, a pigeon and a horse! And say plaintively, 'Don't – don't – not so roughly. Don't give me pain – O leave me, I can't bear it! So protesting, keep talking to the lover. To understanding the way of lover. So play, sometimes soft, sometimes fierce, sometimes fast and sometimes slow; so must the tempo of love be guided.

When passion rises to pitch heat then ask to be left alone. Show yourself to be tired – and for pity's sake beg to be spared. And when the lover exhausts himself finally then shut your eyes, as if you do not remember; even the scratches of his nails. Then in a tired way, relaxing your body, just lie motionless.

When the game of passion is over then quickly cover your body and draw yourself away. Smile with shyness, pretending you have suffered much pain. Look towards him coquettishly.

Then, when the sex bout is all over, then wash yourself well; and sitting relaxed on a mat, arrange your hair. Treating yourself to the chewing of betel leaf go to the bed and in tones of infatuation say to the lover in a clear voice. 'Truly O honoured son of Bhatt, your wife is most dear to you, because the satisfaction which she can give to your passion, no other women can'.

Soul of my survival, the love that you have shown. I pray will not suffer through any misunderstanding which you may have about the life of prostitutes. Just as love, anger, evil, hatred, kindness and modesty are granted to all human beings – so are they the qualities among the prostitutes as well.

Without hypocrisy or deceit, even prostitutes are loving of heart; who can not bear the separation of the lover; and care not an iota for their own life.

In this connection hear a tale, wondrous, the symbol of that tale is the Bangud tree – named after the habitation of the women of lust.

Harlata: The Women of Lust

Told by Vikarala to Malati, that
She may tell in to the son of the Bhatta

There is a great city named Pataliputra; it is the gem which decks the forehead of the world. Sarasvati, Goddess of wisdom and learning, dwells there; high over the residences of Indra towers that city. Above it the moon stretches down her rays like white hands, to steal the charm of its women to adorn her lotus, it is as if she felt shame for the stains upon her face and desired to hide them.

In Pataliputra men grow slack to their wives because of the steel-tipped arrows of the moving eyes of the girls with rounded buttocks.

The noble ladies of that place are famed for the delicacy of their discourse, and of their hands and feet; for the purity of their hearts and the instability of their regard; for the firmness of their breasts, for their exceptional regions, and for the great heaviness of their hair; for their natural inclination to their lords and masters, and for the supple graciousness of their waists; for the depth of their sensibility, and of their navels, which are the quivers of love; for the ample expansion of their hinder parts, and for their ardent veneration of all such men as are worthy of respect.

Here the moon, in order to cover its own blemish. Spreads out its rays like the fingers of the hand. To grasp beauty from the lovely faces of newly wedded brides. Here lovers use the darkness of the night. As veil for stealing their way to the beloved. Wounded by the darts of love from the coquettish looks of the beautiful-bodied women in this city. The travellers lose their wish to return to their wives at home.

Here women of good descent are sweet of speech and have tiny, delicate hands and feet; their hearts are clean and their playful eyes are lustrous. As full-blown as are the breasts, hair and the waist. Is their love for the beloved, and devotion for the husband. Just as a sacrifice is offered in the worship of the family gods. So do the slender waists of these comely maidens become a sacrifice in the Game of Love.

Here the blossoming Harlata creepers alone keep clinging to the crooked Tarl tree; but women do not live with unsteady men. Not looks towards the faults of others. The beloved is cherished and not belittled. Here the fatigue felt by the delicate dancing woman is sensitively felt; but none sympathises with hard labour to which a wrong-doer is subjected.

Here even wily women go straight. For here most women are of good demeanour; slender-bodies and soft of temper, they move like the tumultous river Narmada. Delicate-bodied, they walk like the spirited waves of the river. Even though absorbed in holy teachings they are ravishingly heart-warming.

In that city dwelt men like God Indra, sanctified by a hundred yogas. As learned as Rishi Brahaspati. These Brahmins were known as Purinder. Who, in his time, was held to be the very home of wisdom. He come of a lofty family and was estimable in all things.

Although he was avid to follow the straight way, although he turned from all human frailty and avoided the wives of others, yet he could not prevent his heart from dreaming a little of women.

Therefore he had a son called Sunderasena, whom the creator had formed to be a second God of Love.

He derived charm from the moon, stability from the mountain, charitable feeling from *Megh,* the God of Rain and bigness from the sea. In him was the abode of justice; the refuge of the troubled; seat of honour; source of sweet speech; the home of righteous conduct. Protector of women, resort of the holy of heart; like a tree was he to those who followed the hardy path of seeking. Who kept the company of the good; whose body was golden. Who to the men of Love, was like the mighty Kapila tree and the theatre for the play of Lakshmi, Goddess of Wealth.

Like the sea, rising and falling with the movement of the moon, so bound a friendship to him was the talented Gunapalita. Sitting with him he had heard the song sung by Arya – the songster. He was signing:

"Those who are ignorant of the dress.
Manner and language of other lands
And those who have not served the holy master
Are like oxen without horns."

Having heard this, Sundersen said to his bosam friend: "Gunapatila. This good man has sung the truth."

A man who walks on the earth, surrounded by the sea, he hears people talk of the life of a good man and of the evil deeds of others – the cunning of various people, the merry making of the men of lust, the foul life of bad women. The reading of good and noble books, the tales of the low of birth and knows the ways of tricksters.

"O friend, leave the indolence of staying at home in comfort, and make up your mind to go round the earth with me." Those who undertake journeys.

The traveller is reduced to tattered clothes, travelling whole day; and wearily seeks, by nightfall, a place of shelter. Imploringly, he approaches many homes, saying: "Dear mother and sister, you too have sons and brothers, who go from place to place on work; have pity on me. Would we run away with your precious home in the morning? A good home welcomes all and travellers find rest as in their own home. Dear mother, in your home we will pass the night. The sun has already set; where can we go now?" repeating this, from door to door, he is turned away.

"The master is not at home", says the lady. "Why do you not go to the temple? Look! he is not moving – Truly menfolk are without shame."

And if the owner of any house sneeringly says: "Lie down in this corner of this dilapidated home." Then his wife protests loudly: "Why have you let in a stranger"? and keep quarrelling all night.

"Dear sister." Says the neighbour, "your husband is a simpleton – be watchful. Plenty of thugs and cheats roam about like this." When someone broke into singing, a verse from an old tale:

He whose heart is devoted to the work he undertakes,
The temple becomes his home; the earth a bed,
And the food from the begging bowl nectar from the gods."

And when he had heard this singing, the son of Purandara turned with joy to his friend and cried; "That unknown man has expressed my heart for me, come! Let us set forth together"!

Soon Sundersen with his companion, traversing the sea of the sorrow of separation, left his father's house and went away from Pataliputra. He went along, seeing sights of every type, and the puppet play of life in the light of the shastars, the Holy Books. He seeing the art of painting on leaves, casting wax toys and dolls; learning the intricacies of music and fine arts, he proceeded – experiencing the craft of the cheats and the thugs and listening to the soft talk of seducing women. Sundersen in the company of his friend, roamed round the globe. Thus, knowing the contents of many texts and seeing people of various cultures he decided to go home by way of Mount Arbuda (Abu).

When Gunapalita saw that Sundersen was keen on seeing the other aspect of the mountain he asked: "Have you seen this hilly state? Here lovely women, taking the stars in the sky for flowers in the night. Pine to pluck them.

It is a wonder of wonders that the constellation of seven stars is so near to this mountain. Yet, what is there to wonder about it? All goods things like to be near other good things.

Decorated with green winged birds, and intoxicated with their twitter. Abode of the blue jay and multi-coloured sparrow – it is the home of wondrously beautiful birds. As an ashram is the abode of the sadhus and the saints.

When Sundersen was listening intently to his friend's description, then a passing songster was heard singing:

Who has not seen Arbuda's flanks
Has but his journey's pain for thinks.

"That man has sung very sensibly," said Sundersen. "Come, my friend, let us climb to the highest of these amiable peaks, that we may enjoy the beauty of their prospect in full."

They climbed to the top and saw the abode of holy men. Saw the happy earth, Fields, springs and streams with wonder. In the flower-laden meadow his eye fell on a maiden playing with her companion. She looked like lightning flashing through the clouds. The light descended from the moon like the passion-laden hours of midnight. She was the creator's perfect work; she was the crown, the achieved model of all life, the weapon of Kama, a steel to cleave the shield of holiness.

As Sundersen stood regarding her his heart become disturbed, and he said to himself in admiration and surprise:

Whence come a creator of such exquisite cunning that he could unite these contradictory perfections into one girl?

Desire was welling up in the heart of Sundersen, when the gazelle-eyed maiden looked towards him and become a captive of the Lord of passion. She moved off and sat under a tree, forgetting all that she had to do, and a strange disturbance began to brew inside her.

The fragrance of the garden, which was so pleasing to her under the impact of passion, began to be distressing. Inwardly the fire of passion began to burn her up and her body was bathed in sweat.

Caught in the net of Kamadeva. Through her breathing her breasts were dancing and with desire overpowering, her body had a tingling sensation. Love filled her eyes with hert-throbbing light. Love changed the expression of her face, and the voice reflected the changed beats of the heart. So, the Lord of passion mastered her beyond endurance.

Inspite of the lover by her side, so wanded was she with the arrows of passion that she had no strength to express her desire. At last, seeing her love-filled eyes aflame with passion her playmate said, jokingly: "you of the delicate body, look on the play of passion with all consuming eyes of Lord Shiva, and take the desire not as genuine love but as a play of the women of lust. You with the body charming!

Finally struck with the arrows of Kamadeva he will begin to pursue you. O, one with pointed breasts, the branch of the mango tree never goes in search of a bee."

Having heard this, Harlata – every limb of whose body has been wounded by the arrows of the Lord of passion – spoke to her companion in an indistinct and pain-soaked voice. "O dear one, those who are in suffering need relief rather than soft wards of advice"!

"Such a state is bound to prevail when there is a cool breeze! In Basanta, the month of spring, and a stream flowing by; all these are elements existing passion, O, my loved one"! exclaimed her playmate.

Having realised that Harlata had become, an incurable victim of Kamadeva, Sakhi, her companion, walked over to the son of Purinder and spoke thus:

"Being only a slave I feel diffident of speech, but when the purpose is of common interest there should be no reserve between us. In this world there are only a few, so fortunately born. That their heart becomes restless with the desire of helping someone in suffering. Ever since you have appeared before the eyes of my companion from that moment onwards she is in utter anguish!

The arrows from the quiver of Kamadeva, short by the Lord of passion with his bow, have pierced every pore of her body. What can the poor one do, where can she go, how can she breathe when all her love organs are wearing the jewellery of pain and desire?"

When Sakhi's voice become quiet then Harlata broke her silence with the sweetest of voices. Having recovered from the daze a little then she started to stroll about like a swan gently floating on the waves of a stream. The bee keeps hovering round the blossom in spite of the heat from her burning breath. This is how the play of passion cannot be given up even in moments of distress. Settling on the enfeebled Harlata the bee says to her: "Do not push me away any more"!

She lay on the earth so limp and lifeless that the gold bangles round her wrist fell off. It is a matter of surprise that the charm which she was wearing fell off and of course the losing of anything that the Guru has given had to bring pain and suffering. Truly the garland cannot be made without piercing the blossom; so the Lord of passion does not find rest for his arrow without piercing through the body. The tears mixed with black *Kajal*, falling on. Her delicate breasts, gave the ravishing look of drops produced from the foam of the two waters of Ganga and Jamuna meeting.

Having said this, Harlata's companion left. Gunapalita saw that Sundersen was accepting her word and that the melody of passion had begun to be sung. But he was afraid of getting a bad name through a prostitute, and he said to his friend: Through it is difficult in youthful years to master passion, yet men of good understanding should be careful about involving themselves in the love of a prostitute.

All the exhibitions of the prostitutes – like dancing, music and love – increase and decrease with the quantity of money and jewellery that the lover offers.

How can a man of good breed associate in love with women who can be owned in a short time and yet a lover of long years she can forget quickly! Those women treat the wealthy as the very embodiment of the god of passion and those who have not much to give – they hardly give a look of love to them. They display their bodies in various poses in order to excite passion in the lover. Their makeup and embellishing movements are for increasing the tempo of lust and not just for self adornment.

They eat meat and drink soups to keep their passion at high level. In their rooms they hang pictures of pornographic. Voluptuous excitement. Pain and sympathy are on their lips and not in their hearts. Being straight is the makeup of their arms and not of their temperament. Their breast have got a height – but not their character, which good people may be appreciate.

Their breasts are big – but not their family background. Their movement in the love clasp is slow, but their capacity to draw money is fast.

In makeup they have mastery in the use of colour. But among men make no distinction between the high and low of birth. The word love remains only on their lips. They value a man for what they get from him. And not for enjoyment of the embrace of passion. These prostitutes show their love to the young and old and equally to the impotent and the invalid.

These beautiful-bodied ones behave in an un-Aryan way; they have a smiling face for everyone, selling their body, but not giving their heart. You may call them a flame, but even a flame cannot burn without oil; yet these women of evil life give light of lusty happiness to all even without a drop of love inside them. "But, unfortunate ones who fall in the trap of these money-hungry women end up walking in the streets, empty-handed"!

Just when Gunapalita was giving this advice to his beloved friend, Sundersen, a voice was heard of someone singing:

There is none so unfortunate among
men as one who turns his
Face away from a women who comes
to him
Overwhelmed by the Lord of Passion.

This is the fruit of having been born
And herein lies the joy of living.
This one gets by living in the company
Of happy mates.

Those whose body is on fire with passion
Such women filled with the nector of love
Do not covet men who are not fortunate
by birth."

Hearing this song Sundersen said to his friend: "Dear one, this man has sung just the thoughts of my heart. So Gunapalita, dear friend, let us go and befriend the passion pained Harlata, and waste no more time over fruitless debate."

After a while they saw that at a prostitute's house. A man who had lost everything was recognised by his tattered clothes and was not allowed entry on the ground that already there was a visitor.

Someone got a prostitute, already in bed with another person, to throw him out and secured her with double-fold money for some aged visitor. They heard two other people talking vishaki! Have you seen the amulet on Shashiprabha's arm? Say how did you find that armband I had given her?

Yes Madanaka. Four nights ago I gave her two garments of china silk yet she is talking unkindly. Now, say, what shall I do?

Kalhausak loves me dearly – but that ogress! That old sinner – her mother – cannot be won over even in a hundred years! Kitchkul ! Today it is the day when your beloved girl is going to dance. Put on your robes and flower garlands – why are you sitting silent?

Kandparak! Even if, seeing some display of wealth, she loves you for a few days, she will not give you love for long. O lovelorn fool, say god-bye to Harisena from a distance. She is involved with the son of Vayuprit whom you can by no means beat.

The present which Chandra Drohy Kesara had given on the festival day, wearing that she walks about – see the glory of that net of love! I wish that on the festival day I could be first to make love to Madan

Sena, breaking her virginity. But her mother is demanding too much for it.

Vibhurn! How much worship must be to your credit that, drunk with youth, Madansena given you wine with her own hands and you exhilaratingly receive the cup.

Liladaya! Why have you left the house of Kulwantmala? Dear brother, what good is it keeping a mistress without money?

Managreeva! Everything of Sara Varga is lost. All night long her lover these days presses the feet of Tilakmanjree.

Thus, Gunapalita and his friend heard the talk of prostitutes, the procuress, the maid servant and a lover. An old prostitutes was saying: "My daughter is still not out of her babyhood – yet her charm puts into shade those matured with the passion of youth." The mother of a prostitute told her maid servant, Hara, "Go and ask the music master way he put the tender-aged girl to so stiff a training today."

"Suratdara", said the mother, "What use is your teaching the parrot – your lover is waiting for you." The mother tells the maid servant: "There, Sommerbala has fallen asleep after a tiring music practice. Go and wake her up – say her lover has come."

"Madhuri", said the mother, "how shameless of you; how obstinate in spite of my asking you so many times, to wear the garland given to you by the son of Vigraha Raj, you do not wear it!" "Mother dear, see how careless Indurekha has become. She has not put the nut cutter in the betel tray."

The maid servant told the mother, within the hearing of the lover; "I forgot to given milk to the mongoose and now Kamasena obstinately refuses to eat in spite of my begging her so many times."

The prostitute girl's mother said to the first lover: "Aviram, from the first lover we take a gold coin and later, when Kusumdara comes to like you, then you have a lifelong right to her."

The mother told a new lover: "If you Cherish Chandralekha first make an offering to me and then later, after being with her, you can give what you please." In complainingly the maid servant reported to the mother about the lover: "Madam, Vasudeva's son is getting tightfisted. In spite of being stopped so many times. Again and again he takes off Suratsena's clothes. He's like the sheep that gives no wool now cotton, yet eats up all the seed grains."

One prostitute commenting on the lover of another said: "Sister, this son of Asha Patraj does not leave the house alone and the others do not get a chance – it is like a naked-do-nothing finding a place of Pilgrimage."

So listening to the talk of the pimps and the prostitutes and seeing the gay decorations of the street, Sundersen reached the home of Harlata. Strung with desire and with eyes filled with passion he arrived and Harlata welcomed him.

Sundersen sat on the carpeted seat and having seen him seated comfortably, the maid servant respectfully spoke. "Dear to the eyes, pierced with the pain of love, Harlata, nothing much need be said about her except that her life is dedicated at your feet. The life of you both is without any restriction. Play and enjoy, love and live, one, in joy and sorrow – one with each other. Without fear fulfil your desires; shed shame and reserve, the love welling up inside you – let it be like the torrent of music."

Having so blessed, she departed, and in every organ of his body the sweetness of wild passion began to surge up.

Ancient Art of passionate love! At every stage of a man's life the music of passion bursts forth from within – the laws of love govern enjoyment. Partly some knowledge of sex in inborn, and some cultivated. Some find expression externally, some internally.

As playing with the hair, biting with the teeth, scratching with the nails, pressing the bodies toughly against each other. Kissing with passion filled eyes, pressing the sex organs, gently rubbing them and finding final union in a tight embrace. These poses have been made with depth of knowledge. In exercising them the two bodies melt into each other like milk and water.

The response and fervour on both sides must be well matched – neither tempestuousness, violence, nor quite reserve, nor modesty nor shame – nothing should happen to break the harmony of all sweeping oneness. And, when the stage arrives for the fire of passion to flare up sky high – the joy of that moment is beyond description! The art of kindling the fiercest flame of passion has been described in Holy Books of sex, wherein are mentioned *sixty-four* ways of petting and loving and eighty-four poses for the sex clasp in perfection. When both are locked in sexual embrace then there remains neither good nor bad. Neither bitter nor sweet, neither patience nor impatience. Whatever thoughts were in each other's mind all vanished with the onslaught of the passionate embrace.

When a man and woman are all in oneness, thus clasped together, none in the world can imagine the superb joy of that moment. The delicate-bodies maiden does not get shrivelled up but blossoms by the tought handling of strong bodied man. This is the miracle of Kamadeva, the Lord of Passion. Whether the man entered the woman or the woman entered the man we do not know except that both forgot the separateness of their bodies. Lost in senselessness they lay like the dead with the play of passion over.

Red eyed with sleeplessness, and with fatigue in every limb, Harlata tumbled out of chamber of love.

In the morning Sundersen again started to roam round and began to hear in the street the talk of prostitutes among themselves.

To mandwek an unhappy prostitute was complaining that she was visited by someone who spent all the night in talking and eating, and had only a feeble urge for love. The dissatisfied woman continued: "This fool come to me like the shadow of death in the garb of a pleasure seeker."

One women related the story of a village simpleton: "When my eyes become dark with passion he thought I was dying. He got a fright, left me and ran out of the house."

Sundersen, thus listening to the talk of various women, walked round the town. Thus, spending a life of happy union in fulfillment of passionate love, Sundersen passed a year and a half with Harlata. Sometimes, roaming arm-in-arm with his friend, Gunapalita, he would go and sit in some garden for a Heart-to-heart talk. He saw a postman coming toward him.

He was wearing thick, Hand-woven clothes, and had a rough blanket round his shoulders. In his hand he carried a stick and a fan and an oil can. He had a belt round his waist, and carried a bag. His shoes were torn and his feet dusty.

Recognising the son of Purindar, he drew near, Sundersen joking said to his friend: "Dear one, Hanuman the celestial messenger has come"!

Reaching the sport he placed his forehead on the ground in respect, and handed over the latter. Sundersen opened and read it. From Kusumpur the letter was from Purinder. In quiets eagerness Sundersen read it. The letter said:

> *Purandara, from the august city of flowers, addresses his wishes to Sunderesen, but the words are steeped, even to indistinctness, in the dyes of grief and anger.*
>
> *You have forgotten your stainless race, O one disowned; you have had no thought of what you owed to your elders; you have fallen into the ways of evil, and have not considered the unfavourable reflections which will be passed upon your conduct.*
>
> *How could a pursuer of girls be born into a race where each has always walked most straightly, and where each has displayed such impeccable conduct that no half-thought could be levelled against it, where each has taken pleasure to do wrong to no man?*
>
> *You were guaranteed against all evil by the ritual ceremonies of religion, how could you touch the lips of a harlot?*
>
> *How should these things accord: a face wet with tears because of the smoke of the three sacred fires, and a sea of weeping at the reproaches of a whore?*
>
> *How should these things accord: the sacred formula that is murmured during the sacrifice, and the voluptuous whispering, the inarticulate cry of a woman who belongs to all?*
>
> *How should these things accord: the respectful trembling which seized you when your master beat you with his switch, and resignation under the petulant kicks of an angry girl?*

How should these things accord: the antelope vestment of one who gives all his life to pious endeavour, and a garment stained by contact with a public woman?

You split wood for the sacrifices in your childhood; whence come this art to you of tearing mistress' lips?

You practiced unwavering obedience to the priest; whence have you learnt this conquering manner over loose women?

Your perfect pronunciation in reciting the syllables of the sacred text became a by-word; whence have you such virtuosity in speech with raging girls?

I have recalled your family to you, now I go pray.

Sundersen took note of the contents of this letter, and then fell into a hesitation as to what he should do! Then it was that someone sang these most appropriate lines in the metre *Arya*:

"To be caught in the snare of a

Prostitute's love, and tread
A wrong path, and ignore the advice
of elders –
The words of the elders are like bitter
medicine –
Distasteful in the beginning, but beneficial
in the end."

Finding the moment opportune Gunapalita said: "Good people do not take ill whatever their dear ones say out of love. Not listening to the friendly counsel of your companion, you are sunk in the sea of a prostitute's passion. Now the sorrow – laden message of your loving father is the only lifebuoy for you. Gunapalita whispers, have you forgotten the family members are all around?

Thus, having heard his friend talk Sundersen began to think more feelingly about his own family.

"The command of the father," said Sundersen, "Cannot be disobeyed, and without Harlata I cannot live! Therefore, death is the only answer – how it shall happen I don't know. He who desires no wealth and wants only love a man can only leave her if either the gods will it or iron shackles bind a man's feet."

Finally he decided to go to Kusumpur and told this to his beloved. When he departed, Harlata come out of her chamber of sorrows, and started to walk behind him, mournfully.

She leaned forgetful against the root of a tree detail. Haralata and Sundarsen the Women of Lust > Courtesy 'Book of Eastern Lover' (1927).

Coming of the shade of the *Banyan* tree Harlata stood tearfully and Sundersen spoke to her with a voice shattered with pain.

"Dearest, come either to this tree, or farthest upto the village pond yonder, and no further. So, enjoin the Holy Texts, the Shastras. Dear, dear one, where the gods are striving to cut the knots of love what can an unfortunate one like me do? Beloved, I have left my heart with your heart. Take care of it with all your might lest you lose it."

Hearing the sweet and loving words of Sundersen, Harlata spoke with a voice faint with sorrow: "How compare me, born of a low home, earning bread through voice, with you, born an embodiment of virtue, talent and nobility? You had come on a pilgrimage to see the country, and on the way you stayed at my humble abode so long; it is the fruit of my good actions in past life. My Lord, what ill or well I committed out of love for you, I beg pardon for it."

Having heard her say this Sundersen said: keep well and be happy! Then turned his face and slowly started to walk away.

Harlata, who was holding the branch of the Banyan tree, and whose lips were parched with the heat of her own breath, stood watching the path which he was treading. She dishevelled her hair and turned her garland back to front. Her eyes were filled with tears and her body had become so weak that she could barely carry her own weight! She was quickly holding her heart with both her hands. She gave up all joy in life, wore no ornament nor precious clothes.

She was surrounded with sorrow and faced an inner struggle to live or not to live! From her heart come a voice choked with pain: "O my breath of life! Part not till my beloved is out of the dangers of the jungle" – Disregarding this prayer, her breath, too, departed.

After a short time, from a traveller who had overtaken them, Sundersen enquired – "Did you see on your way a sorrow-stricken woman?"

He said, "I had seen the motionless body of a women under the Banyan tree and non else!" Hearing this Sundersen like a stone fell to the ground. His friend lifted him and Sundersen said sorrowfully:

"My father's ill advice and your inducement has led to this that I, the sinner, and her own life both departed from her at the same time. "O my fate, you are dead! The play is over. O love! What will you do now? The township of the heart is desolate, having no objective; wandering aimlessly in the land of pain. In sorrow at our separation she gave up her life. I must go back for her funeral with the rites of the Holy Fire."

They reaching the place where Harlata lay dead! Sundersen too fell to the ground, and began to mourn loudly. "See…we have come back now. Why are you angry and why are you soiling your body with earth? Get up, dear one, and say… something. The gods had given her birth after churning the ocean of beauty. She was the most prised pearl of creation."

Without paying further attention to the lamentions of his friend, Gunapalita now raised a pyre and burnt the body of the courtesan. In his despair the lover would have thrown himself among the flames, but at the moment a man felt these most appropriate lines rising within his soul, and so gave voice to them:

Only a madman follows into death
The girl who seemed more dear to him than breath,
Whose passing put his sole into confusion;
Since, though in women such an end is meet,
Man has the fortitude to clear his feet
Of every grief, for grieving is illusion.

These words drew Sundersen from his prostration, and he said to his friend: "My spirit is enlightened by this wise man, for he has shown me what is fitting. What man of sense would fall into any passion because of this circle of existences? He is bond within it to the pain of losing; he is bond to birth, to age, to sickness and to death!" Sundersen said: "Let us go now towards Kusumapur, for I vow to find my refuge in the last stage of life which is asceticism, so that freedom from ignorance may be my portion."

To this his noble young friend made answer: "Since earliest childhood you have not left me. What need is there, even for one who dreams of complete renunciation, to abandon a friend? I have not one desire which points towards the world of sense."

"It is well" cried Sundersen, and led his friend in the direction of the forest of penitents, of resolution and abiding vows…

The story of the tragic end of Harlata having been related stressing the constancy of the love of a street-women, now Vikrala, the teacher of the temptress Malati, instructs her in the art of dramatishing a situation so as to give the lover the impression that his mistress has sacrificed a great deal in accepting his love.

Story of Manjuri from Harlot to Heroine

O one with the beautiful waist, remember what Manjari, the daughter of Parvacharya. The famed prostitute of Varanasi, whom she had begotten of Kamleshwar Padswami, a Brahmin of renown had done to the crown prince. Having drained away all his wealth, she just cast him aside.

When the first movement of dance, following the modes and postures of *Ratnavali*, starts, who is there whose entire body does not begin to quiver with sexual desire? So Manjuri too be-feet a Swirl of Passion.

Vatsraja's technique of acting is so superb, that the admiring audiences cannot discern whether they are seeing play – acting or witnessing a real-life situation. Acting like Vatsraja, Manjuri is swept off herself into oneness with her role, her hand becomes full of sweat and she gets numb and limp – so forgetful does she become of the physical living self.

She so expresses with her eyes the hope of meeting the lover, and the despair of not finding him. That the audience forgets whether they are watching a drama or witnessing the real torment of a women parted from her lover.

So that art critic was describing the talents of Manjuri when the prince, looking at her, with amazement exclaimed: "So that is she"! Having understood the meaning of the prince's words, the minister started to talk about the character of women, denouncing the prostitutes and praising the nature and conduct of slave girls.

"One loves one's wife for having children, and one keeps slave concubines for pleasure – and such propitiation of the Lord of passion one seldom gets with women of other types."

Having heard this, Manjuri replied to what was said about other women: "I keep busy with my own work, and do not worry about others. Today my mind is much disturbed. If I had known his home, and if I had the strength, I would have broken with a stick the back of he who poses as the *maker of Destiny*."

Manjuri says, he has made my body so beautiful, yet not matched it with an equally unique lover, he has made my life without the fruits of joy…

Then, thus hearing words said in favour of her class, Manjuri's mother contradicted what the prince's minister-in-waiting had said. "An ignorant lout who cannot control his passion at the sight of women carrying, water from the well – such a man, for sure, will run down singing and dancing woman. Those who have studied the art of love, and are wedded to a bad wife, their passion never gets aroused to the highest pitch. Putting the water pitcher on the ground, and spreading grass on the earth – thus men and women in the village make love.

The sons of Bharat have given instruction in the art of drama to the dancing girl at the court of Raja Nahush; yet even they could not vie in their art with the excellence of this performance. "*Ratnavali* is being praised as the highest creation of dramatic technique for its beauty and music. The most accomplished critics have nothing but admiration for it."

The prince, having been so pleased, was thus praising the performance when someone burst into the chanting of an Aryan hymn. "Not to run away from battle, a knowledge of dramatic art, its perfection of speech, excellence in hunting – these are the essentials for the education of princes."

Hearing this the prince started to talk about the art of drama itself, and on various acts of the drama in a masterly way. "With the practice of Akhet the most tantalising objectives are achieved like roaming round to various parts of the earth, riding a sprited horse….

Thus, the son of Somer Bhatt was holding forth on the art of hunting when someone in the audience started to speak loudly and said; "Whoever gets caught in the Swirl of hunting gets so obsorted in that he even forgets eating and drinking."

Taking this as a hint for ending the performance, Somer Bhatt, the prince, beckoned his treasurer to reward them suitably. Casting loving glances on Manjuri, the prince got up. After reaching home and having had his food, he was struck with passion for Manjuri. Took counsel with his minister. "How does Kamadeva, the Lord of Passion, vibrantly live in the beauty, sweet speech, smile, coquettish glances, all at the same time?

The benefit which Lord Brahma got in creating Tilotoma, the celestial nymph, was that the Orgres, Sundh and Upsundh, were destroyed. But what good did the gods see. In creating Manjuri, the beautiful one, who is killing people with her charm?

A Look at Manjuri Excites Passion: With eyes lovely, like a baby deer, long slender arms – a look at Manjuri excites passion in any human being. Sparkling with virtues and faultless her beautiful face like the sweet lotus, only the dwellers of paradise can aspire to enjoy her.

Those men who are overwhelmed with passion, worship the lust-filled body of Manjari for fulfillment. Her delicate waist has three curves in it, and her slender arms have two curves. That doe of a woman is so passionately warm. That the heat of the sun bears no comparison to it.

Manjuri, she is like a poem, beautiful of body, joy-giving to passionate desire-slender waisted, with sweetness of speech and loving words. With these five qualities is there a man born, whom Manjuri cannot confound with desire?

While performing *Ratnavali,* Manjuri's glance at Vatsraja. The actor, was like a thousand arrows shot forth, from the bow of Kamadeva, the Lord of Passion. Even old men get passion struck by the arrows of the glance from Manjuri.

Her beauty shines when she acts, like rays of light from a lamp. Is there anyone in whom the movements of her body do not excite lust? Just as the body of Kamadeva burns like fire with passion, it cannot get cool, even through the fear of the blue-necked god, Shankar. So the burning passion of the celestial nymph, Paramda takes possession of Manjuri's body and makes her beauty blaze.

O recluse, if you aspire to Paradise, go fast to the place where dwell the women of lust. If we think we can only conclude that when God created Manjuri, he cast her from lumps of salt. Her blossoming, youthful breasts are robbing lovers of all their peace. But when they have been played with by hands of lust, who will care for her? Why should men of lust not lose their heads over the heart-ravishing body which the master of creation cast with his own hands?

He who is born just when he is thought of, arrows which become as welcome as blossoms, he whose power protects the helpless, he who has no strength and yet comes to battle – all are manifestations of the mysterious deeds of the almighty. Leave done others – even Lord Brahma, who is above all, forgets to reveal the holy knowledge of the Vedas, and then blames himself for it.

If Lord Shiva had a look at her, then he would turn his face away from all other women. Even the fire in his third eye is not more scorching than the heat of Lord Kamadeva's passion. Then Lord Shiva blames the fire in his own eye.

The beautiful Manjuri has breasts so exquisitely attractive, that even Lord Vishnu loses faith in his abstinence. With the graceful gait of a she-elephant, how can she fail to move the hearts of the pundits. And the young people are in a tumult of passion anyway. Who knows to whom will belong her golden-hued body, and on whom will fall her blue eyes which are enchanting, like saffron fields.

No women can match her, and men cannot enjoy her. So neither men are happy, nor women. The eunuchs along are content. People of low nature are not worthy to praise her breasts. For both her breasts are covered by the garlands of precious pearls, which causes havoc in the hearts of men. There is nothing more wondrous on earth than that, having got Dhritrashtra, the valiant Pandav chief, the slender-waisted Draupati still did not give up sex union with the other Pandav brothers.

This woman's waist needs no ornaments. Lord Brahma has girded her waist with such a garland of passion that she is irresistible. Her lips always quiver, her eyes remain drunk with passion, and her eyebrows remain arched. She looks as if she has conquered the whole world. Her strong body does not overshadow, the beauty of her breasts, which look like two cleft mounds in the hills.

Knowing the art of love and the postures for exciting passion, in spite of her delicate body she gets the better of even strong men. So the prince was waxing eloquent over Manjuri, when Manjuri's maid arrived with a message. She respectfully presented the basket with betel leaves to the prince, and then began to unfold the purpose of her visit, as deputed by Manjuri.

Manjari Wants to Own the Moon: "Foolish Manjuri wants to make Lord Vishnu's lotus an ornament for her ears. From the sky she wants to own the moon. She wants to make the nectar from heaven. Her food and of the tender leaves of the sandal tree. She wishes to make a bed for herself. From the tree of heavan she wants to pluck blossoms, and in her sorrow she wants to put her head on the chest of a god.

Manjari, who has now fallen in love with you, used to scoff at soft-tempered Sarojini, and used to talk ill of the recluse with godly qualities. She is one who is born once in a hundred births. I, a slave worthy of only five mean coins, am not praising her for the sake of praise, but am only saying what she deserves.

The snakes which entwine the sandal creeper and suck sweetness from its fragrance – them to do not praise; for the embodiment of passion, Fie! I have no ward of praise even in my dreams. She understands the music of the sex organs, as well as the music of an instrument. But just as foolish men do not understand the difference between a Brahmin, a cow, an elephant, a dog and a low caste man, she does not understand men.

She does not honour Rambha, the celestial spouse of Nalkubar – and she slanders the heaven born Urvashi. She robs men of their hearts, but her heart, she never loses to anyone, she given joy to others, but never gets satisfaction herself. Through her art of love she captures the passion of others, but in spite of men giving her thousands of presents, she does not give her heart to them.

She seems brimming with love, but knows love by name only. She gets passionate with men, but only hears from others about the joy of sex union, never experiencing it herself. Knowing the art of love she speaks sweetly, but is not swayed by love. She does not know the ills of passion, but the pains born of youthful passion torment her.

Like Chandralekha, the young and vivacious hymph, the impudent Manjuri robbed Ravana, the king of Ogres, of all his possessions. Oh Lord of he-men, even Shiva, the ruler of the three worlds, could not extinguish with the might of his third eye, the blazing fires of passion ignited by Kamadeva, the God of Love. Having set her eyes on you, the anger of suppressed passion began to shoot arrows at her heart. In whatever way you happened to touch her, that become the arrow of Kamadeva for her. When the play began she locked longingly at you. This disturbed her acting, which made her – a laughing stock among her co-stars.

Not caring for the violation of Bharat Manu's laws for dramatics, the stage master asked her to spread out her part and portray her feelings in full. "After the ending of the play does she continue to feel as emotionally disturbed as when the play began? Or was it only a part of play acting on the stage?" he asked.

"She who never praised even a man of high knowledge, now fills her mind only with admiration for you. This way he sits, this way he talks, this way he walks – forgetting everything, thus she think of you.

O God among princes, even Janaka has not got your talents, Nor is he cultivated in as many arts. Then with whom can I compare the preciousness which belongs to you?" – this the maid messenger said with an air of sad despair. "Sometimes coming, sometimes right here, sometimes going, sometimes in her arms – thus she keeps thinking of you all the time."

"O Lord of her Soul," said the maid: Leaving everything else alone, with one heart bent on her happiness, she keeps repeating, like a hymn, your good qualities as the center of her thoughts. To her you are unique, owner of her heart, worthy of worship, giver of joy ravisher of the heart, one sunk in her heart, a god, master, protector, lord of her soul, bestower of beneficence on all in distress.

"Shameless one – go to the one with whom, you were sitting till now; no use talking senselessly to me." Thus, repeats in her heart, the slender waisted one, what she will say to him when he comes. She does not dare look at her own face in the mirror. Not to talk of looking at the moon. She despairingly tosses her arms about. Then how can she restfully place her arms on her soft bed?

Even the touch of her own hands she cannot bear – not to talk of the trunk of the banana tree. She cannot rest even on the tender banana leaves. "O Manjuri, are you yourself? Is it the same town, full of the same people? Is it the same Kamadeva, Lord of Passion? Then from where springs this desolation of the heart? She asks herself.

"One whose passion has nothing to give, whose love is like straw – have you reached that stage of life? What is a human being not subjected to in this world!

O one with the beautiful body, all that is learned, whether of the real or the unreal, the inner meaning only those know who have understanding.

This anger in love, so saddening to you makes you look more beautiful. It makes your friends worry, but it is heart-warmingly lovely – rather it adds to your bewitching charm.

O women of lustful pleasures, fortunate is the man, who has reduced you to this plight, who used to rob men of peace and wealth with the trickery of words. We must find his whereabouts, for the healers find a cure for every ailment." Hearing her companion say this, for a while she started at her blankly – then with a voice filled with pain said 'yes'!

Therefore, O one with the manly body, if the dust from your lotus feet touchers her, then all the prayers of her well wishers will doubtlessly bear fruit. Hearing the thunder of the clouds the pea-hen feels happy and the fish keep looking intently love, and thanks clouds. I am not vainly praising Manjuri, nor am I trying to seduce your heart. I am just describing the qualities which nature has bestowed on her.

Manjuri is tired with dancing but the soft-bodies one is distressed with overwhelming passion. And you are the hero of the battle of love. May the gods beless you both." In the heat of passion, as the women leads, the man joyously follows. When the bed-chamber was quiet, then with modesty and fear the singing girls said, "what are you doing to me"?

"I am doing that which confers bliss – that which is the desire to every man's heart." So saying, the prince began the love bout. Then the women of the lust with all her artifices sucked him dry of all passion, and left him as a mere skeleton of skin and bone.

Thus, Ended Vikrala, the Arch Temptress, by practicing what I have thought you of the art of squeezing money from rich lovers, your name will live forever. Having received this teaching, with heart full of the happiness of knowledge, Malati, who was thirsting for love, touched Vikrala's feet as a homage to her wisdom, and returned home.

All men who read or hear this poem, and understanding it learn a lesson from it. Never shall they be caught in the snares of procuress, a temptress, a pimp or a prostitute.

Mithuna or the ceremony of Union, attended by two maids. Kandariya Mahadeva temple of Khajraha 10th Century.

Chapter Six

Sringaramanjuri

Raja Bhojadeva

In the city of Dhara there lived the King of Kings, Maharajadhiraja Parameswara Sri Bhajadeva, who was a glorious king, a valiant king, a learned and just king, a king who was the source of Dharma.

In the court of Sri Bhojadeva reigned supreme the courtesan Sringaramanjari. She was the embodiment of beauty and the abode of Love; she vanquished the treasures of beauty of the heavenly damsels by her own Loveliness; she was the envy of not only the fair women in the kingdom of Bhojadeva, but also of the courtesans of the neighbouring kingdoms.

The mother of Sringaramanjari was Visamasila, the retiring courtesan. She was respected by all. She was anxious that her daughter should hold her own in the court of Sri Bhojadeva and should excel in all the arts.

One summer evening, seated by the bedside of her daughter she spoke thus: "Child, being intoxicated with your good fortune that is on par with your beauty, do not err. Generally speaking, many courtesans have been deceived and ruined by dhurtas. You can practice your art successfully only by propitiating the minds of others and this is possible only if you study and comprehend the emotions (ragas) that rule the minds of men. I shall relate to you the stories of other courtesans who employed their knowledge of the art to climb the dizzy heights of glory, so that you may enrich your learning by their experiences, Listen."

Fall of Ravidatta

In the town of Kundinapura dwelt a rich and learned Brahmana called Somadatta. He was a renowned scholar, as he was well-versed in the Vedas and Sastras. He had reached the pinnacle of fame and had amassed great wealth. He was growing in years, but was not blessed with a child.

The learned Brahmana propitiated the Sun, the giver of desired objects, by observing the *vijayasaptami*. As a result, he begot a son whom he named Ravidatta, after the Sun God.

By the time Ravidatta grew to be a boy of sixteen, he was given the sacred thread and was initiated in the studies of the Vedas and the Vedangas.

Ravidatta avidly studies the rich literature of the Vedas and almost equalled his father in the depth of knowledge he acquired. The father was conscious of the wealth that his son would inherit and being anxious to protect his son from the danger of being ruined in future, he taught him all the arts; he taught him the secrets of harlotry as laid down by *Dattaka* and other learned men.

One day he called his son to him and said:

"Son, youth is dense darkness and it cannot be avoided by living beings. *Madana* is wicked and wealth is the one abode of intoxication. The mind by nature is as inconstant as a drop of water on the lotus leaf; senses are as unrestrainable as untamed elephants; the objects of pleasure are naturally fascinating and among these especially young damsels. The beginning of the monsoon and the autumn and other seasons are great excitants. And who can possibly resist Love, their friend? Therefore, you should conquer the group of six enemies: the senses, the inspiration of wicked people in proximity, and the contact of wanton women.

"Son, remember, that the teachings of the elders slip away from the infatuated mind. The study of sastras is brought to naught your self-respect and pride of class is trampled upon by people around you, your courage fails, your power of discrimination vanishes and ultimately your character melts and brings about your complete ruin, if you fail to conquer your senses.

"Therefore, my son, be cautions and act according to your position. As a rule avoid wicked company, shun the sound of the triple harmony of instrumental music, singing and dancing. Disregard the impassioned glances of young women and do not frequent the neighbourhood of dancing houses and gambling halls. Bear in mind that one who acts contrary to his rank and position will be reduced to the state derision. Let the examples of the powerful kings like *Pururavas* and others who were brought under subjection by courtesans like *Urvasi* serve as an object lesson to you."

Ravidatta was a dutiful son and followed his father's advice in letter and spirit. He come to be greatly respected and Somadatta had the satisfaction of having done his duty by his son.

A few years, after the death of his father, his mother also died. Now, Ravidatta, led almost a lonely life, stricken by sorrow. As the years passed the sorrow lessened and he received and entertained friends to dissipate his loneliness.

Many a spring come and many a festival of youth was celebrated in the park called *Kusumakara*. But Ravidatta did not even visit the park once, though he was a blooming young man, and all the passions and exotions of youth demanded satiation. Following the advice of his father he scrupulously avoided all places of revelry and festival.

But now long could he suppress the feelings and emotions that surged within him, as he grew to be a healthy and strong young man? Nature's forces demanded expression in a natural way and Ravidatta had not the will to break the laws of nature.

It was spring. The air was thick with the sweet fragrance of varied flowers, that wafted freely in the gentle breeze of the park. The mango groves were inlaid with clusters of buds and the cuckoos announced the spring by the melodious songs they sang from the branches of the trees and bushes, the *Madhavi* creepers crept low, burdened by the weight of the blossoms.

Everywhere young people walked lightly laughed heartily and talked merrily. The festival of spring (Festival of Youth) was being celebrated in the Kusumakara park and all young eyes and minds were turned in that direction.

A group of revellers come to Ravidatta and said:

"Dear friend, today is the festival procession of the fish-bannered God. If it is not seen what is the use of life! What is the use then of this fruitless pair of eyes if they cannot witness such festivities? We know, you have no curiosity, but can you not gratify our wishes by accompanying us? Therefore, come along, we shall go."

Ravidatta remembered the advice and the instructions of the elders and did not wish to go. But strangely enough he felt he was being forced to go forward by youth, and pulled in front by the senses – the friends.

The Kusumakara garden was a house of pleasure of the fish-bannered God. There were pleasure lakes, the sides of which were adorned by *Tiloka* trees with thickly grown sprays of blossom; there were pleasure hillocks where the *Kurabaka* trees stood like lovers with hair standing on ends due to the opening of innumerable buds and there was a mansion of *Madana* (passion) built of white crystalline stones.

In the house of *Madana* Ravidatta espied a woman looking like the presiding deity of love. Seeing her, he wondered at the skill of the creator and spoke to himself:

"Oh! in creation this is an unparalleled achievement of *prajapati*; a matchless type among the class of women, a new sea of loveliness; an elixir of the life of love; a magnet for a attaching the hearts of people; the stage for the teacher of cleverness."

Now and then be directed his glances into the mansion of Madana and he was almost startled to find that the wondrous creation of the creator was throwing furtive glances in his direction.

Vinayavati was the name of the damsel. She was a courtesan of matchless beauty and high accomplishments.

On seeing Ravidatta, a youth of charming form and opulent appearance, she became enamoured of him. As Ravidatta lingered about the mansion, she frequently glanced at him with affectionate eyes and exhibited her love for him by amorous gestures. Inferring his affluence from his form, she thought: "Ah! After a long time a treasure has come my way; after a long time the tree of hope has bloomed, desire has flowered and ambitions have borne fruit."

Vinayavati started talking to a friend nearby and smilingly looked at Ravidatta, making graceful movements and gestures. Ravidatta, who till now had not experienced the charms of love, felt a strange sense of happiness and thought the wondrous damsel was enamoured of him every moment and the gestures and smiles were intended for him.

At the close of the festivities he entered the mansion and after performing the worship of *Kandarpa (Manmada)*, wended his way to his house through the garden. There was only one thought in his mind – "the wondrous damsel"!

Towards the close of the evening that day, Vinayavati, sent her friend *Sangamika* to Rabidatta's house. At the threshold of the house, she hesitated for a moment, then boldly entered. Ravidatta's friends who where in the house recognised her and introduced her to him.

Taking her seat, she said: "Ravidatta, I have something for your ears only. Give me a private audience."

Ravidatta was very, much pleased to know that she was Vinayavati's companion. He recollected having seen her in the mansion of *Madana*. He gestured to his companions to move away from the room, and when they had done so, he addressed the lady:

"Well, beautiful one, what news do you bring, fair or foul"?

"Good one", said Sangamika, "though this is against your rank and position yet I am afflicted by anguish because of my mistress." Please listen to what I say:

"Since your Lordship come within the sight of my mistress during the festive procession of *Madana*, you have entered her heart cleft by hundreds of arrows of *Samara*. Since then her heart is pierced by a shaft, her mind is intoxicated, her body trembles and her breathing is heavy; her eyes are anxious to look upon your youthful form, her ears are eager to hear your virtues, her speech is pregnant with your name and her desires are to be united with you. You are a learned and righteous man. Therefore, give my friend the boon of life. In your smritis and other sastras it is said that the killing of a woman is a great sin.

If you do not oblige my friend by coming to her now, then she will end her life this day."

Sangamika stopped in her speech and looked at Ravidatta questioningly, as if to say, "On your reply depends the life of the most charming young woman on earth."

Ravidatta was perplexed. He was torn between two conflicting forces. He was greatly agitated due to the intoxication of youth and his love for the 'Wondrous damsel'. Then there were those instructions from his elders and his sense of discrimination.

After struggling with his thoughts for some time he decided to go and meet the Beauty of Beauties at her house.

Guided by Sangamika he reached the house of Vinayavati, as the Sun had disappeared behind the tree tops and dusk was fast approaching.

After the first visit, Ravidatta become a habitual visitor to her house and gave her riches, bit by bit. Disregarding the elder's instructions and divesting himself of all sense of shame, he become a victim of Vinayavati's harlotry.

The courtesan understood Ravidatta's *Niliraga* and she arranged picnics, festivals and religious pilgrimages. She received valuable presents from him on all these occasions and gradually took from him all his wealth and made him a pauper.

Now the time come to discard him like a rotten apple.

One evening Sangamika told him: "Learned friend, a merchant Prince and an old acquaintance of Vinayavati has come to town, after having amassed huge wealth. He is head over heels in love with her and goes about saying that he would give her all his wealth even if she calls him for only one night. Her wealth is your wealth, as you have given all your wealth to her. And any addition to her wealth will benefit you. Therefore, do they away for a day or two." So saying, Sangamika made the servants drive him physically out of the house.

Ravidatt's degradation was complete. Thereafter, he never secured access to her house. Whenever he went there he was insulted and abused by the servants.

Neither Vinayavati nor Sangamika cared to recognise him.

Because of his infatuation for her, he spent the rest of his miserable life, thinking of her and considering himself fortunate if he could catch a glimpse of her at a distance.

The Matchless Courtesan Devadatta

One of the towns that flourished on the banks of the Ganga was called Hastigrama. It was a town of Brahmanas.

Except the parents of Suradharman, all the other Brahmans were wealthy and learned. Suradharman's father as well as grandfather were so poor that they could not boast of a square meal a day.

When Suradharman grew to be a young man his father died leaving him to shift for himself in an unkind world. He saw the wealth of other people and felt miserable. He was poverty itself and the contrast between himself and his neighbours was so striking as to make him look almost non-existent and this smote his heart very badly. He wondered by what means he would obtain wealth. "Riches help to gain more riches, but I have nothing," he ruminated, "I would like to serve a king, but I do not know how. I shall worship the Lord of the Sea: I shall torture this body of mine that proclaims my poverty to the world, if need be," he decided.

He left his town and wandered far in search of the sea, and when he sighted it at last, his heart swelled with joy. He espied the vast blue expanse fringed with shining bubbles of foam. The waves rolled on in never-ending succession and lashed the earth in majestic fury, but beyond the breakers was the all-embracing calmness of the blue kissing the sky-line.

"There is nothing so sublime, so enchanting, so awe-inspiring and so ennobling as the Lord of the Sea," he thought. And to such God be started paying homage.

Every morning, wearing a short leather loin-cloth and taking a staff in his hands, he would go and offer a handful of flowers to the sea, and bowing down he would move forward and backward with the tide and the ebb. Spending the whole day thus, in the evening after paying his salutations to the sea he would return. He spent many years thus, sustaining himself on alms.

The Lord of the Sea was moved, yet he wanted to test the tenacity of the poor Brahmana. Assuming the form of a small boy, he went to the Brahmana and asked, "Oh! Brahmana, why do you inflict such pain on yourself? The Lord of the Sea cannot be easily moved by your austerity. So give up this painful living and return home."

The Brahmana replied: "Young man, why do you worry about it ? Go your way. Nothing in this Universe moves without a purpose. No creation of the Lord expends itself in wasteful energy."

But when the boy persistently asked him the purpose of his offering homage to the Lord of the Sea, the Brahmana replied: "I am much afflicted by poverty and the pains of penury are more severe than the physical pain that I impose on my body. The poverty has come down to me from generations. Therefore, I am worshipping the sea. I believe no other power can relieve me of this curse of penury."

Seeing the Brahmana's firm resolve the boy said: "I am the Lord of the Sea. I am pleased with your sacrifices and homage. I have come to give you indestructible wealth." So saying, the boy, assuming the form of the Lord of the Sea, gave the Brahmana an invaluable jewel, and disappeared.

Suradharman heaved a sigh of relief. But now worry gripped him. He wondered how he could carry such a priceless jewel on his person. After much contemplation he hit upon a novel plan. He slit open his thigh, put the jewel in and healed it up. He then dressed like a madman wearing rags and winding a dried up garland round his head. He wandered about eating whatever he got on the way, sleeping anywhere, and staining his body with dirt and uttering no other words than "Mother Knows."

After months of wandering Suradharman reached the city of Ujjain. This city was the abode of pleasure and leisure, mirth and merriment. It was said that the Lord of the three worlds, Sri Mahakalanatha, prompted by pleasures and fascinated by the glory of the city, took up abode there having given up the lofty heights of Kailasa.

In this city ruled the great King Vikramarka, who by the valour of his arms destroyed all his enemies. One of the precious possessions of the king was his courtesan Devadatta.

Devadatta was as beautiful as she was artful; as charming as she was crafty; as famous as she was wealthy. She had a particular caprice. She used to travel in pomp searching for someone wealthy and fit to be fleeced.

Once she mounted a carriage drawn by horses and accompanied by five or six hundred foot soldiers and a retinue of clever maids rode through the outskirts of the city.

At the foot of a mango tree, just outside the eastern gate of the city, sat Suradharman, uttering "Mothet Knows." As the procession passed by he blinked at the soldiers, the maids and "the matchless beauty" in the carriage. He seemed unperturbed and unconcerned, but Devadatta's intuition told her that the Brahmana's madness enshrined some precious treasure, for securing which she resolved she would renounce the three worlds.

The madman did not realise that the jewel, though it was hidden in his thigh, radiated its brilliance through his body and no observant eye could fail to detect it.

Now Devadatta decided to rope the Brahmana in and resolved that she would employ every stratagem she could conceive of to deprive the man of his treasure.

As her carriage came opposite the mango tree, she halted it, alighted from it with the dignity of a queen, and walked slowly with the gait of a swan towards the Brahman.

She stood before him, with her bewitching smile and her inviting looks for a moment, and then addressed him respectfully.

"Oh! learned Brahmana, whence do you come? Where do you wish to go? It is a pity that such a noble face, with those sparkling eyes, the proud nose, the broad forehead, should wear the mantle of madness. You are certainly not born mad; perhaps no one bestowed tender affection, enduring love and soothing kindness on you. Come, come with me. I shall make you more noble than you were ever before."

Speaking thus, she lovingly touched him on the shoulder, and taking him by the hand led him to her carriage.

The madman was apparently unmoved by Devadatta's amorous gestures. But he ungrudgingly followed her muttering the words, "Mother Knows."

When they reached the abode of Devadatta, the madman was attended by her servants as if he were one of the nobles of the land. The courtesan bathed him, clothed him with the finest garments and fed him with delicious sweets. Every night she adorned him with ornaments, smeared unguents on his body and enjoyed with him every kind of pleasure.

Six months slipped by. Devadatta continued her loving and tender ministrations day after day, giving up her harlotry and even neglecting her services to the king.

But the madman showed no signs of improvement. He spoke nothing but "Mother Knows," though he never showed the slightest dislike for the enjoyment of sensual pleasures. This behaviour confirmed Devadatta's belief that the Brahmana was really more of a rogue than a madman and there was a method in his madness.

Suradharman had his own reflections. Once or twice it occurred to him that the courtesan must have divined his secret and his prolonged stay would induce him to surrender his treasure to her out of infatuation for her. Now he planned to leave that town.

One day while he was seated on the couch beside the courtesan, he gesticulated. He folded his hands and pointed in the direction of his country, as if to suggest that he wished to go home. He frequently uttered "Mother Knows."

Devadatta somehow divined the madman's design. He was trying to slip away. But she could not just hold him by force, for that would not make him part with the treasure he hid somewhere. As natural to all women, she started with lamentations.

"Oh! my lord," she said. "Have I not given up myself entirely to you? Have I not neglected my obligations and services to the king? Have I not given up harlotry? – All for your sake. How can I bear the pangs of separation from you? I love you dearer than my life. I shall not continue existence without you…."

Tears streamed down her pretty cheeks. She held him by the hand and implored.

"Don't go away, my lord. Is it money that you desire to obtain? Then you should not give a second thought to it, for all my wealth is yours. Here, take all these this very moment." So saying she unloosened her necklace from round her pearl-white neck, removed the jewelled armlets from her shapely arms, brought out gold from her strong box and placed all that wealth in his lap, and sobbed bitterly.

Between her sobs she spoke, "My—my lord, if it is the attachment and affection for your parents that draws you homeward, be not anxious on that score. I have servant who would bring your kith and kin here, and my maids will attend to them all and make their lives full of cheer. Tarry, my lord, don't desert me; if you do so, it will be my ruination, my end and the end of the rich and sincere love for which I sacrificed everything."

The Brahmana was mad indeed! Now he was mad after home. Devadatta's laments, pleadings and weeping were of no avail. Suradharman folded his hands, as in supplication before her, and pointed to the same direction and repeated, "Mother Knows."

When Devadatta discovered that the Brahmana was resolved to cheat her, she allowed him to go, but did not give him any inkling of her future plans.

The Brahmana quietly started for his country, thinking as he walked homeward, how methodical he was with his madness, and how cleverly he escaped from the clutches of the courtesan.

Devadatta wiped her tears. And she reflected thus: "What a great fall! A great defeat, that too at the hands of a mad rogue. My life is lost; this beauty of youth on which I pride so much is worthless; I cannot use my wealth to any advantage; in spite of all my knowledge and artifice, I am outwitted by a rogue; the secrets of harlotry as taught by bawds and handed down through generations have come to nothing…"

She was silent for a while. Then stood up, walked up to the window and looked out. She espied the madman walking, nonchalantly. Her blood rushed to her face; it reddened, but it was proud, graceful and majestic as the full-blossomed lotus petals. Perhaps she was more attractive when in a temper than when mild and pleasing. She clenched her fists and resolved: "If I allow myself to be cheated by that rogue, then what use these magnetic breasts for me? I shall chop them off and throw them into the fire."

Devadatta summoned two of her maids and said: "My dear girls, the madman has got the better of me. If he escapes it is a disgrace to the very profession. You must entrap him and bring him back here with his hidden treasure. Do as I bid you.

"Avoiding his sight, you two should go two yojanas by the by-path. After you have covered two yojanas, one of you should come from the opposite village towards him. The other should walk slowly behind him. When you come near to each other enact a scene of recognition as best as you can and entice him back to this place. Your training, your service and your loyalty are on trial. Tarry not, hurry away and show your mettle."

Suradharman had covered two yojanas. His thoughts were confused. All these years he was methodically mad, and no finer sentiments ever bothered him. His association with Devadatta had no doubt kindled in him all finer sentiments natural to human beings. He had successfully hidden these sentiments, but now his thoughts were getting confused. He was sorry to have left Devadatta. He almost believed that the courtesan was sincerely in love with him. But his anxiety to hide his treasure got the better of his love for Devadatta.

Hardly had he turned the first bend on the highway, he espied a lovely damsel coming from the opposite direction. From her mode of dress he could judge that she belonged to the servant class. Suradharman was not conscious of the other woman following him at a distance.

When the women came close, they rushed into each other's arms in joyful embrace, and with astonishment reflected on their faces, began to converse thus:

The one who came from the opposite direction said: "What a good fortune to have met you. Oh! Priyangika! It seems it is ages since we met last." Clasping the other in affectionate embrace, and wiping the tears of joy that gushed out of her eyes, she inquired: "Whence do you come, Priyangika?"

"I come from Ujjain," replied Priyangika. "But Lavangika, how long is it since you left Ujjain? Perhaps it is ten years now—or is it twenty? You have aged a little since then, but you have maintained your youth and grace. You giggle as of old, but one or two lines are perceptible on your cheeks. Have you worked hard? Whence you come now and whither are you bound?"

Lavangika — "I come from yonder village. Many days have passed since I left Ujjain and I am dying for news from that wonderful city. Tell me, Priyangika, how is our great King? What is the condition of the State? and What is the latest news."

Priyangika — "Walk a few steps with me and I shall tell you something wonderful: something that is unheard of in the history of the renowned city of Ujjain."

They talked aloud within hearing of Suradharman, as they walked.

Priyangika continued: "Sister Lavangika, you remember Devadatta, the famous courtesan who was the favourite of the King and the talk of the whole town! That courtesan gave up harlotry, neglected her obligations to the King, but fell madly in love with a madman. All the tricks of her trade and her bewitching beauty failed to hold the man and he had deserted her. Devadatta could not endure the pangs of separation even for a day, for she loved him truly. And so, broken-hearted, ended her life immediately the madman deserted her. Now all her maids and servants are preparing to end their lives, for they cannot any more live in pride and pomp."

On hearing these words Suradharman abruptly stopped in his walk and turning to the ladies enquired whether what they were talking was true. Priyangika repeated everything, when the madman bemoaned: "I am the sinner, I am the cause of the ruin of a famous courtesan."

He turned his steps and briskly walked towards Ujjain resolving: "I will end my life as well."

Devadatta's house was grief-stricken. Maids, servants and retinues were wailing in sorrow; on one side was a heap of sandal-wood pieces and pots of ghee.

The body of Devadatta lay prostrate on the floor, her once jewel-bedecked neck, arms and ankles, now bare and her body clad in plain white.

On seeing Suradharman, Makaradamstra, the mother of Devadatta, who sat holding her chin in her arms, raged: "Oh! wicked sinner, why have you returned? After having killed my daughter, who was my life and the ornament of the whole world, what sinful motive brings you back here? Do you want to gloat on the misfortune you have brought on us all? Tell me, by whose favour will this family subsist now?"

The servants lifted Devadatta's body and placed it on a bier.

Now Suradharman said sharply: "Mother, why do you reproach me? Inevitable is the curse of Destiny. What purpose is served by scorning me? It is your Fate that this calamity has befallen you. Be it so. I too do not desire to live without her."

Before the maids and servants could divine what was coming, Suradharman tore open his thigh, took out the jewel and handed it over to the bawd, Makaradamstra, saying, "So long as this jewel remains with you, poverty shall not haunt you."

Holding the invaluable jewel in her hand the bawd addressed her daughter: "Rise, Oh! perturbed one, you have won the battle, you have won the battle, you have upheld the tradition of the courtesan."

Devadatta awoke as if from a long slumber. Everyone rejoiced and the mad Brahmana was welcomed as her son-in-law by the bawd.

A fortnight later, when Suradharman sat talking lovingly to Devadatta the words "Mother Knows" escaped his lips due to force of habit.

Devadatta asked him: "Ah, does your mother know or do I know?"

The Brahmana replied: "Mother does not know anything, but you know everything."

Devadatta ejaculated: "If I know everything then out with you," and the Brahmana was kicked out of the house.

Lavanyasundari

Lavanyasundari was the dutiful wife of the oilman Ghuda who was in affluent conditions because of his rich patrimony. He lived in the city called Ahicchatra, where resided rich merchants and great poets.

In that city ruled for a long time the King Vajramukuta enjoying the pleasures of kingship. This king had defeated the circle of neighbouring princes, had conquered all the arrogant enemies, and ruled almost unchallenged. Gradually, due to the sense of security and the lack of serious problems that taxed his time and energy, the king took to pleasures.

Lavanyasundari was young and beautiful. Her beauty was not unparalleled in her own class of people, but as it surpassed the beauty of all the other women in that city, she was an object of wonder.

One day King Vajramukuta during his usual prowl along the streets of the city happened to get a glimpse of Lavanyasundari who stood near the window looking down the street. The King was struck by her matchless beauty and he resolved to possess her by hook or by crook. Through his spies he came to know who she was, but as the oilman was wealthy and as he enjoyed a position of rank among the citizens, it was a problem to tackle him.

The King arrested the oilman under the pretext that he had practised adulteration in oil. Though the oilman offered to pay for in lakhs, he was not freed. On the other hand he was tortured and made to live a wretched life in prison.

Lavanyasundari, by intuition, guessed the King's motive in subjecting her husband to such harrowing and humiliating treatment. She went to the prison and told her husband: "My lord, you must free yourself from this hell by agreeing to pay any price the king demands." Gudha accepted her suggestion and told the King accordingly. The King asked for a hundred elephants knowing fully well that the oilman would not be able to get them.

Lavanyasundari, hearing of the King's impossible demands, heartened her crest-fallen husband by saying: "Do not lose courage, my lord. Accept the demands of the King, but ask six months' time to fulfil the demand. I shall procure you hundred elephants."

The oilman did as he was told and became a free man once again. King Vajramukuta was yet hopefull. He should at the most wait for six months at the end of which period Lavanyasundari would be his.

When the oilman was sunk in sorrow, he lamented: "What good this life to me when I am to pass every hour in anxiety and worry? Where can I get the hundred elephants? Why did you ask me to accept such a demand?" he asked his wife.

"My lord," replied his wife, "You have not fathomed the evil import of the King's design. It is cruel and against Dharma. He is like a king to me and I will not satisfy his lustful wish. He holds your life at stake hoping that you would surrender me to him to save your life. I tell you that it is an idle dream of the King to possess me. If you do as I tell you without questioning my conduct, I shall procure hundred elephants and save you from the clutches of the cruel King. Your life is more precious to me than my wealth and honour."

The oilman was immensely pleased with his wife's devotion to him and said: "Oh! dutiful wife, virtuous women are rare in this world and when your virtue is impregnated with devotion and love for me, I will do everything you bid me."

Lavanyasundari thought of King Sahasanka who ruled in Ujjayini, the city of all adventures. There was no king other than King Sahasanka who could give her the hundred elephants, and she resolved to please that king.

Taking with her five hundred best horses and carts and a retinue clad in liveries, she started for Ujjayini. She took up her residence in a palatial mansion in the outskirts of the city and got a rumour bruited that a courtesan of unrivalled accomplishments and matchless beauty was attracting the nobility of the land; she spent her days in ecstatic pleasures and distributed gifts adequately to suppliants, but did not accept anything from anyone.

When the news about the courtesan reached the ears of the King, he sent his spies to verify the rumours. They reported back to him saying that the courtesan was more beautiful than the damsels of heaven, and that to win her smiles and keep her company the elect of the land vied with one another.

The report of the spies roused the curiosity of the King. So pretending to be on a hunting excursion, the King followed by a small retinue of select guards went out of the city, passing by the courtesan's mansion.

Being informed of the approaching hunting party, Lavanyasundari draped herself in gorgeous robes and showed herself gracefully to the King, standing at the window. The window-sill, painted in golden hue, framed her figure so superbly that, viewed from the distance where the King was, her figure appeared to be a wonderful portrait in life painted by an artist of unparalleled skill and imagination. The sweet fragrance that issued from the flowers with which she had adorned her braided hair pervaded the atmosphere. The inviting smile that played on her ruby lips captivated the King so much that he felt that his heart was pierced by the arrows of Madana (Cupid) and then and there he resolved to possess the courtesan.

Returning to his palace the King sent for his clever and affectionate entertainer and said:

"Makharaka, in all my life, I had not set my eyes on a courtesan, who by her refulgence has enslaved my heart. Go to her residence and tell her of my desire and report her reply to me."

Makharaka was cordially received and honoured as befitting a king's messenger, by the courtesan. During the conversation, while Makharaka talked of various things, he inquired of her purpose in coming to Ujjayini, and casually said: "While the King was returning from the hunt he saw you and he wanted to know to whom you belong."

Good Makharaka, it is good news that you have brought me. Who has not heard of the great King Sahasanka, who has conquered all his enemies, and who reigns justly. For years I have been pining to meet him and gratify him.

Though I am a courtesan, I have not set my heart on anyone except your King. I have been encamping in this city with the hope that the great King would meet me and on hearing of my love for him would accept me. All these days I have been anxiously waiting to hear from the King and your coming here fills my heart with boundless joy. Tell the King that I have come all the way from a distant land to win his favours and to win his love. Also tell him that if he rejects me, I will cast away all the riches that I possess and end my life in the hope that I may be born in my next birth as his slave, only to nurse him and serve him."

King Sahasanka was immensely pleased with what his entertainer told him. He prepared himself to meet her on an auspicious night.

The spring season set in. It was a glorious night. The Lord of the night-lotus giving life to the cluster of Kumuda flowers, shone in all his silvery radiance. The stars glittered brightly dispelling darkness in the sky. The moon light produced the fire of love, agitated the sea as well as the hearts of lovers. On such a night the King sent for her and enjoyed amorous pleasures in her company.

When the yellow rays of the morning sun peered through the ventilators of the Royal Bed Chamber and gently touched the King's cheeks rousing him from sweet slumber, he felt sad, for he had to let Lavanyasundari go.

Next morning the King told his wise and good adviser Bhattamatrgupta all about Lavanyasundari and how he could enjoy ecstatic pleasures in her company and how true her love was for him.

Answering the King, Bhattamatrgupta said: "Sire, different kinds of selfish women move about the earth and to gain their selfish ends they employ various means. This is harlotry."

King Sahasanka was a little ruffled by the remark of his adviser. He thought to himself: "Bhattamatrgupta is venerable. I shall not cross words with him. But do I not know what is natural love and what is harlotry?" Therefore, disregarding his adviser, the King confidently spent many days in the company of the courtesan.

But Bhattamatrgupta, as in duty bound, reminded the King of his warning. The King, rather irritated by his adviser's persistence, asked him: "How can true love be known? When I test her, she does not even protect herself. On the other hand all signs of love are visible in her. She does not seem to think of anyone else except me even in her dreams."

"Then your Lordship should test her by rustic methods," replied the adviser.

The King, following the advice, derided her by vulgar methods as cutting off her nails, teeth, and hair. But he found that her love for him showed no abatement; on the other hand she became more attached to him.

When the King met his adviser next he told him: "Venerable Sir, you always scoff Lavanyasundari saying that her actions are that of a harlot. I treated her rough, degraded her, disfigured her, yet her love for me shows no signs of lessening. I think it is cruel justice that I show to her in return for her unstinted love."

Bhattamatrgupta observed: "I am doubly convinced now that it is nothing but harlotry. She is a clever rogue, this new friend of yours. She has succeeded in producing an illusion of love in your Lordship's mind."

Lavanyasundari came to know how Bhattamatrgupta advised the King. Therefore, she was apprehensive and looked upon the venerable adviser with great awe. She became conscious of the fact that days and months were slipping by and soon six months would be completed and her mission would remain unfulfilled.

Now she resolved to beard the lion in his lair and take the drastic step of self-sacrifice to accomplish her object. One morning she came to where the King and his adviser sat chatting and pointing to Bhattamatrgupta said: "Great King, this is the fruit of your favour that having come from a distance out of love for your merits, that person says it is all harlotry. Let it be so. Perhaps this consideration, you think, is the proper return for my unstinted love. Now I know that you, a King famed all over the world for righteousness, is in unison with a devil, who has caused my degradation and shame."

The King was taken aback by the forthright accusation by the courtesan and he asked rather indignantly: "Who told you this falsehood? Whom are you accusing, me or my adviser?"

Lavanyasundari only smiled a reply. She went to the bed chamber of the King and snatching the sharp sword that hung on the wall, severed her head.

When the courtesan did not emerge out of the bed-room for some time the King, with his mind full of misgivings entered the room, and was stunned to find her lying in a pool of blood, with her head cut off. The King felt that he was all ablaze that he was severely bitten by a poisonous snake, that he was struck by lightning.

The King called his adviser and pointing to the body on the floor cried angrily, "Venerable Bhattamatrgupta, do you see the end of harlotry?"

The adviser, in his unruffled, serene voice replied: "What else can I call it? This is harlotry *par excellence*."

The King was wrathful. Unmindful of the adviser's words, he ordered his servants to lift the body of the courtesan and take it to the temple of Goddess Asapura. He marched in a grand procession to the temple, followed by his entire retinue and prepared to cut off his head. As he raised his sword, the very sword that severed the courtesan's head, Goddess Asapura appeared on the scene and caught hold of the King's hand and said:

"Tarry, my son, do not be rash. You are not an ordinary person and it is not just that you should end your precious life, just out of compassion for an ordinary woman."

The King folded his hands and saluted the Goddess and prayed: "Oh! Divine One, leave off my hand. I shall present you today a delightful offering." Saying this the King again raised his hand.

Now the Goddess said: "I am pleased with your extraordinary valour. Ask any boon that you desire and it shall be granted."

The King was pleased and asked the Goddess to bring back to life Lavanyasundari. The Goddess granted his wish and vanished.

The courtesan rose as if from a deep slumber. She rubbed her eyes and finding the King near, fell into his arms and clasped him in affectionate embrace.

Lavanyasundari returned to the palace with the King. Everywhere felicitations were offered and the citizens were happy. The King spent the next few days very happily, contented in mind and attached in love, and leaving the affairs of the State in the hands of his Ministers.

One evening when the King was chatting with Lavanyasundari, and was enamoured by her excessively fascinating, beauty and charm, he told her:

"My beloved, I am very much pleased today, and I feel I have not had the peace of mind and joy of heart, as I have today, for the long years I have lived. I am minded to give you anything you ask. You are only to speak."

"Whatever is yours is mine as well," replied Lavanyasundari. "But if you want to please me, know that since childhood I have great fascination for elephants, and in those days I played only with toys of elephants. So what else can I ask except a hundred elephants."

"This is nothing, ask for something more," said the King.

"My Lord, it will be an honour to me if you can announce the fact that you have gifted me with elephants."

The King did accordingly.

After two days, when the King was in the best of cheer, Lavanyasundari told him her story and begged his permission to return to her home town.

She said: "Good King, I am a courtesan, and I have done everything for you as befits my profession. Give me leave to depart." The King though heart-broken, granted her wish.

Lavanyasundari returned to Ahicchatra, gave the hundred elephants to King Vajramukuta and led a happy life thereafter.

Love is Dangerous

Pundravardhana is a city that outshines all other cities in its neighbourhood by its heavenly mansions, gardens, tanks, lakes and its rich and great men.

In that city lived a wealthy merchant Vasudatha, almost a king of its class, doing a flourishing and prosperous trade with kings and nobles far and near.

One sorrow that afflicted this merchant prince was that the Gods did not bless him with a child for many years. So he observed vows, offered prayers, went on a pilgrimage to all the holy places and as a result begot a son in his old age. He named his son Ratnadatha, lavished all his affection on him and gave him everything he desired. Ratnadatha grew up as a spoilt child to the dismay of his father. But the father was wise too. He put the child under the tutelage of a famous teacher called Vasubhuti.

Ratnadath aa was a gifted child. He learnt the secrets of gambling, the science of harlotry, the art of painting as well as warfare. In a short time he learnt all that the great teacher could teach him.

Now he found that his father's profession of trade was not suitable to him as he could not profitably employ all the arts and sciences he had mastered and so he desired to seek out a sovereign king and serve him. When he as expressed his wish to his father the merchant lamented and said: "Oh! my only son, how can I live separated from you for long; you have all my wealth to spend as you like. Where is the need that you should seek wealth for service outside, when you can be a prince among merchants?"

"No, father, I do not wish either to squander your wealth or add any more to it. What is the use of my learning all the arts and sciences if I cannot put them to proper use? The more I expend my knowledge, the more I gain in them. Therefore, permit me to travel far and wide and gain glory and fame, wealth and pride as befitting my accomplishments."

The father reluctantly agreed and gave his son one thousand gold pieces to help him in his travels.

Ratnadatha accepted the money just to please his father, but had no intention to spend it. He took his sword 'Vasumandaka' and accompanied by his servant Subandu started on his journey.

On the way Ratnadatha visited gambling houses and won the gamblers' wealth which he utilised for buying provision and meeting other expenses on the way. Those who met him and came to know of his valour and wisdom spread his fame. So when he reached the city of Vidisa he found that his fame had preceded him though there was none to identify him.

It was a bright morning in spring that found Ratnadatha on the bank of a tank offering worship to the God. The clear water of the tank glistened with the radiance of burnished gold in the morning splendour of the rising sun. The swans glided majestically on the water, jerking their uplifted heads from side to side and at times diving their beaks into the water to catch and swallow a wee fish that came playing merrily in the ripples that spread around as they swam noiselessly.

To that tank came the renowned courtesan Lavanyasundari to play with the swans, to gather lotus flowers and dance before the God. Going down the steps of the tank, she seated herself on the second step and dangled her lovely, white feet into the water and splashed them gently so that they made a sound as if the swans were beating the water with their wings. As if responding to a call from one amongst them, a troup of six snowy white swans, came swimming in snake-like formation, clucking love music as it were, and clambered over the steps. Lavanyasundari picked up the smallest of them with water dripping from its closed wings and set it on her lap. She gently patted its back, ran her soft palm over its neck and head, bent low and peering into its round eyes whispered a few sweet words and then laughed. Her laughter rang through the air like the jingling of silver bells.

One of the swans, a roguish one perhaps, suddenly fluttered up in the air and perched on the head of Bakulika, friend of Lavanyasundari who had come to the tank to fetch her friend (Lavanyasundari) to the dance mandap, where the dance teacher awaited them.

Bakulika screeched with fright of the wet-footed crown. Subandu, who stood watching the scene a little distance away, loudly 'shooed' away the swan.

The screeching of Bakulika and the 'shoo!' of Subandu so frightened the swans that they all fluttered in the air, beating their wings furiously and clacking loudly and then settled on the water and swam away. The uproarious noise startled Lavanyasundari; she sprang to her feet and looked in the direction from which the 'shoo' came. And she saw Ratnadatha standing knee deep in water, with uplifted face towards the sun, with handful of water raised over his head, ready to offer '*arghya*' to the Sun God.

Her eyes took in his youthful form, his powerful sinews, his radiant face and his calm, resolute composure; she felt that the whole of him pierced her heart. It was as if her heart was pierced by the arrow of Cupid (Manmatha). She was immediately caught in the spell of love and fell unconscious on the ground.

A few minutes later she regained her consciousness, and followed by Bakulika went to the dancing mandap. She told the teacher that she was unwell and could not dance that day. Bakulika understood the nature of her friend's illness, but lied to the teacher saying that Lavanyasundari has had a severe headache since early morning and that he should allow her to go home and added that she (Bakulika) would dance instead.

The good teacher agreed. And Lavanyasundari reaching home, threw herself on her bed and shed tears of sorrow or joy, she could not say which. But her heart beat furiously and her mind was gripped by a craving, which she had never experienced before. She knew she yearned for him, the stranger who charmed, her eyes and heart at first sight.

After the dance Bakulika went to Lavanyasundari and said: "You always laughed at us and said that we were like hogs. What is this now? We are more refined, for we accept a man's company only after knowing his charms and conduct. You are meritorious indeed that without knowing the man's place of residence, conduct and wealth, you have fallen in love with him at first sight and have been reduced to agony."

Lavanyasundari replied: "True. I am now stung by love as I had never been before and I cannot account for it myself. At such a time when my vitals are stung, is it proper that you should speak such jocose and cutting words? Is this the fruit of our friendship?"

Bakulika — "Excuse me. I did not mean to hurt your feelings. I shall only be pleased to serve you as you wish to alleviate your misery."

Lavanyasundari — "You think I have acted rather impetuously, but I am positive that on seeing his radiance you will make him your own."

Bakulika — "Don't have any misgivings. Now that I have known your mind, I shall seek him and bring him to you."

So saying Bakulika embarked upon her mission. "Where can I hunt for strangers? If he is a student, he should be in a monastery, if he is a prince he should live in disguise in deserted temples," she reflected. Now she remembered the "shoo" that frightened the swan that perched on her head that morning.

She went to the temple where she had danced, and searched for him in closed corridors. Then she went to the tank and walked round it going to the *mandaps* built at the corners. In one of them she found him sleeping on the floor waited upon by his servant.

Approaching the servant she said: "Is it meet for your master, who looks to be a fortunate man and a man of accomplishments to sleep here, and that too in the evening. If my eyes are not liars his face seems familiar to me. Please wake him up for I intend to converse with him."

The servant woke him up, and Ratnadatha sat facing Bakulika. She rubbed her eyes as if to wipe off something that dimmed her vision and then looked straight into the stranger's face and said: "Oh visitor! whence do you come? I have a feeling that I have seen you before, but don't remember where and when."

Ratnadatha — "I have come from another Country and I am on my way to join the services of a sovereign king."

Hearing this Bakulika started weeping. "Now I remember, now I remember," she lamented. "You cannot be anyone other than my brother, who, they say, was kidnapped by a cruel bandit three years before."

Between her tears she said, "Oh visitor! you remind me of my brother, you are so like him that I cannot think you are anyone else."

Ratnadatha — "Do not lament, sister, I shall truly be a brother to you, not to spend your wealth, but to stand by you in your difficulties."

Bakulika — "Then come to my house and be my guest that is the place for you and not this *mandap* where only vagrants take shelter."

Thus, Ratnadatha and Subandhu went to the abode of Lavanyasundari.

Meanwhile Lavanyasundari stood on the terrace holding a cup of poison in her hand. While her friend was away seeking Ratnadatha she had been thinking thus: "The stranger's radiance is so magnetic that there can seldom be a woman who would not take him to her house and if Bakulika does the same, I shall no longer live in this world. What is this life worth if I cannot be the wife of that stranger whom I have loved at first sight? If I see Bakulika taking the stranger to her house, I shall drink this cup of poison and end my life."

When Bakulika returned with the stranger, Lavanyasundari's hope revived. Feigning ignorance she asked Bakulika: "Who is this stranger with you?"

"It is my brother, friend," said Bakulika, "welcome him, as fitting his position."

Now Lavanyasundari's doubts cleared. She gave Ratnadatha bath, meals, etc., according to her wealth and love and kept his company that night.

Early next morning Ratnadatha woke up before dawn, he tied five hundred gold pieces to a corner of a coverlet; he told the maid of the courtesan to search for the coverlet, and then walked out of the house, accompanied by his servant.

Having been awake late into the night, enjoying amorous pleasures with her lover, Lavanyasundari was deep asleep and was not aware of Ratnadatha's departure.

When morning had advanced and the sun's rays were beginning to be bright and painful she woke up and found to her amazement that Ratnadatha had gone. When she made enquiries her maid brought her the coverlet at the corner of which was tied five hundred gold pieces. Seeing this she reflected: "Ratnadatha is generous, besides being handsome and talented. If I lose him I lose a precious gem which I cannot acquire all my life."

Again consternation gripped her mind. Doubt assailed her. "Will he not return?" She asked herself. She sent for Bakulika and said to her, "Dear friend, he has gone away somewhere, please search for him."

Bakulika "mounted a she-mule and with her retinue went to the gambling house, where, she thought, he might have gone to gain wealth. Her surmise proved correct. There he sat playing boldly amongst the rich men. She knew that many women were under the power of gamblers and so she stood silent at the entrance of the hall.

After some time Ratnadatha perceived her and said: "Sister, how long have you been here?"

"Since a long time," she said.

"It is not proper for people like you to come to such places," he remarked. He continued his play for a few minutes more and defeated his opponent. When the keeper of the gambling house settled accounts Ratnadatha had won fifty thousand gold pieces.

He told the keeper: "Give to my sister Bakulika four hundred pieces and send sixteen thousand to Lavanyasundari." He distributed ten thousand in charity. Then accompanied by Bakulika he returned to the mansion of Lavanyasundari.

After having spent a few days in joyous pleasures in the company of the lovely courtesan, Ratnadatha decided to proceed to Manyakheta where ruled the King of Kings, Pratapamukta. He told his intention to Lavanyasundari, who tried her best to persuade him not to leave her, saying that all her riches would be his and there would be no need for him to seek wealth elsewhere.

He replied: "Wealth I seek not. Nor Love. All I thirst for is glory, that begets glory, in the service of the King. Come back I may, but go I must."

Now that Lavanyasundari was certain that she could not dissuade him from leaving, she sought the advice of her mother, a bawd called Dhonda. The bawd said that she would devise some means by which Ratnadatha would be compelled to return.

Thus, it came about that Lavanyasundari and the bawd accompanied Ratnadatha. Travelling slowly, after many days they came to the town of Purnapathaka. They were very tired and so Ratnadatha sat under the shade of a mango tree outside the town. Feeling sleepy, he laid his head on the lap of Lavanyasundari and slept, while his servant, Subandhu went to the town to bring food and other necessities.

Now the bawd thought that Lavanyasundari was determined to go away with the stranger and therefore, she should go to the king of the town and make a complaint to get him killed so that she could take back her daughter.

She collected some flowers and went to King Suradbarman and said: "Oh! good king, it is just possible that you have forgotten me. Sire, in my youth, I had kept your company for many a day, and a daughter was born to me by you. Now that daughter has become the most beautiful damsel, full of bloom and youth, whose company is desired by kings and nobles of the land. But now she is being lured away by a thug, who is resting on the outskirts of the town. I have come to ask you to do justice."

The king became angry and asked his police-officer to arrest the man who had cheated his daughter. When the officer with his men came to the mango tree, he found a handsome young man sleeping with his head resting on the lap of a beautiful damsel who looked happy and cheerful. He could not believe that the man was a thug hence they stood looking on, thinking that the bawd must have lied.

When the police-officer did not return, the bawd was perturbed and she said to the King: "Sire, I told you that the man was a great rogue and he must have cheated the police officer too." On hearing this the King sent a senior officer of his guards to get him information about them. The officer of the Guards, learning the truth from the police officer, stayed on too.

Now the King got impatient; he decided to go himself and punish the scoundrel. Followed by a band of armed guards he went to the mango tree, only to find his men standing stupefied.

Lavanyasundari, seeing the King coming, woke up Ratnadatha and said: "My Lord, you told me that you could fight sixty-four men single-handed. Here are thirty-two armed men led by the King. You can do what you think fit."

Ratnadatha woke up, took his sword 'Vasunandaka' and charged the men, while Lavanyasundari looked on, a sweet smile playing on her lips.

When the King beheld the valour of Ratnadatha and the animated look of Lavanyasundari, he was convinced that the bawd had lied, and that the beautiful courtesan was following the handsome youth of her own free will.

The King retired to the palace and sent his Master of Ceremonies to fetch Ratnadatha with honour to the Palace. So Ratnadatha rode on an elephant, with Lavanyasundari seated behind him. The King received him as he would receive a King of the neighbouring State and asked him-"Good man, whence do you come and whither are you bound?"

Ratnadatha told him that he was going to secure high office with the Sovereign King. Pressed by the King, Ratnadatha stayed as his guest for a week and enjoy royal honour.

Now the bawd also welcomed Ratnadatha as her son-in-law and told him that she acted as she did only to make the King recognise his valour and virtues.

Taking leave of King Suradharman and receiving many gifts from him and accompanied by Lavanyasundari Ratnadatha started for Manyakheta.

On reaching that city he took up residence with a courtesan named Chitralekha. He wanted to meet King Pratapamukta and exhibit his valour before him so that he might take him up in suitable employment. Ratnadatha thought he would need at least four days to convince the King of his mastery of the various arts. So he said to Lavanyasundari:

"Devout wife, I am going on the mission on which I had come all the way from my country. I will start tomorrow morning and shall be back within four days. You shall live with Chitralekha and be happy."

"My Lord, it pains me much even to part with you for a day, for there is always the dread of evil men trying to possess me or even the

King sending for me. So try to return at your earliest after successfully accomplishing your mission," pleaded Lavanyasundari.

On the second evening after Ratnadatha's departure, Lavanyasundari was seated on the terrace with Chitralekha talking about the panoramic beauty of far-off mountains with the peaks glowing fire-red in the rays of the setting sun, and with the green valley below looking white as meal as the evening mist was settling on the shrubs and grass.

King Pratapamukta followed by his friend and trusted servant Sankamaka came that way returning from the hunt in the thicket at the outskirts of the city. Coming near the mansion of Chitralekha, the King heard sounds of ringing laughter which made him turn his head up and look at the terrace. Then his eyes rested upon a pair of long lotus eyes fringed with long lashes and crowned by bushy brows meeting in the centre of a blond forehead; captivated between the lashes were the two black crystal-line pupils swimming hither and thither on a sea of white as if trying to find a way to climb up. The eyes were immediately turned away by its owner, but while she stood up and turned to walk away, the glow of the evening sun brushed, her cheek and made it shine like burnished gold.

The king rode off, but his heart felt like being pierced by those eyes. When he reached his palace, he told Sangamaka:

"Good friend, there is a newcomer in the house of Chitralekha, an object worthy of becoming a King's acquisition. I charge you with the responsibility of securing that object for your King."

"There is nothing that I will not do for you, My Lord. I know of whom you are talking. I have had news only yesterday that a new courtesan from another country who has given up harlotry and followed a very handsome man out of love for him, has come to reside with Chitralekha. This night she shall be with you."

Sangamaka then proceeded to the abode of Chitralekha.

His knock at the door of the courtesan was answered by Chitralekha herself who perceiving the King's servant welcomed him suitably and led him in.

Thereafter asking him to be seated on a cushioned chair, asked him what good tidings he had to convey.

Sangamaka said: "Oh! beautiful one, the Beauty of Beauties, who has sought shelter under your roof has not escaped the King's eye. The King has ordered that I should take your guest to him this night failing which he would kill me and order his guards to chop off your friend's nose and ears. Thus, I am commanded and seek your assistance in carrying out the King's orders."

"Oh! Good one, perhaps your King is ignorant of the facts. It is no courtesan who resides here, but the wife of one who is as handsome as he is courageous, as learned in arts and the Vedas as in the sciences. He has gone to seek service under the Sovereign King, leaving his wife under my protection. How can I play false to him?"

Then turning to Lavanyasundari, she said: "My friend, I can live and continue my profession only if I will have the favour of the King. The King's displeasure will bring ruin upon me. If you will take my advice, you can go and meet the King, now that your husband is away and you shall come back before his return. In this way you can please the King and save me as well."

Lavanyasundari reflected: "How can I bring ruin upon one who has offered me hospitality? Well, Ratnadatha will understand and respect my intentions."

So she went to the King and enjoyed his company that night. The next morning the King sent to her one thousand pieces of gold and other gold ornaments embedded with precious stones.

But Lavanyasundari accepted only seventeen gold pieces as her fees, and rejected the King's gift to the great surprise of the King.

The next day the King sent for her and asked her to give a performance in folk dance. She accepted to do so on condition that she should be free to leave any time she liked even in the middle of the dance. The King consented.

Before going to the palace for the dance she told her friend thus: "Let my necklace be with you. When my husband comes, you come and stand at the entrance of the Elephant Gate and show me this necklace and then I shall leave the dance and come away."

Lavanyasundari then went to the palace dressed suitably for the dance. The dance was in progress and the King and the nobles applauded the skill and grace of the dancer.

While taking a forward step for the next dance, she glanced at the Elephant Gate, and there stood Chitralekha with the necklace in her hand. As if gripped by sudden consternation she stared at the King, dishevelled her hair, disarranged her attire and ran out.

Going to her house she fetched a bowl of water and started washing her husband's feet. But noticing her dishevelled hair, and tight-fitting attire he said: "Tarry, my lady, you are my mother as you are my master's wife, and it is not meet you should wash your son's feet."

Lavanyasundari stood stupefied-at Ratnadatha's words.

In the palace, immediately after the dancer left it, the King and his trusted servant followed her bent upon knowing and meeting the person for whose love the beautiful damsel turned down a King's favour and gifts.

They reached Chitralekha's house and waited outside the latticed window overhearing Ratnadatha's conversation with Lavanyasundari.

Rather surprised at the way in which he spoke to her, the King and his servant made bold to enter the house through the door, when Ratnadatha, seeing the King coming, cried out in a loud voice:

"Whoever you may be, you enter at the risk of your life."

And he brandished his sword so that the King could see it.

The King said: "A while ago you spoke to the lady in one way, now you show a different attitude. What does it mean?"

Ratnadatha said: "I am the master of my household and the place of the King is the Palace and when I am there I am bound to obey my King's order."

The King retracted his steps. The next morning Ratnadatha was taken to the Palace on a decorated elephant, in a procession led by the palace guards and he was given a high place in the councils of the King and there he lived crowned with honour, fame and wealth.

Lavanyasundari lost everything, place and position, favour and gifts and led a life of servitude.

Muladeva Distrusts Women

In Avanti Ruled the great King Vikramaditya, who was acknowledged as the sovereign King by many a king of the land, because of the valour of his hands and wisdom of his judgment. The stories of Vikramaditya's miraculous adventures had reached all corners of the country and people eagerly looked forward to the news about the Kings of the Sovereign.

In Avanti lived a gentleman-scoundrel by name Muladeva. He was clever, a master of roguery, skilful in all arts and an object of King Vikramaditya's affections. He brought under subjection the smart, cheated the clever, and deceived the intelligent. He augmented his wealth by every foul means he could think of.

Many years' experience had taught Muladeva not to trust any women. He frequented the houses of well-known courtesans of the city, enjoyed amorous pleasures with woman of all types, yet held women as a class in contempt and therefore never married.

King Vikramaditya was not unaware of the doings of Muladeva, but his attitude to women rather puzzled him. Whenever the two met, the King used to ask him why he remained unmarried, but Muladeva declined to give a straight answer and found some excuse to change the topic.

Once Vikramaditya asked Muladeva: "My friend, you have many a time been evading the answer to a simple question. Though it is a matter of personal interest to you, your firm attitude makes me curious and I have come to believe that you have very strong reasons to assume this attitude. And your stubbornness only makes me very inquisitive to know your reasons. So I command you to speak."

"Sir, if you insist, I shall speak out my mind. I only wish you should not press me to do something against my wish," said Muladeva.

"There is no question of bringing undue pressure on you just to please my fancy. But so long as a thing is not reasonably proved false, it should be accepted as truth. And if I can reason out with you that your attitude is not substantiated by facts, you have to accept my advice," said King Vikramaditya.

Muladeva agreed and said: "Sire, women, according to my belief, are very difficult to please," he began. "On the whole they have bad intentions and they are fickle-minded by nature. They are difficult to be protected for they become detached very soon and very often cherish love for the lowborn. It is said in the Srutis and Smritis that a woman is the half of man. Therefore, even when a man is not himself a sinner, he becomes one when his woman sins. This is the reason why I am not willing to take a wife."

King Vikramaditya laughed on hearing his friend's unequivocal denunciation of women and said: "My dear Muladeva, you have seen the ghost, without seeing the person. Perhaps you must have been toying with certain false notions of yours, which have now become an obsession with you. And to justify this obsession you are quoting Srutis and Smritis. Listen, I shall correct you. Know that woman is an instrument to the attainment of the three goals of life. She is the abode of happiness, the root of fame, wealth and offspring. The householder's life is the mainstay of all the other stages of life. Without begetting a son a man never frees himself from the debt of his ancestors. Therefore, you must take a wife, you should not fight a ghost where one does not exist."

"Sire, your argument, though not completely convincing, at least has brought about a change in my attitude." said Muladeva, "I have decided to take a wife at least to verify the truth of all the ennobling qualities you attribute to a woman."

Muladeva's married life was not unhappy, yet his suspicions about women in general persisted and he watched every movement of his wife. He found her very clever and she appeared very faithful and loyal but there was a particular twinkle in her eyes that he could not comprehend. And this twinkle brightened up when she was alone, when she seemed to be engrossed in her own-thoughts.

It was the spring season when trees, plants and birds were merry, when the young minds were joyous and young limbs were springy, when every young heart had a happy thought and when every young lip had a sweet song. Now it was the time for young women to be out under one pretext or the other.

Muladeva's wife evinced great interest in going to the temple to worship the Fish-bannered God. Donning the best of garments and taking articles of worship accompanied by the neighbour's wife she would wend her way to the temple every evening. Late in the evening she would return, trying to look pious and religious as if inspired by a spiritual fervour. But Muladeva's cunning eyes detected the play of amorous pleasures in her eyes and he decided to follow her to the temple unnoticed.

A week later he followed his wife on her way to the temple, keeping himself a few yards behind. She went to the temple and finished worship within a few minutes. On her way back she directed her steps not homeward, but to the house of a merchant named Dattaka.

At the threshold of his house, Dattaka stood waiting for her. He led her in and they were closeted together for nearly half an hour.

Muladeva took his position at the corner of the street and entered into conversation with a gossip who lived in that street and who chanced to pass by. Without disclosing his identity he asked the gossip: "My good woman, what is the latest breeze that has blown your way?"

"Oh! citizen of Avanti, there is nothing breezy these days. Only the usual goings and comings. Haven't you noticed the family-woman who entered the house of the merchant a short while ago? She comes to pray to the God in the temple, but finds pleasure in the house of Dattaka. It is the common talk that Dattaka, though a miser, lavishes valuable gifts on this lady ; he has rejected the company of many a courtesan fearing that they, will fleece him of his wealth yet he has no scruples in giving away his riches to this family woman," said the woman.

"Perhaps you are mistaken, my good woman," said Muladeva. "You must have seen the merchant's wife returning from worship, and you must have taken her for some one else."

"I ! mistaken!" she exclaimed and laughed mockingly at him. "I am as much mistaken here as I am mistaken with the Queen. Who has not heard or seen the queen Ehillamahadevi that lives in this city of Avanti? Fair woman — they say she is the wife of the clever rogue Muladeva — has been carrying on with this merchant as the Queen, the wife of the great King Vikramaditya has been carrying on with the elephant-driver, Batharaka."

Muladeva was astounded, yet he was glad for he could now triumphantly demonstrate to the King that his evaluation of women in general was true to the core for even one so highly placed as the Chief Queen could not be trusted. But before approaching the King with such news he had to secure solid proof to convince the King. Therefore, he decided to watch the nightly movements of the Chief Queen.

One of the attendants of the Queen's palace had a big family to support. He was always in pecuniary difficulties. Every time he approached the Chief Queen for help and every time she helped him just to tide over his immediate troubles, but promised further assistance later. This way the Queen exploited the poverty of her servant to make him her confident. In her nightly journeys this servant accompanied her.

Muladeva, through one of his hirelings, threatened death to the servant if he accompanied the Chief Queen on the next night. Instead he disguised himself in the clothes of the servant and stood waiting for the Queen at the appointed place.

It was a moonlit night. The streets were empty, except for the barking of the dog at a distance, the scurrying of rats among the dry leaves and grass on isolated parts of the palace garden, and the measured beat of the sentry's steps at the main entrance, no sound of life was audible. But it was a splendid night for young lovers, for the Kumuda flowers blossomed in clusters and the Moon, in her silvery spoon walked along her heavenly path playing hide and seek among the fleecy clouds that came across her way.

According to the directions given him by the Queen's servant, Muladeva waited patiently outside the wicket gate expecting the Queen to emerge. The servant had told him that the Queen was very punctual and would step out of the palace compound exactly at the stroke of 12 in the night. But something seemed to have gone wrong some-where, for fifteen minutes had already elapsed since the striking of the appointed hour by the sentry at the fort, but there was no sign of the Queen.

"Perhaps the servant has outwitted me," thought Muladeva. "Perhaps he has warned the Queen of my intention. That scoundrel, if he cheats me, I will destroy him and his clan," he cursed.

Then he heard a gentle rustle of dress, the sound of latch being lifted. He stood attention with his back to the wall. The wicket gate opened and out came a figure covered completely from head to foot with a grey shawl. But the smell of sweet champaka fragrance exuded from within the grey shroud and Muladeva recognised it as the same that followed the Queen wherever she went.

Once the figure was out in the street, it seemed to be in a hurry. Without turning her head either backward or sideways, the Queen walked briskly and as she walked, she said.

"Servant, are you following me? I am already late and I have to return two hours before the cock crows. The King is in deep embrace with sweet slumber and I have administered him a herb tonic that will make his head giddy with the rising of the sun. This will keep him in bed till late in the day. But you should be in your place of duty at the right time. And tomorrow evening you can tell me fresh stories of your financial troubles."

"Obediently yours, my Queen," said Muladeva in truthful imitation of the servant's tone and form of address.

The Queen reached the elephant-driver's house situated at the farther side of the stables abutting on the southern wall of the palace garden. It was almost an isolated place hardly frequented even during day time by anyone other than the elephant grooms.

Reaching the house the Queen gently pushed the door which yielded to the touch as it was unlatched. Then she closed the door and bolted it behind her.

Muladeva sat outside with his ear glued to the door with the hope of overhearing the talk.

But to his surprise and horror he heard sound of lashings with a whip.

Then he heard the rough voice of the elephant-driver saying: "Oh! Queen, you are late tonight. You have put me to worry and anxiety and have made me keep awake late in the night to gratify your sensuous pleasures. Allow me to teach you a lesson or two, with this whip of mine, which I judiciously use on the black hard skin of the King's elephant. Your soft velvety back can certainly take a few. There, one, two and three. That is for late coming, as the school master says to the negligent pupil."

Muladeva's ear could detect no sound escaping from the lips of the Queen. Then all sound died.

Like a dutiful servant Muladeva conducted the Queen back to the palace two hours before cock-crow.

Next morning found the glorious city of Avanti as gay as a lark, but for two individuals who complained. One was the King who complained of giddiness and the other was Muladeva who complained of sleeplessness.

When these two met as usual at dinner time, the King said to his friend: "Good friend Muladeva! It is for the first time since you have taken a wife that I see you with swoollen eyes. Your gay spirits have deserted you today. You appear to have wept all night for some long-forgotten 'lady-love.'

Taunted thus by the King, Muladeva said: "Sire, it is true that my eyes pain and swell for want of sleep, but my back severely hurts as if lashed by a cruel hand."

"Explain yourself, friend. I am not quick at comprehending riddles," said the King.

"Sire, I dread to speak plainly lest I should incur your wrath and suffer punishment. I have often heard that cruel are the ways and fantastic the fancies of Kings who permit their queens to drug them to giddiness. Therefore, Sir, if I have your assurance of forgiveness for any errors of judgment or observation I shall tell you the truth."

The King agreed. Then Muladeva suggested that the Chief Queen be present at the dinner. The Queen, ordered by the King, took her seat next to Vikramaditya. While they were half-way at dinner, Muladeva said aside to the King.

"Sire, the dishes are many in number and variety and are delicious indeed. But I notice that the Queen cannot relish such good food when her paramour is not here to partake of it. Sire, will you order your elephant-keeper Batharaka to be brought to your presence?"

The King gave orders that Batharaka be summoned to his presence immediately but asked Muladeva what villainy he was contemplating.

"Sire, the drama cannot begin before all the actors are ready. I crave your patience."

When the dinner was almost over and when Batharaka stood before the King in all humility, Muladeva cried out, "Sire, will some one bare the body of the Queen so that the King may look at a wondrous thing."

The Queen's face turned deadly pale and her body trembled, while Batharaka's knees gave in and he almost sank to the ground. The King was quick to notice everything. He heard the Queen and saw her back swoollen with the markings of the lash and then turned to Muladeva for an explanation.

"Sire, have I not told Your Lordship that women are sinful and wicked of conduct. Here, this Chief of Queens, has deceived a great King, the great Sovereign Vikramaditya and has made love to the elephant-driver. And what a pity the Queen takes gleefully the whip-lashes from her paramour," said Muladeva.

"Sire, I have fare as badly as you have. Much against my will, but at your command, I took a wife and how has she loved me? She has been carrying on with the merchant Dattaka," concluded Muladeva.

King Vikramaditya ordered the arrest of the merchant and the confiscation of his wealth. He chopped off the nose and gouged out the eyes of the Queen and threw her into prison.

"Such is the result of love, true or untrue, divine or devilish," said Visamasila to her daughter. "Therefore, oh Beautiful one, to uphold the prestige of our house and our noble profession, you should eschew love of all kind at all times."

Chapter Seven

Courtesan in Bombay

K. Raghunathji

Bombay Dancing Girl

"There's a Shadow in her eyes,
A languor in her frame" —HERVEY

The Dancing or Nach Girls of Bombay are either Hindus or Muhammadans, and are known by the name of *Kalavantis* or women possessed of the arts of *Kala* of dancing and singing. Some call them Kulavantinis[1] or 'Women of genteel birth, and Naikins, a term applied to women who are born Naikins, and who have undergone the ceremony of *Seja*. While mere children the females are called *Chedvas* and the males *Chedas.*

The ceremony of *Seja* is compulsory be form a woman can style herself a Naikin. She places herself generally under the protection of some individual, as an ordinary married women, and passes the greater portion of her time in dancing and signing. The money she earns is her own property, and her protector has no claim to it. But the money she earns by singing and dancing on Mondays, in the month of *Sravan* (July – August) and on holidays in considered as charity money, to be applied towards charitable purposes, such as giving dinner to her caste fellows, or feeding Brahmans, and in case this latter is not attended to, excommunication follows. This is not made known to the party excommunicated till the heads of the caste, when invited for any ceremony, refuse to go to her house, and when asked the reason tell her what her offence was, and fine her from Rs 150 to Rs 200. On the fine being paid, the whole caste is invited to the feast, and she, coming before the dining table, with her hands joined, makes a low bow and begs forgiveness. This is granted, and then she dines with them, observing the caste of her master of the time being. A Naikin in the keeping of a Musalman will not dine in the same line with one in one in the keeping of a Parsi or a Banya, and so on. And in this way there may be seen a number of rows of these women at their feasts. Their castes are not fixed, but change with their Masters. One may be a Musalman today, and tomorrow a Prabhu or a Brahman, and again on a latter date a Parsi or a Musalman again.

Steels says these girls are sometimes purchased on a deed of sale, *Kharid patra*; given from friendship; or taken on receiving a presented. They are taught the usual accomplishments of the profession, and sometimes eventually rise to the head of the establishment. They cannot leave their purchasers without consent of the latter, and the parties generally live harmoniously together. They exchange the appellation of 'mother' and 'daughter' and support each other; sometimes the girl's liberty is purchased by an admirer. At others, from rivalry, ill-treatment, or attachment to a favourite lover, they abscond, and the master becoming a loser in consequence complains to the Sarkar. Under the Native Government then Girls was restored with remuneration for the injury sustained, unless a compromise was entered into by the seducer NPA. A purchased girl is under the orders of the daughters and manager of the house. Naikins may purchase girls, their age and number not being limited. All property acquired by them is taken by their mistress, though a purchased girls sometimes is heiress, to her companion. The son or daughter performs the funeral obsequies, and in default, the caste – which also may purchase a girl and establish her as successor to an heiress Naikin, with the ceremony of lighting a lamp in the house. The property is not taken either by the caste or government.

Among dancing girls, a boy is married, and a girl may either be married or introduced to her profession at her parents' pleasure. Marriage is concluded according to caste custom, and the wife may remain creditably in private, under her husband's protection. A girl born of such marriage is under the orders of her parents, and need not follow the profession unless from choice. Children of Dancing Girls are of their mother's caste, and are entitled to inherit her property. During her life the mother has a right to the daughter's gains. They have no claims on their fathers, though occasionally a girl's husband or paramour will provide for her. But a son is heir in preference to an adopted girls. The latter is heiress, if neither son nor daughter is alive. Daughters inhereit the mother's property in preference to sons. They can not inherit other property, but may acquire it. If one in a family die, leaving a young child, the rest provide for its maintenance until of age and understanding sufficient to conduct its own affairs. Partition is not customary among them, a daughter of ability conducts the affairs of the family, and sometimes a son is the manager. Should one of the family separate, the rest provide maintenance. In girls, in sales and pledges of property, it is customary for the manager to consult the Naikins before concluding the engagement. A family consisting of a mother, son, and daughter, on separation take *Farkhat* the girl living separately provides for her own subsistence, but if in distress, her family will assist her. A temporary separation sometimes takes place. A mother dying and leaving a son and adopted girl, they may separate, sharing debts and property, but it is usual for a family to live together. Debts of all daughters contracted on account of *Sansor*, during community, are defrayed by the rest.

Hindus extol music as the language of heaven and greatly enjoy it, but it is considered sinful to teach it to either men or women who are to lead a married life.[2] They invite these women on extraordinary occasions such as the thread or marriage ceremony, birth-day, and house warming, for it is said that without the jingling of their feet bells, a house does not become pure. A *Kasbin*, though she has learnt to sing and dance well, will be allowed to sing only in a few houses, but not to dance in a respectable Hindu house neither will she be allowed to dance in the temples before the gods, as she is considered, impure, and not a fit object for the performance of *nritta*. A Naikin will on no account dance or sing at a Bhavin's house though offered a large gratuity.

The several performances of the dancing girls are:- *nach*, a dancing with singing; *baithak*, or singing while seated; *Karba*, dancing in a male head-dress; *Jalsa*, singing and sitting in turns; *pachamba*, singing while sitting at the houses of leading members of their own community;

and *phugadi*, dancing in a sitting posture and jumping in circles, before the idol Ganapati.

The Hindu dancing girls are of four sects, viz. – Naikins, Bhavins, Murlis and Kasbins. Of these the first two belong to Goa and villages round it, being natives of that district; Murlis belong to Jejuri in the Poona Zilla; and Kasbins are recruited from all places.

The Naikins, otherwise called *Goekarins*, or women from Goa, are regarded as born for the purpose of singing and dancing and this is supposed to be in keeping with the practice in heaven, where the *Rambha* are for the entertainment of Indra and the other gods.

A young courtesan > courtesan in Bombay (5th edition) 1890.

In Goa and the places round it, none but these women have a licence to dance. In lieu of marriage the perform the ceremony of *Seja* or marriage with a dagger; and until they have done this, they are debarred from performing before the gods in temples. As everywhere else, the Portuguese laid their hands on some of these women when they took possession Goa, and forcibly converted them to Christianity, and not content with such conversion they kept them as their mistresses. Their descendants have ever since been free from caste prejudices in respect to carnal intercourse with people of other than their own caste. They do not observe Christian rites, but Hinduism in all its details. Their sisters, who either escaped from Goa or screened themselves from the Portuguese, will not dine with them. These and the other Naikins come to Bombay with the express object of carrying on their profession, and when they have succeeded in making a fortune, they either return to their native country or establish themselves as permanent residents.

Dancing girls as a rule are handsome, with open smiling countenances, large sparkling eyes, regular features and an intelligent pleasing appearance. They are fair, with a softness of face and features, a gentleness of manner, with a peculiar grace and ease, which one would little expect to find among them. A lady-like manner, modesty and gentleness, beautiful small hands and taper finger and their ankles neatly turned as to meet the admiration of the connoisseur, — they draw all eyes on them to the oblivion of all else; whilst they themselves are under the impression that they have taken to a most honourable profession by following which they are honouring the gods and are appreciated both by gods and man."

They are brought up in schools, and read and write Marathi fluently. They not only sing but compose songs as well. They all speak Musalmani, and a few of them English also. Formerly when their lovers forsook them they had to go to *Pantajis* and Pry them from writing letters. But now some of the dancing girls do the writing themselves, sometimes filling their letters with the most obscene expressions, ending with abuse of their mothers, sisters and daughters. Some of the older Naikins are of a religious turn of mind. They have Brahman priests in their service, who read to them the sacred books, and in return for such services receive handsome gifts. They visit temples and mosques, observe fasts and feasts, and feed Brahmans and Fakirs.

Excepting the head, dancing girls shave themselves clean, not allow even a hair to grow on the temples near the ears. Like other Hindu women, they divide the hair in front along the centre, comb it from both sides back – words, and tie it in a knot resting loosely on the neck. They dress like others in a long robe and tight fitting bodice, generally of English cloth, and sometimes of silk or other rich stuff with borders and trimmings of different patterns. When going out they muffle themselves with Kashmir Shawls, and put on China velvet slipper. Except that it is costlier, the ceremonial dress of a dancing girl does not differ from that worn on ordinary occasions. The bodice is richly ornamented with gold, silver, and velvet, lace or pearls. The shawl is worked with flowers, birds and beasts in gold and pearls. As a rule they are wealthy and load themselves with jewellery. Daily they decorate the head with garlands of sweet-smelling flowers and perfume themselves.

The following are among their ornaments:- For the head *Chandani,* Mor, and Naga; for the ears *Balya, Ering, Kap* and *Kudi*; for the neck *Aidora, Chinchapati, Gathle, Gop, Pot, Kaligathi, Sakli* and *Vajratik* for the hands *Bangdia, Tode, Jode, Patlia, Vela, Ruiphul, Gajra* and *Nilachyapatlya*; for the fingers rings of sorts; for the feet, Sokla, and sometimes a *Bedi,* and for the toes *Sale*. Except the feet ornaments, which are always of Silver, no Hindu, excepting Rajas, who are considered incarnations of a god, ever think of putting gold on the Feet, — the others are frequently of gold.

The food of the dancing girls consists generally of rice, pulse, vegetables, fruit, and butter; and of animal food – fish, mutton and fowls. Their drink is water, milk, coffee and sometimes liquor. They take two meals a day, one before twelve and the other before 6 P.M. In the night they are fed at the cost of their masters on spiced milk, fruit, and sweetmeats, betelnut leaves, and tobacco – for they are always chewing. They rub lime on the rough side of betel-leaves and make them into small packets filled with betelnut, catechu, cardamam, cloves; nutmeg, mace, saffron, cinnamon, musk and almonds, and either spiced or simple tobacco. They smoke once or twice a day, and sometimes drink.

They speak Goanese, which differs from the language of Bombay, and on first arriving they are somewhat shy to sing in public, their pronunciation being strange; but they soon learn to sing both Marathi and Hindusthani songs with taste and it is difficult sometimes to distinguish a Hindu from a Muhammadan dancing girl, from her voice. They are taught to sing and dance at the early age of five the older girls learning after they adopt the profession. The lessons are given daily two hours before day-light, one of which is devoted to singing, and the other to dancing. In the evening after five the same time is given, so that each has to practice four hours a day, and in about three years she is supposed to have mastered both singing and dancing. By beginning their studies at the age of eight these girls are able to appear at about 12 or 15, very rarely earlier. They practice the art till they are 40 or 50, if not previously rendered unfit by disease or premature old age.

Their dancing masters or called *Vastadjis,* and are paid for teaching the girl from Rs 50 to Rs 500, with other presents according to his ability. A contract is made which is dependent on the wealth and position of the party. The dancing masters belong to the same caste as the girls, and are the sons and brothers of other dancing girls, both Hindu and Musalman. They live by themselves, and are generally in poor circumstances. Their earnings they spend as fast as the money comes to hand, being addicted to drinking, smoking intoxicating drugs, and debauchery. They dress in tight-fitting, fine cloths, bright coloured turbans, carry sashes of fantastic colours, either on their shoulders or

Nautch girl of Ulwur > India and its native Princes. Louis Rousselet New Delhi (1882).

in their hands, and allow their hair to fall in ringlets on the back of the neck. They wear caps of silk and embroidery when they have not turbans on, English or Native shoes, whalebone or other rich walking sticks, and gold or silver watches with Albert Chains, — all the property of the dancing girls or their masters. Like their mothers and sisters, they are good-looking and quiet, but timid. They seldom offer prayers to their gods, and are so expert in singing and playing music that should a dancing girl err, while performing before her quests, they put her right by their playing, ask her to go on, and with a nod of the head and smiling faces, encourage her to sing.

Is so great esteem is a Naikin held by the Hindus that it was a compulsory practice amongst them to have marriage string *mangalasutra,* strung by one of these women, for the reason that she is considered a married woman all her life, and the ceremony symbolised the wish that the girl about to be married may live and die a married life.

The *Seja* alluded to above is the marriage of a Naikin with a dagger, from the age of 8 to 11, or before she arrives at purify. But before the performance of the *Seja* ceremony the girl is taken to the temple of one of the following gods and goddesses, viz. Shanta-Durga, commonly known by the name of Santa-Crus, Mahalakshmi, Vetal Vira, Ravalanath or Mangesa, and there taking a flower, she sticks is slightly on the breast of the idol and prayer to be informed what she should become – a married woman or a Nakin. If the latter, the flower falls to the right, but if the former to the left.[3] And accordingly as it falls to the right or the left or does not fall the omen is interpreted.

When a Naikin wishes to perform the *Seja* of her daughter, she consults a Brahman priest as to the time and hour when the ceremony should be performed. The Brahman consult his almanc, names the lucky day and hour, and a procession of Naikins addressed in rich clothes starts, accompanied by music, to the houses of their caste-fellows and friends, inviting them to the ceremony.

On the *Seja* day, another girl, older than the one about to be married is feasted and dressed in male attire, coat, turban and waist-cloth, and decked with jewellery to represent a bridegroom, and made to stand on a heap of rice with a dagger in her hand, the girl dressed in the garb of the bride is new brought and made to stand on another heap of rice in front of the first with a garland of sweet-smelling flowers in her hands, and a cloth is held between them. The priest repeats verses from the *Puranas,* and the guests throw on the heads of the pair of few grains of rice at the end of each verse. At the proper time the curtain is dropped, the bride thrown the garland of flowers round the dagger in the quasi bridegroom's land and they are wedded. After exchange of gifts and distribution of betelnut and leaves, coconuts, and money to the Brahmans, the guests leave. In the night a procession starts accompanied with music, and a number of Naikin guests, generally in this order: A bullock cart with a band of pipers and drummers, a row of carriages full of well dressed children, buglers walking, a band of Muhammadan drummers, a band of Gujarati drummers, two richly harnessed horses abreast ridden by little children in gay fancy dresses – the favourite sorts being English uniforms, and English, Parsi, and Bania ladies' costumes, a brass band of Goanese, behind the band dancing girls walking in a line, and immediately behind them the bride and the bride groom, each on a richly caparisoned horse with gold and silver trappings, or in an English carriage and two, or even four horses, on either side a couple of men wave silver fly-flaps, another couple fan

A innocent young courtesan > courtesan in Bombay (5th edition) 1890.

them with silver or gold fans, and another holds ever him a long-handled large read or green silk umbrella. After the couple walk the dancing girls and guests. On either side and behind the bride and bridegroom are the women guests, and wooden frames are carried with pots of artificial trees laden with fruit and flowers.

Should such processions meet on the way the tarbers lower the umbrellan, and hold them in front of the bride and bride groom's faces, that they may not see each other. At each turn in the street coconuts are dashed on the ground to appease evil spirits, and then thrown away, and as they go, fireworks are let off.

In older times, aikins say, celestial choristers form *Svargo*, who form the orchestra of the gods, come down to marry them, but since the Kaliyug, they do not expect these *Gandharvas*, and hence their marriage with the dagger.

The marriage expenses generally amount to from Rs 200 to Rs 500 and are shared by her mother, sister or lover if she has already got a promise. Some of the well-to-do Naikins, besides their masters, have a gallant whom they feed, clothe and give monthly pay to, besides depraving? their household expenses.

When a virgin is of age and first begins her profession, if Muhammadan, the ceremony of *Misi* is observed, when cardamums are distributed to the guests, turmeric is put on the girl's person, and a religious ceremony performed in honour of the *Pirs*. The *Misi* (a powder made of vitriol) is applied by several Naikins, one of whom holds hereditary office in the caste, who takes the girl on her lap and present her with a robe. The *Misi* of adopted girls is performed after that of born daughters *(palak-kanya)* but in other respects they have equal rights with the born daughters in a manner analogous to adopted sons.

The women of the community are invited to a feast, and they in turn dance and sing; but if Hindu, the *ganbhadhan* ceremony is observed.[4] The girl is made to sit by herself during three days, and in the evening her house is lighted, and she is dressed in rich clothes and her head encircled with garlands, and takes her stand in a window fronting the street. Musicians play, and offers are made for the hand of the maiden, the highest bidder being the winner. Offers sometimes are made before hand, that is when the girls is five or seven years old and a score or two rupees paid in advance as earnest-money. On the evening of the fifth day, dancing girls collect at the maiden's house, and the winner of the girl's hand site side by side with the virgin on low wooden stools, and the Brahman priest officiating, performs a short ceremony. Then they rub one another with sweet-scented powders, and drink from one another's hands silver goblets full of spiced milk, and he presents her with a rich suit of clothes, consisting of a robe and bodice, and if well-to-do or fast-going, with jewellery; and the girl, dressing in that suit, he lifts her up taking her in his left hand, leads her into a room, and seats here on a bed spread with sweet – scented flowers. Here he gives here the promised money, and she makes it over to her mother or sister; he then takes her to bed. Before closing the door, the mother addressing the lover says, "Sir, son-in-law (*Javayajibowa*) the girl is made over to you, and you take care of her." He has here in his keeping for a mouth or two, and if after that he wishes to retain the girl, he has to pay her from twenty to a hundred and fifty rupees a mouth.

A Naikin is sometimes as faithful as she is fascinating, and will help her protector in his difficulties. The following story is told in illustration of the faithfulness of Naikins:

The true one is the false one,
The false one true;
The Patel the dog of the town;
The Raja the ass of the crown.

There once lived a man who had a Naikin of great beauty. The man, doubting his wife's integrity, one day took home a goat's head covered under his waistcloth. On entering the house, he ordered his wife to lock the door after him. He then handed her a parcel containing gold and pearl ornaments and told her that he had robbed them from a child's person, and cut its head off, and brought it home to be buried in an inner room to avoid detention. The husband begged her, and the wife promised him, to keep the crime secret. But, like a woman, she spoke of it to a neighbour, who was her friend, and the neighbour spoke of it to her husband, and thus the story spread until the man was apprehended by the Patel and taken before the Raja who ordered him to be hanged the next day. A *bataki* was beaten, and the inhabitants invited to see the *tamasha.* The wife felt sorry, but she thought she had enough to eat for the reminder of her life, and therefore did not move in her husband's behalf. But his Naikin, hearing of what had happened, repaired to the Raja's palaces, and previled with him to suspend the sentence until inquiries were instituted. The result was the honourable acquittal of the supposed murderer.

The money usually paid to a Naikin for dancing during ceremonies and on other festive occasions varies from 30 to 60 rupees a night, and she pays here two *fiddlers* at the rate of two annas to each, and three annas to the *drummer* out of every rupees, the balance remaining to herself. Generally, Naikins in well-to-do circumstances decline accepting a *vida*, unless a condition is made not to demand their presence in processions. This objection is more from pride than – as alleged – that the evil eyes of the passers-by might not fall on them and cause them loss of beauty.

Dancing girls or Naikins live either in *Chals* or in *banglas* furnished after the European fashion, according to the means at their command. These women sing all night when disengaged, and persons who visit them to hear their singing pay from one to twenty or more rupees per night. On Saturday nights their houses are full of visitors. This night is called the pleasure-loving people the *golden night,* and Sunday the *silver day,* but Monday is called by them the *black* or the *iron day,* as on Monday they have to attend to business.

When a dancing girl is wanted for an entertainment, a person who is in the habit of frequenting their houses is employed to make an engagement, and he goes with a rupee from one house to another for a few nights, although he has already determined which he will favour. This he does for the purpose of hearing the singing in different houses *gratis.* At last he goes to the one he has fixed upon, and from whom he expects a commission, and gives her the rupee wrapped up in betel leaves which she accepts as earnest money. This is called the giving of the *Vida*. There are several kinds of vidas, but the *vida* given to a Naikin means that her singing is beyond any money value.

If the engagement be for a Thread or Marriage Ceremony, the girl so engaged attends the house for few hours on the night previous to the ceremony, and this is called *Mujura*, or singing by way of paying a compliment; for this purpose she site down upon a carpet. On the day of the ceremony she dances according to the appointment, and sings before the host and his friends. No females are present, the audience is entirely composed of males and children; but the females look through windows in the walls, which do not open but have holes or *Jalis*. If the women becomes ceremoniously unclean after the receipt of the earnest money, she does not attend, nor does she return the earnest money, but the party engaging her is left to make a new engagement with some one else.

Muhammadan Dancing Girls

The Muhammadan dancing-girls are known by the name of *Kasbis* and *Randis,* and come from Punjab, Gwalior, Sindh, and Hyderabad, the remainder being girls of Gujarat. Musalman prostitutes, or else stray waifs from honest households. In Northern Gujarat, living chiefly in the *Gaikavad's* villages, are a tribe of prostitutes known as *patars*; in their own villages they are cultivators, possessing lands, and during the hot and cold seasons making tours in the neighbouring towns and Native States for prostitution. They do not pretend to be either good singers and dancers. Neither do they belong to the regular guild (*jamat*) of other Musalman dancing girls but from a community of their own. They speak Gujarati and dress like Hindu women. Another community that swells the ranks of prostitutes is that of Mirasis (Gujarat Musalmans p. 48).

The foreign Musalman Prostitute is generally a dancer and Singer. She is by courtesy termed *deredar* and *tawaif,* and has from two to four *naurichis* or girls. It is not considered disreputable to be seen in her dwelling. Some of them are considered respectable, as they confine their favours to a single person, to whom they allow a pension. The girls in her house may either be her own daughters, or others obtained by doubtful means. They are taught to sing and dance, and their prostitution is not regarded as casting discredit on the head of the house. If the girls are her daughters, the *tawaif* exercises more control over them, their love connections and their caprices, so as to preserve the prestige of her house. The first connection of a girl of the above description is celebrated as *Sarfaraz-hona* (to be exalted), or *misi lagana* (to apply the black dye). There are however, no very pompous ceremonies attending this event. A girl is considered to have attained her maturity on the first signs of puberty. She then waits for an offer from some well to-to-do person, but if she has waited any length of time without an offer, her patron goes a round of the neighbouring Native States with her – the surest mart for barters of this kind. The price of the loss of virginity varies from Rs. 100 to 2000, according to the beauty and accomplishments of the girl. The master has a right to the company of the girls for two months, during which time he is expected to present her with clothes, jewellery and money. The celebration of the event begins eight days before it actually take place. Dinners are given by the girls relations and friends to people of her tribs, at nights they dance and sing at her house. The cost of the feast is defrayed by the master. That night the girl, richly dressed, is sent to the house of the master in a carriage attended by either a man or women-servant, when she passes the night with him and returns home the next morning, when a sumptuous breakfast awaits her. On this occasion, near friends of the house are feasted. This concludes the ceremony. Pregnancy, child birth, and other occasions of rejoicing are observed as among other Muhammadans in the usual way.

Their is a story among the Musalmans to the effect that if faithful, a dancing girl is more faithfull than a wife, and if false, she is so thoroughly; but she does not possess either quality beyond mediocrity. She is generally ready of wit, is more cuttivated than a married women, and owes much of her fascination to the fact that in a country where wives are not considered fit for society, she is a most charming and pleasant companion sometime it has happened that a dashing, wicked dancing girl, has married and tamped down to the routine of Muhammadan daily life, and taken the marriage veil with constancy. There are others of them who though admired, courted, or flattered for their beauty, music and dancing, have led a comparatively virtuous life.

The Muhammadan *naikins* are the best singers of Muhammadan and Marathi Songs, and are adepts in paying all respect and compliments to visitors. They sing Hindustani Songs with taste and delicacy, and their general demeanour at entertainments is most agreeable and cheerful (Munshi. F. Lalfulla).

With regard to the class of dancing girls who come from the Mufasal and Goa, a brief account may be given of the manner in which women of this sect come under the designation of Bhavins. These Bhavins, before they take the veil, are called by the name of *Zil,* and the men are Zilgas. The term [Bh] Bhavin is applied to women in the service of the idols in temples in Goa and places round about, and women from Goa who have forsaken their lowful husbands call themselves by that title, asserting as their reason that in olden time married women were in the habit of forsaking their lawful husbands and joining the service of the temples. Some of these women have been presented to the gods in infancy by their parents, as a *Murlis* are in *Jejuri.*

As a Naikin has to obtain the permission of her gods before she performs *Seja* so also has a Bhavin to ask here gods whether she may take the veil. She has recourse to a flower omen, and prior to dedication her parents invite the head-men of the caste to a temple, and there tell them of there intention to offer their child to the god. A flower is stuck to the image in their presence, and the girl goes to the burning lamp, takes a handful of oil, and pours it on her head, and declares herself a Bhavin. The guests are presented with betelnut and leaves, and they depart. The parents then take the girl with them to their house, and a feast to the castemen ends the affair. The girl from that time should place her full faith (*bhav*) in and give herself to the service of the god and not practise prostitution, but live as an ascetic, and should the temple not be able to maintain her, she is fed at the expense of the caste.

The ceremony undergone by a married women who forsakes her husband to be styled a Bhavin, is to go to a temple and take a handful of oil or dip her fingers in one of the lamps continually burning near the idols, then to place the same on her head, and declare herself by that act to have become a Bhavin in the presence of worshippers in the temple.

As a servant in attendance upon an idol her business is to attend the temple lamps and to keep them trimmed, to sweep and cowdung the floor, the turn the *chauri* over the idol, to serve the *huka* to the congregation, to keep the furniture in order, and to serve the visitors to the temple. A Bhavin's name always ends with the name of the place of which she is a native for instance, Emni-Pednekarin i.e., Emni inhabitant of Pedne. A Bhavin always trims a lamp with her fingers and not with small sticks as other Hindus do. The trimming of lamp with the fingers by any other than a Bhavin is supposed to bring poverty, and this is particularly observed in all Hindu houses.

These Bhavins, tried of servitude, leave the temple, and try to enjoy their liberty as independent mistresses, and this course is eventually preferred. Such a one gets away from the temple by becoming the kept mistress of a person or persons who have the means to protect her; but others in the temples also are at liberty to hold illicit intercourse with persons of their own caste, these women being commonly known as *chedvas* and the men *zilgas*. Such of the female descendants of these women as lead a moral life, adhere to the profession of there mothers, viz., attending to the indoor duties of the temple. In their Native place they are fed from the temple funds, and those who have young sisters, daughters, or other relatives with whom they can live, establish themselves as *Kasbins*. A register of these Bhavins is kept, but as a rules, formal permission is obtained before any of them quits the temple and establishes herself in any persuit, and this permission she obtains whether the persuit be honourable or not provided she annually sends a present however trifling, to the temple.

No Bhavin would consent to contract matrimony with a person of her own caste or remain in his keeping, as prostitution, in their view, is more honourable; it enriches and makes them sole mistresses of their liberty and property, and their protectors are ever ready to be at their command.

Some of these Bhavins, like the Naikins, learn to sing and dance, but they are not allowed to do so in Goa, as they are all considered low and the most debauched of their sex. The utmost a Bhavin can earn in Bombay per annum is about Rs 600, for they get no opportunity of forming connections with men of the higher classes, who generally visit the houses of Naikins. A person visiting the house of a Bhavin is regarded as disreputable, for the only object of his visit apparently must be debauchery.

It is the general understanding amongst Natives that whoever has a Bhavin in his keeping reduces himself to proverty, for he is said to expose himself to the rage of the gods, by having carnal intercourse with their servant. Bhavins are descendants of pure Marathas; but as they have degraded themselves to the post of 'temple casts', they have seats allotted to them behind the temples, whilst a Naikin dances before the gods, and amidst the gatherings of the great, and has a seat allotted to her before the gods.

The Bhavins, properly speaking, have only one dance, called the *ghumat* dance, which is accompanied by a kind of drum called *ghumat*. This dance generally takes place in the month of *Shimaga* (February – March).

To celebrate the dance, Zilgas[5] raise a sum of money by subscription and hire a place in the neighbourhood of their dwellings where a canopy is erected, and on the floor is spread a carpet on which the members sit encircled by the spectators. At one end, one or more Bhavins stand dressed in bodices and *sadis,* which are so tightly worn as to display their forms; their hair is tightly twisted into a khot behind, and sweet smelling flowers encircle it. Behind stands a drummer with the drum called ghumat, made of clay having one end small and the other large, covered with leather, a *Pakhwaj* and *Zanj* or metal cups. On both sides stand Zilgas beating cymbals, and clapping their hands, and the women dance. The dancers are led by the drummers, for they move their legs up and down, according to the rhythm of the beats or the drum. The dancers jump frantically about, singing licentions songs. None but the Zilgas attend this entertainment, but if prevailed upon, a respectable person might enter the gathering, but only for a few minutes. For these dances subscriptions are raised by the Zilgas among themselves. The dancing girls are paid about five rupees per night, and the balance is spent on a feast. This dance is cultivated by the Zilgas for their own amusement.

A Bhavin is an cunning as a fox, and will rob her protector of his last farthing and be done with him as soon as she can, or when she finds him not so libereal as before, or his purse empty, — with a rod, in her hand, she will show him out. She will be on terms of intimacy with some of her many visitors without her protector's knowledge, while he is by her side. In fact, they are a class of pick-pockets and cut-throats.

A certain Bhavin possessed of an engaging form and face, it is said, attracted the notice of a householder, and attached herself to him. After sometime he become aware of her infidelities, and giving her a large sum of money he ordered her out. The money was soon squandered and she applied for more, but was refused. She then told him that if he did not grant her a settlement for life she would burn down his house. He persisted in his refusal, and ordered her out. That night his house was burnt to the ground. He then quitted the place, and went some hundreds of miles away, and hoped he had done with her, but the woman followed him, and wearied out with her importunities for a settlement, he at length granted her an annuity for life. But she continued her supplications to be restored to his house. He however, fell in love with a beautiful young country-women, who come to the place where he then resided. He proposed to her, and the wedding day was fixed. The Bhavin heard of this, and forcing herself into his presence she asked him if the report were true. He replied in the affirmative, when venting her rage in curses, she imprecated tremendous disaster on his head and heaped on him every insult that language could command. At length he reminded her of his settlement on her of a sum sufficient to place her in affluence for the remainder of her life, and that her annoyance would provoke him to retaliation. She replied by declaring in fury he would die within six weeks of his marriage. She then quitted his presence. The singularity of the meance somewhat startled him, but it was soon forgotten. The days after his marriage he sickened, and before six weeks had passed he was dead. He fell a victim to slow poison administered by his personal servant, who, strange to say, was the Bhavin's brother, and the day before the man died they both decamped and were never again heard of.

There is another class of Kasbins, the *Murlis*,[6] or girls wedded to Khandoba the lord of Jejuri. If a low caste Hindu is childless, he vows that if Khandoba blesses him with offspring male or female, the same shall be set apart for life to worship and attend upon the deity, and he accordingly dedicates it. Others again, forsake their little ones under the plea of a vow made by them; while grown-up women leave the protection of their husbands and become murlis on the pretext that Khandoba had appeared to them in a dream and told them they ought to become Murlis.

Mangs and *Mahars* have also Murlis among them. These Murlis hang about the temples of Khandoba, and loiter in the streets with a bag of turmeric powder, which they apply to the foreheads of passers-by and ask for charity. They dance will bells in their hands, and sing songs in praise of their lord, and obscene *lavanis*, for the entertainment of visitors. They do not live in Jejuri alone, but scatter themselves in distant towns and villages and under the clock of religion carry on the profession of prostitution. An ordinary Hindu may keep one of these women under his protection, but generally they are the Kasbins of Marathas and low caste Hindus. Without shame they take free quarters for a few annas or so with any one, not excepting the Musalmans. The standard of their morality even in Jejuri is very low, so much so, that gentlemen visiting *Jejuri* with their servants have either to stay out of the place for the night with their servants, or to accommodate them in their own house to keep them from mischief at the hands of these women. "That a Murli should be a women of abandoned character is understood to be a matter of course, even more than a Kasbin should be so." The term *Murli* is applied by Hindus to a loose and flirting women. The life of these Murlis is "openly a life of prostitution, prostitution under the supposed sanction of religion."

And a majority of diseased and ugly kasbins in Bombay are the Murlis of Jejuri and other like places.

The other Naikins from villages in the Mufasal are chiefly women who have forsaken their husbands to lead an immoral life. Muhammadan and other prostitutes, as a rule, when they express a desire to live under the protection of one individual and lead a married life, are obliged to undergo the ceremony of *Nika*. This ceremony is performed by a Qazi, and is equivalent to marriage, and the man and woman are considered as having become husband and wife. Hindu prostitutes who undergo the ceremony of *Misi* are supposed to have accepted Islami and are not readmitted into their caste or society. But a Musalman woman performs the ceremony of *Nika* as often as she likes, or becomes a prostitute according to her capricious fancy. A Hindu women, if once expelled, is renounced for ever, and no offer of bribes or gifts can restore her to caste. It is to be understood that Muhammadan dancing girls have to undergo the ceremony of *Misi*, like the *Govekarins*, who undergo the ceremony of *Seja*, to be style regular Naikins.

Talukdari household lady in the harem in 18th Century >
Courtesan in Bombay (5th Century) 1890.

Besides these, there is another class of women in Bombay who come under the title of Kasbins. These are either the wives of husbands or were purchased in infancy by chiefs or persons in well-to-do circumstance in Goa. By caste they are Kunbis, and after their purchase they are considered as the permanent servants of the family. Their business is to attend to all household work, and to serve their masters as wives. The children they get are either provided for by their fathers or are left to earn their livelihood as they can.

Some get their freedom, says a writer in the *Literary Society's Transactions*, from their masters, in consequence of good conduct, and occupy a separate house and cultivate on their own account. Other are inmates with their masters and their treatment is very good, they are clad and fed in the same way as the members of the family, scarcely any difference being observable, except in their taking their meals apart. They get pocket money on holidays, if they behave well, and their masters are at the expenses of their marriages, which may cost a hundred rupee. The men labour in the fields, the women serve their mistresses and do all household work, cleaning rice, cutting vegetables etc., except cooking, and worshipping the family gods, and when unmarried are sometimes the concubines of their masters, or they are married to Marathas. The present race are no doubt all home-born. Freedom is given them from religious motives for good conduct, and sometimes from their becoming burdens some; such persons take the name of sindes, and are looked on as inferior, and others rather avoid intermarrying with them. Boys are rarely brought to market, but girls are frequently so, and if beautiful, are bought by the rich as mistresses, or by courtesans to be taught to dance and sing; they are sold for from Rs 100 to Rs 500. The less favoured ones are bought as servants in Brahman families. Among Mahammadans too, a women who takes to prostitution is called a Kasbin. They are raised from all classes of Musalmans and Converted Hindus, either from their own children or by girls adopted or kidnapped.

There are six kinds of dancers, three of which are performed by Naikins at houses on payment, and the others at their own quarters. When a dancing girl is not performing, she wears a *Sari*, but when she prepares for an entertainment, she wears a short gown, or *Peswaj*, with short tight sleeves. As soon as the drummer and the two fiddlers commence to play, the former standing behind, and the fiddlers one on each side of her, she puts on a thin embroidered muslin *dupeta*, in graceful folds and an embroidered bodice, or *Choli*, and her neck is encircled with a gold and pearl necklace; on her wrists and finger she wears rich jewels, and has a silk handkerchief in her hand; she has also two silver rings on each great toe. When called into respectable Hindu houses to perform before guests, they do not by speech or conduct offend in the slightest degree against propriety. Many of these women are of remarkable beauty, but they are as abandoned as they are beautiful, and "although generally accompanied by the most debauched of their sex, they are nevertheless continually engaged at large entertainments." But there can be "nothing more modest than their dress and demeanour", and in their movements they are considered unrivalled." The great charm of their dances consists almost wholly in the elegant and graceful attitudes which they assume." You see no violents swings of the arms, no unnatural curving of the limbs, no bringing of the legs at right angles with the trunk, no violent hops and jerks and dizzy gyrations. The *nach* girl adrances gracefully before her audience, her delicate arms moving in unison with her tiny naked feet, and her footsteps making a soft music. She occasionally turns quickly round with a burst of song by which the loose folds of her thin short gown are expanded, and the heavy gold border with which it is trimmed opens into a circle round her neat little finger, showing for an instant the beautiful outline of her form, draped with the most becoming and judicious taste."

When dancing the *Kerba* dance (which is performed in male head-dress) she lets her long black hair fall on her shoulders and back and round her breast. She puts on a Maratha turban (as worn by *sipahis* in public offices) or a gold embroidered skull-cap, inclined a little to her left ear, and with her thin small hands imitates the flying of the kite, and her eyes are turned upward.[7]

When performing this part of her dance her tightly knitted drapery shows the form of her round limbs. At times she rolls a part of her *dupeta*, holding one end between her teeth and the other in both hands the fingers indicating playing on a flute. She does not exactly dance, but revolves in the midst of the audience, and sings with a charming simplicity, which is the supreme effort of these Muhammadan and Hindu women:

"She leaps forth with a burst of song
From the glittering crowd,
Like a Sunny glimpse of autumn light
From behind a darkening clod.
Her oft-suspended foot doth throw
It's shadow on the earth;
And her burning eyes are turn'd to heaven,
As to the region of her birth.

That bound-that bound-when venus sprung
Out of the waters, into light,
And round her breast her tresses clung
A garland of delight;
With lip and cheek, and eye, like thine,
And motion breathing music sweet,
She made the purple sea her shrine
The white foam lilies for her feet.

Once more! once more! the silver fawn
of moon-light through the sapphire sky,

After the fading summer eve,
With lighter feet doth never fly,
Thy wreath of dewy blossoms shakes
Its perfumes rich around,
And they bird-like footstep makes
Soft music on the ground.

Rest, sweetest, rest, for faint and weary
The spirit of thy feet must be;
Rest, sweetest, rest, and give repose
Unto thy melody.
The flower-bird floats not all the day,
But when the red son gilds the west,
Like a bright summer evening ray,
It creeps into the lily's breast."

Much excitement prevails among the audience when she dances the *Kerba*. The promised money is then handed her by the head of the family, folded in betel-leaves, she respectfully make *Salam* and then retires.

These dances, which commence between nine and ten in the evening, last till three or four o'clock next morning, and sometimes till daylight.

The dance called the *Jalsa* (singing and sitting in turns) is performed at the houses of the Naikins themselves during holidays, such as the Ganapati festival and like occasions. Nach girls assemble in numbers on such occasions, and each in turn sings a song or two. Invitation are always issued for these dances to friends and acquain-tances, but strangers have free access to them. The dance commences generally at nine p.m., the hostess opening the ceremony of the evening by singing herself a song which is prayer to Ganapati to assist in carrying out the programme with success. A relation of the hostess prepares betel leaves, and distribute them with hosegays and rose water to the audience. A silver plate is placed in front of the naikin, who sits to sing, in which the moneys given by the visitors are placed. The money thus collected often amounts to Rs 200 a night, and to this the hostess alone has a claim. The fiddlers and drummer, if engaged by the night, have no claim to any of it, but if otherwise, the Naikin is bound to share with them at the rate above named. Visitors about to leave are treated to a cap of milk prepared with sugar and spices supplied in an inner apartment, specially furnished for their reception.

Pachamba is a kind of *Baithak*, held in the mouth of *Sravan,* on Mondays, in the houses of Naikins, the chief in the community, on this occasion they gather together in the afternoon. The hostess places on a raised stool a water pot and covers it with a cocoanut, and dressed it in a rich waistcloth and Brahman's turban, and worships in honour of Honaji the founder of the tribe, with the help of the Brahman priest. In the evening the men and women friends of the hostess meet at her house and sit singing by turns one or more songs each. Invitation[8] are issued to the friends and acquaintances of the hostess, and the money paid by visitors and others is not appropriated the hostess, as on *Jalsa* nights, but is applied to sacred purposes, such as feeding Brahmans, & co. This *Pachamba*, like the rest of the dances, commences between nine and ten and is over by six o'clock or next morning.

Phugadi is a kind of dance held at the house of Naikins or their friends during the Ganapati holidays and sometimes during marriage and *Seja* ceremony. A few friends only of the hostess are invited to this dance, as it is solely for their own amousement. Their nearest relatives assemble and form themselves into a circle before Ganesa, each carrying in both hands a brass drinking vessel or *tambia*, and another holds a metal plate full of bells, which she strikes with a small strick so as to enable the pebbles (*ghagrya*) to sound, and they dance up and down with violent swinging of the arms, and singing loudly most charming songs. The drummer alone beats his drum as no fiddler is required for this dance.

In Madras, (Encylopaedia India Vol. p. 36) Tamil girls of certain castes are dedicated to some of the temples and brought up to the profession of dancing. They do not marry, but are permitted to live in professional concubinage; such practices is no way degrade them from the right to caste privileges, provided they do not form intimacies or cohabit with outcastes. *Dasi* dancing girls are either the daughters of such, among them like other Hindu Castes, the profession descends by hereditary succession, or should these women have no children, which is more frequently the case, they adopt girls of tender age. All girls intended for the profession of dancing are connected with some Hindu temple, to which they dedicate their persons; and in confirmation of the same a nominal marriage ceremony is carried out of the marriage of the girls to the presiding deity of the temple.

Sometimes a Hindu vows in sickness or other affliction to give one of his daughters to some particular temple, to be brought up as a dancing girl, and the vow is scrupulously kept at the proper time.

In the selection of girls for adoption in this profession, good looking, well-made girls are chosen. The art of dancing is said to be exhibited in sex different ways; by the movements of the eyes; the action of features; attitude of the breast and chest; position of the hands; action of the feet; and by tumbling, somersaults.

When attached to temples, dancing girls receive wages, the amount of which is dependent on the income, sanctity and popularity of the particular temple which they have joined. The salary they receive is nominal, seldom exceeding a few annas, and sometimes a rupee or two a mouth.

The chief object in being paid the sum as salary is to indicate that they are servants of the temple. In addition to this, one or more of them, receive a meal a day, consisting of mess of boiled rice rolled into a ball. They are required to dance six times a day at the temple, before the god, while the priests are officiating, but this duty is performed by turns.

Their dancing dress consists usually of the short jacket or *Choli*, a pair of *rarake* or string drawers tied at the waist termed *Paijama* – or *Pavadai*, — both these are generally of silk – and a white or coloured muslin wrapper or *Sadi*. One end of the *Sadi* is wound round the waist, and two, three, or more feet, according to the length is gathered and inserted into the portion encircling the waist, and permitting of a folding fringe or gathering of the cloth in front while the other end, taken after the usual native fashion over the left shoulder, descends towards the waist, where the end or *mundani* is opened out and allowed to drop in front, one end of it being inserted in the waist on the side, and the other left free. This portion of the *Sadi* is usually ornamented with gold thread, tinsel, etc., the free end descends to the middle or lower half of the thigh, the other free end of the *Sadi* is then passed between the legs and fastened to the tie round the waist at the back, and the whole bound by a gold or silver waist-belt. By this arrangement a fold of the muslin *Sadi* forms a loop round each leg, and descends nearly to the ankles, whilst the gathering hangs in front. At home they wear the *Choli* and *Sadi* with a petticoat or *pavadai* this is their usual dress, except when about to perform they exchange the *pavadai* for the *Paijama* or *Sherai*. The *pavadai* is made of chintz or silk, according to the means of the individual. A string of small brass bells is tied round each ankle.

The dancing girl's caste has peculiar laws for adoption and inheritance. A dancing girl can adopt a daughter with the permission of the authorities of the pagoda to which she belongs, but she cannot adopt a son for the transmission of property, it being immaterial whether she have a son or not. The adopted girl cannot share her mother's property during her lifetime, and although she may be the heiress, she is not bound by the laws of caste to support her brother's widow. Among dancing girls, property descends in the female line first, and then in the male as in other castes. On the failure of issue, the property of a dancing girl goes to the temple to which she belongs. A simple recognition on the part of a dancing gird of a child as her daughter in the presence of one or more individuals is sufficient of constitute her claim to adoption.

Dancing girls are respected by the Hindu castes, and are allowed to sit in the assembly of the most respectable men, such honour not being accorded to their own wives and daughters. As a rule, it is seldom that these women have children of their own, unless when they live in concubinage with some single individual, consequently they are always anxious to adopt girls, not only to become their successors in the temple, but that they may likewise inherit their property.

Formerly, a large trade was carried on by kidnapping good-looking girls from large towns and remote villages, who were sold to these women. The practice of selling minor girls obtains largely under suppression. The recent famine in Ganjam, Orissa and Bengal, was taken advantage of, not only by abandoned characters, but also by immoral native princes, for the basest purposes. At a criminal session in Calcutta two women were sentence to seven years imprisonment each, for having purchased a girl under sixteen years of age, for the paltry sum of one rupee ten annas.

In some station there are said to exist two kinds of dancing girls. The dancing women differ from the pagoda dancers, and the latter are said, as a rule, to live in concubinage. These women are recognised as *Dasi* and *Devadasi* [See Mrs. B. Marcus Fuller's Devadasi]. The Dasi or dancing women belong for the most part to itinerant bands, and are frequently made up of women of low caste, who practise their professional accomplishments and prefer living in concubinage.

The Saiva temple of the Suvarnamukhi (Kalastri) a Zamindar of North Arkad district, maintains a large establishment of what is termed *devadasi* or temple dancers, forming a distinct community there, who live exclusively in concubinage. Their sons, who know no father, pass by the appellation of Nagari Kanada, or son of the country, and are slaves to the Zamindar. Of the daughters, after supplying the vacancies in the temple staff, the reminder are brought as drudges into the palace.

The dancing girls when about to perform are accompanied by two men singers, termed *Nattuvan* and *Padowen*, who while singing also play on cymbals. These instruments are of two kinds are sizes. While the symbol is played with the right hand, the left hand open is generally applied to the left ear they sing, bowing their bodies and swaying from side to side contorting their faces and making grimaces. In singing they scream as loud as they can; one or more old women – superannuated dancing girls – join in and frequently clap their hands during the performance some of these girls are good looking, handsome, with open countenances, large sparkling eyes, regular features and intelligent appearances. They are perfectly self-possessed and assured in manner starting at onlooker with their large eyes. They possess much courtesy and polish, tempered, with languid grace and unembarrassed bearing, having all the teaching which experience of the worst side of human nature gives, they know but one form of pleasure, — vice, in which their lives are spent; and their countenances often assume a sodden, pale, and unwholesome aspect. They seldom possess any conversational powers beyond the usual laugh and giggle and monosyllabic replies to common-place questions.

When their services are required outside the temple, larger sums of money have to be paid for them, the charge being increased according to the position of the girl, as some will not go to any one less than a Raja or great man. Some visit other districts when they are required by petty rajas or zamindars, and they are engaged for as many days as they have to perform, and are well paid. Should they please the master of ceremonies, they frequently received valuable presents in money, shawls, gold ornaments, which are bestowed during the performance. Every village of importance has a temple with some of these women attached to it, and in larger towns having temples noted for sanctity, they are numerous.

Author Notes

1. These Kalavatis are one of the fourteen precious things or gems obtained from the churning of the ocean. The names of these fourteen gems are: Lakshmi; Kaustubha; Parijatak; Sura; Dhanvantari; Chandrama, Kamadhenu; Airavata; Rambhadidevangana; Saptamukhiasva, Halahala, Haridhanu; otherwise called Sarng; Panchajanya and Amrita.
2. In the *Harivansa* we read however of a pleasure party in which Baladeva, Krishna and Arjun with their families spent the day in feasting, singing, and dancing. The Yadavas too are said to have not only allowed their wives and daughters freely to sing and dance, but themselves joined the pleasure party and indulged in the presence of parents and seniors.
3. It is left to the girl to demand whichever side she likes. Some stick two flowers on both sides of the image and demand that either the right or the left one may fall, and accordingly as it falls to the right or the left or does not fall the omen is interpreted.
4. Besides *garbadhan*, the Naikins perform the fifth and the twelfth day ceremonies of a newly-born child. The *Seja* ceremony and the birth of a female child are hailed by them with delight and the ceremonies are performed with great *aclat*, and at much cost – *Educational disabilities of the children of dancing girls in India* (Bombay, 1879). A member of the same community says, that the dancing girls are not married, because that would be offensive to their family deities.

5. The Zilgas are good-looking fellows, and generally hold employment in public offices as *Patevalas* and in cotton mills. They have a peculiar way of wearing the hair and dressing in caps or turbans cocked on one side, and tight-fitting polkas so as to show themselves to advantage. But the sons and brothers of Naikins dress in plain but tight-fitting clothes, and in a way to reveal at once who they are.
6. The real *Murlis* are those barren women who become lean at the feet of the god *Khandoba,* with the object of getting children only low class women become *Murlis* [see Mrs. B. Marcus Fulter's Muralis].
7. This is because she is acting Krishna Kannya, tradition ascribes so ancient a date as the time of Krishaa to the *Kerba.* It is said this was a mode of dance Indian, it may be noted, are essentially *ragas* and *ragnis* set to action and motion.
8. ासा िसढ !ासाज्ञप!ढसड़ !ह्यझे प!ह्य; सस्र रसौ ढसा िर्त्तै ढुस प! साप?सचसा !उअ!ासझसा ट ध्सछ चसछेझा! िसढम ढ ! वढध्स उ ा िसा ढस चर्झा ढसेड़ !ू सा फ्ढस ⁄साप्इ कढ्म !ू साजे ा सा ध्सा िजा कसढत्पा! म यअ! कसो सड़ र सढ्तसघ! ⁄सढ्सछ स्क प्ू सा जर्त झसछी ! ढसाज् सा जढ्सडस सछ सा!; सा-सी साढ !ा प!ह्यउहे ठ

उवस

लझासा प!अस्ढ म प्ढ !लसढजा ासढस

Bibliography and Notes

Ch. One: Ascetics and courtesans: Jan Gonda Selection of studies, Vol. 4 E.J. Brill, Leiden 1975 'The Chanter of the *Samaveda* and the courtesan of somadeva – The ocean of story, Vol. 1, Ed. Penzar Norman Mosley (1924).

Ch. Two: Jataka (Stories of Courtesans): Kanavera No. 318, Book IV, Sulasa No. 419 Book VIII. Atthana No. 425 Book VIII, Jataka, collection of tale forming the 10th book of the *Kuddaka Nikaya* of the *Sutta Pitaka* dealing with the previous birth of Buddhas. The Jataka trns. Robert Chalmers, Ed. E. B. Cowell. Cambridge University Press (1885).

Ch. Three: Kamma Katha – Sagara: Marriage of Carudatta and his Entry into a prostitute's House *(Sarira)* and Samba and his Lover for a Courtesan's Daughter *(Pedhiya)* > The Vasudevahindi (Vh), A authentic Jaina version of *Bharatkatha.* LD Series: 59, Ed Jagadish Chandra Jain. Ahmedabad (1977). Story of Rupinika (Brahman's Courtesan Lover) of Somadeva > The Ocean of story. Ed. C.H. Tawney 2nd ed. 1968 (1880).

Ch. Four: Caturbhani (Four Play). In one volume Caturbhani first appear in 1922 by M. Rama Krishna Kavi and S. K. Ramanath Sastri, Pub. D. G. Sarma and Krishna. Bakerganj, Patna > The Ubhayabhisarika of Vararuci trns. Dr. Sukumar Sen. The Calcutta Review, 3rd series. July – Sep 1936. Calcutta University > Caturbhani. A Collection of four Bhanas, *Srngarahata* (Hindi) ed. Motichandra and Vasudeva Sharan Agarvala. Bombay 1959 > The Ubhayabhisarika of Vararuci Ed. and trns. T. Venkatacharya, A. K. Warda. Madras 1967 > Three Sanskrit Lighter delight (Ubhayabhisarika): Mehta, C. Bombay (1969) > The Ubhayabhisarika of Vararuci, trns. Amiya Rao and B. G. Rao

Printex. New Delhi (1979) > Caturabhani > Glipes of Sexual Life in the Nanda-Maurya India, trns. Ghosh, Manmohan, Manisha Pub, Calcutta (1976) > The Quartet of causeries (The Bhanas) trns. Ed. Csaza Dezso and Somadeva Vasudeva. New York University Press (2009) > Caturbhani (Bangla): Sanskrita Sahitya Sambhara, Ed. Gourinath Sastri 26th Vol. Calcutta (1983).

Ch. Five: Kuttanimahatmayam *(Kuttanimata)* of Damodara Gupta. Primary source "The Art of the Temptress", poetry form of work translated by B.P.L. Bedi, Bombay 1968 > The lessons of Bowd (Eastern Love). Vol. I. trns. Mathers, Edward Pawys. London (1927) . Feet, J.F. Corpus. Inscription Indicarum III, Kalhan's *Rajatarangani* > Sastri, Ajoy Mitra: India as seen in Kuttanimata. Calcutta (1975) > *Rasadipika* (Commentary). Guzerati Printing Press. Also, in Bangla, Kuttanimatam, trns and Ed. Tradib Nath Ray Calcutta (b.era 1360).

Ch. Six: Sringaramanjuri Ed. Kalpalata Munshi. Singhi Series, Bombay (1959) Sringaramanjuri (The Courtesan who inflamed Love): Ayyer H. R. Bomaby (1961) > Sringaramanjuri of Raja Bhojdeva. Malwa (Studies in Indian Library) Singhi Jain series No. 30, Bombay (1959) > Sringaramanjuri of Saint Akbar Shah, Sanskrit MS. in Devanagari and Telagu Script. English trns. And Ed. Dr. V. Raghavan. Archaeological Dept. Hyderabad Govt. Publication (1951).

Ch. Seven: Courtesan in Bombay. The castes and classes of these female dancer of courtesans in the ancient traditions described in detail in the publication of the *Bombay Presidency Gazetteer* of Bombay and *Ethnographical Survey* of Bombay. K. Raghunathji's article: Bombay Dancing Girls (Same as our version) pub. in the Indian Antiquary. Ed. Jas Burgess (A journal of Oriental Research) Full text Vol. XIII (1984). Also printed in book form by Bombay Family Printing Press, (5th edition) 1890.

Glossary

ANATHAPINDIKA: Pra. Skt. (also called Auathapindada in Skt.) literally "one who gives alms (*Pinda*) to the unprotected or needy (*anatha*)." Eitel's etymology "One who gives without keeping (anatha) a mouthful (Pinda) himself" is not tenable. A wealthy lay devotee famous for his liberality and donor of the *Jetavana* Vihara.

ARBUDA MOUNTAIN: Is situated in the Gujarat and at the time of Mahabharata it was known as *Arbudachala.* According to a legend, Arbuda is the son of Himavanta mountain and a person who spend a night here gets the *punya* of gifting one thousand cows to a Brahmin. Mount Abu is famous for its beautiful Jain temples, most famous among them being the marble temples of Vimalavasahi and Lunavasahi.

BHAVIN: (Skt. *bhavini,* a handsome, wanton woman) devil (Skt. *Devala,* an attendant on an idol) or *naikin:* Mistress, procuress. They are said to be descended from the female servants of the Savantvadi or Malvan chiefs, but some of them are of earlier origin, and their rank have been recruited from the households of the chiefs – women of other sudra castes, besides Marathas and Bhandaris, who may become *bhavins* by pouring water from the god's lamp in a temple over their head.

BRAHMADATTA: P. Skt. (elym. Given by Brahma) name of a mythical king of Kashi. "In former times, there live at Benares a powerful king whose name was Brahmadatta of Kasi."

BROTHEL: Originally meant an abandoned woman, *i.e.* a prostitute, but it also was used synonymously with bordel and by the sixteenth century brothel had replaced bordel as the common term for house of prostitution.

COURTESAN: The term was originally applied to a person attached to a princely court and was derived from the Italian *cortigiano*. From this original usage it came to include the court mistress, a high-class prostitute, and has since the sixteenth century been applied to the more expensive prostitutes, especially those who work so hard to deceive their customers or patrons.

DARIKA: (Initiation): A harlot was called *darika* before she launched on her profession. The darika of a maiden as a hetaira was an occasion to be celebrated. The man who had the first sexual intercourse with the initiate had to pay a very heavy fee which was within the reach of the rich alone. This was an age-old custom and is referred to in other work also. The custom is reported to have been current among the prostitutes of Varanasi till recently.

DEVADASI (Slave-Girl of the gods): Whose patron saints were *Annapurna* and the *Upsras* (Celestial Courtesans), held as her symbol *Sooee* the parrot: bird of the free love, counterpart of Cupid's dove, upon which *Kamadeva* (the Hindu Cupid) rode. The temple prostitute, born and bred into sanctified whoredom, was known by many names, among them *Muroli*, *devakunya* (daughter of the gods) and *devastree* (Wife of the gods).

GANIKA: Among Indologist the Sanskrit term is not yet a household word. A *ganika* is a special type of courtesan. She is not prostitute. Indeed, the Indian tradition seems to have classified, and specified, the difference between the two. The civilised public women, proficient in the arts, winsome in her ways, and endowed with exceptional beauty and taste is called a *gonika*. Below her are ranked women who do not possess the talents of a *gonika, vesya, rupajiva, pumscali, dosi* etc. are some of the terms applied to women who are considered prostitutes. The *Ganika* of ancient India, like the *hataera* of ancient Greece or the Japanese *geisha* is the exceptionally refined and cultivated courtesan.

HARLOT: Like so many other words applied to prostitutes, this term started out as a masculine word meaning vagabond, beggar, rogue, rascal or villain; it was probably derived from varlet meaning a young man, servant, or even young noble. In the fifteenth century, it was applied to women as a term of execration; in the sixteenth century it tended to replace the word whore in the various English translations of the Bible.

HETAIRE (hetaera): The Greek (and, Latin) term for prostitute still used. In ancient Greek, hetaerae were courtesans, that is to say, highly educated, sophisticated companions. They are often regarded by people today as simple prostitutes, which is an incorrect assumption, although most of them did, in fact, have sexual relations with their patrons.

HOT HOUSE: At one time this was a brothel in which the clients could call upon the prostitutes to do anything at any time. Now it usually refers to a house, apartment, or message centre where the call girls receive or keep their appointments.

JETAVANA: A Vihara. Anathapindika took the land and Jeta the trees, and they placed them in trust of *Sariputra* for the Buddha. This vihara was called Jetavana, and the friend of the orphans invited the Lord to come to Savatthi and receive the donation.

KAMA (*Kamadeva*): The god of love, about whose origin many legends are told. In the Vedas, desire is said to have the first thing that stirred in the deep at the dawn of creation, and the *Atharva-veda* Kama exalted as a creator. In one legend Kama was directed to arouse love-thoughts in Siva who was so absorbed in meditation that the demon Taraka assumed control over the universe. Kama succeeded in his mission but incurred the wrath of Siva who reduced him to ashes with a flash from his third eye. Kama's wife, *Rati* (sexual desire) was a daughter of the arch – mage Daksha. In another legend says that Siva finally relented allowed Kama to be reborn as Pradyumna son of Krishna and Rukmini.

KUSIKA: A *rishi* who founded the Kausika family of Kanyakubja. The term *Kausika* means sexual love, and in combination is used for a courtesan. Kusika's mother was said to have been an *apsara* or heavenly nymph, which may account for the name. The descendants of Kusika the rishi established an important vedic school known as the Kausitaka, which was responsible for the composition of a Brahmana, an *Aranyaka* and an Upanishad, called Kausitaki after them.

MISTRESS: Derived from the French word *madame*, literally my lady, which was a French title given to women of quality and now commonly applied to all married women. In English, however, the term madam has been used derisively since the eighteenth century to refer to a kept mistress, a courtesan, or a prostitute. It came, however, to refer primarily to the female head of a house of prostitution, although occasionally the term is still used as a euphemism for prostitute. Since the fifteenth century mistress has been used as a term to refer to any woman who illicitly occupies the place of the wife.

PATALIPUTRA: The name of Modern Patna which is situated near Pataliputra is derived from the same source. Earlier, the city had been known as Kusumadhvaja or *Kusumapura*, and later Pushpapura.

It was originally a fortess founded by Ajatasatru (480 B.C.) in place of Rajagriha the earlier capital of Magadha, and the site selected was at the confluence of the *Ganges* and the *Son,* although the latter river has now changed its course. During the time of Chandragupta Maurya it was a timber and brick city nine miles long, and its massive timber fortification were pierced by sixty-four gates and crowned five hundred and seventy towers. The royal *sugangeya* palace was built partly of stone and partly of teak, with rich carvings, and ornamental designs in gold and silver.

Megasthenes, Greek envoy at Chandragupta's Court, declared that the palace at *Palibotra* was more splendid than the palaces of Susa and Ecbatana. About a century later the Chinese pilgrim Fa-hien visited Pataliputra, but by this time it had been virtually abandoned. Wandering among the majestic ruins of the Great City.

Another Chinese visited Pataliputra, Hiuen-Tsiang in 629 AD. He recorded:

"In old days when men's lives were of immeasurable length, then this town was called Kusumapura (Explained to mean the city of the palace of fragrant flowers); because the kings palaces had so many flowers, it was so called. Afterwards, when men's lives dwindled down to a thousand years, then it was called Pataliputra, after the Pataliputra (the trumpet flower – tree)."

PIMP: The origin of this word is obscure but it is probably related to or derived from the verb *pimper*, meaning to render elegant. By 1607 the term meant one who provided means and opportunities for unlawful sexual intercourse.

PROCURER: Procuress. A person who procures women for the gratification of lust. The word was first used in this sense in the seventeenth century. Originally it meant one who brought about something or induced it to be done by the agency of another.

PROSTITUTE: From the Latin *prostatuere*, to cause to stand up, or set up, the past participle of which, *prostitutus*, means place before, expose publicly. Since the sixteenth century this has been the most often used English word to describe the selling of sexual intercourse and the woman who sells it.

PUMSCALI: Sanskrit term for a ritual prostitute among the early vedic *Vratyas*, who were a precursor of the later ascetic and yogis of Siva, but with clear bacchantic, orgiastic connection.

PUMSEALI: Sanskrit term for a ritual prostitute among the early vedic *Vratyas*, who were a precursor of the later ascetic and yogis of Siva, but with clear bacchantic, orgiastic connection.

RATNAVALI: A popular Sanskrit play written by king Shriharsa or Harshavardhan who ruled in the first half of the seventh century A.D. The king also wrote three plays. Most popular of these plays, *Ratnavali* a natika in four acts. In the first act of the play the celebration of the *vasantotsava* or Holi full of dancing, singing, drinking and merry-making is portrayed with full gusto. We come to know from Kuttanimatam that this act of the play used to be entacted by the beautiful courtesans of Varanasi in the temple of Kashi Vishvanatha.

SACRED PROSTITUTION: Temple prostitution, or religious prostitution is a sexual ritual consisting of prostitution or other sexual intercourse performed in the context of religious worship, often as from of fertility rite. Sacred prostitution had a wide distribution in canaanite religion, in Egyptian religion, in the cult of the Great Mother of Asia minor. There is a survival of sacred prostitution connected with certain temple in modern India.

STREETWALKER: A common prostitute whose field of operation is the streets. The term has been synonymous with prostitution since the seventeenth century.

SULA-PALA (brothel-keeper): Normally a courtesan worked singly and independently; but there appear to have existed some brothels, possibly with more than one inmate, under the charge of a man. The keeper of a brothel was called *sula-pala*. He looked after arrangement of theatrical performances given by harlots belonging to his establishment. He exercised strict control over the inmates of his brothel. A verse refers to his not allowing a harlot to act on the stage saying she was passing through the menses.

TAWAIF: The word tawaif is derived Iron the Arabic *ta'ife* and includes in its definition: "bands or trupes of dancing girls." She was by far the most popular among the entertainers. As the tawifs were singers and dancers by profession. Some of the tawaifs managed to enter the royal harem and become favourite begums and women of great importance and influence. The most prominent among them was all, was Begum Hazrat Mahal, a wife of Wajid Ali Shah who played a heroic and noble role in the freedom struggle of 1857-58. A tawaif (Urdu) also *Kanjri* or *Kanjari* was a courtesan. The tawaifs excelled and contributed music, dance (*Mujra*), and the Urdu literary tradition considered and authority on etiquette.

THE BOWD: This word originally meant bold, lively, gay, merry, but at the same time it could mean wanton, licentious, unchaste. No account of prostitution will be complete without a reference to the mother, real or adopted, who was a *sine qua non* of the establishment of a hetaira. She was variously called *mata, janani, kuttani* and *sambhali*. She was normally an elderly Lady with a found of experience to her credit and as such served as friend, philosopher and guide to prostitutes. Some of these women, who had been successful courtesans in their youth and had thereby developed deep insight into the nature of men and things, were highly respected in their community, and a number of harlots flocked to them for instructions into the intricacies of the profession.

UJJAIN: (Pali for the Sanskrit *Vijayani* victorious), known to ancient Greek, geographers Ozene, is situated on the Sipra river in central India. Throughout its long history Ujjain was a meeting ground of nations, associated from remote antiquity with foreign races. It lay in the direct line of the great trade routes leading from the Seaport Broach (Barygaza) to the western markets of Sind and the Gangetic trading centres as far as Pataliputra.

In the epic and early historical period the city and surrounding country were known as *Avanti* or Mahishmati. As Mahishmati (from Maghas) it was the home of the heterogeneous Haihaya tribe, who were notorious, among other things, for their sexual lexity. The *Mahabharata* states that the women of Mahishmati had the privilege of free sexual relations with anyone they pleased without restriction. Subsequently it passed to the Bhoja tribe, who were classed as *mlechchhas*, descended from Druhyu son Yayati. Under Chandragupta it was absorbed by the Mauryan empire and become Asoka's capital when he was viceroy (275 BC) during his father's reign.

VARANASI: Formerly Benares and later Banaras, a city in India, in Uttar Pradesh. It is situated on the River Ganga. Hindus regard Varanasi, which they also call Kasi (Kashi). According to legend it was in Varanasi, at a spot now called the Dasasvamedha (Ten Horse-Sacrifice) Ghat, that Brahma in ages past once offered, a sacrifices of ten horses. The name of this luminous city is frequently mentioned in ancient Indian literature.

VESA-SANNIVESA (Colonies of Prostitutes): According to our evidence there were regular colonies of prostitutes *Vesa-Sannivesa* at Abu and Varanasi. Life in these colonies was very busy and business quite brisk. A reference to a harlot from Kerala at Abu being visited by a Southerner. The other story features Rupinika, a prostitute stay at Mathura. The Padma-prabhrtaka and Padataditaka prove the existence of such a colony at Ujjayini, is the venue of the scenes of these monologues. The Dhurta-vita-samvada and Ubhaybabhisarika at Pataliputra, is the venue of the plays. In many stories of Sringarmanjuri set in Ujayini, the ancient capital city of Gupta empire and later at the time of Raja Bhoja of Dhara. The courtesans hailing from Saurastra, Pataliputra, Kasi. Surparaka (Modern Sopra), Simhala, Surasena. Lata, Dravida and Barbara and of the Yavana extraction.

VESHYA: Tantrik / Sanskrit term similar in content to the Near Eastern concept of the Sacred Prostitute. In a passage of the Niruttara Tantra takes pains to state that the *veshya* are not common prostitutes, who bear the same name, but are so called only because of the independence they have in common. Another specific type of *veshya*, not mentioned in the Niruttara, is the *Veshya Kumarika* or 'Virgin harlot' who takes part in the Kumari *puja*. A different interpretation of some of the *veshya* type is given under the entry Deva Chakra.

VITAS: Mention in most of our stories. The *vita* character frequently in Sanskrit plays and is described at length in the texts on dramaturgy and erotics. We may chose *pimp* as *vita* in English word, which seemed to be a suitable name for someone whose favourite haunt is the red light district and who arranges rendezvous between prostitutes and their clients. According to Bharata, he was to be skilled in pleasing prostitutes, sweet, courteous, poet, proficient in argumentation, bold and shrewd. Vatsyayana defined a *vita* as a man who has exhausted his wealth in enjoyment, is endowed with good qualities, is married and is respected among harlots and in *gosthis* and earas his livelihood thereby.

WHORE: Probably the oldest term in the English language referring to a prostitute. Originally it was equated with adultery but by 1100 its prime usage was to describe a woman who prostituted herself. It has been spelled in numerous ways: hore, heore, hoore, houre, hourir, hoare, whoor, whoar, huire, hure, *et. al*.

Index

L

M